A GUIDE FOR THE PERPLEXED

Vegetarianism

KERRY WALTERS

continuum

Continuum International Publishing Group

The Tower Building	80 Maiden Lane
11 York Road	Suite 704
London	New York
SE1 7NX	NY 10038

www.continuumbooks.com

ISBN: HB: 978-1-4411-0350-5
PB: 978-1-4411-1529-4

Library of Congress Cataloging-in-Publication Data
Walters, Kerry S.
Vegetarianism : a guide for the perplexed / Kerry Walters.
p. cm.
Includes bibliographical references (p.   ) and index.
ISBN-13: 978-1-4411-0350-5 (hardcover: alk. paper)
ISBN-10: 1-4411-0350-3 (hardcover: alk. paper)
ISBN-13: 978-1-4411-1529-4 (pbk. : alk. paper)
ISBN-10: 1-4411-1529-3 (pbk. : alk. paper) 1. Vegetarianism–Moral and ethical
aspects. I. Title.
TX392.W325 2012
179'.3–dc23
2012002888

Typeset by Newgen Imaging Systems Pvt Ltd, Chennai, India
Printed and bound in the United States of America

For my students over the years in
Philosophy and Food
and especially for
Sara Tower
and
Chris Wolf

Vegetarianism

CONTENTS

INTRODUCTION
The ethics of diet

Mr. Leopold Bloom ate with relish the inner organs of beasts and fowls. He liked thick giblet soup, nutty gizzards, a stuffed roast heart, liver slices fried with crustcrumbs, fried hencod's roes. Most of all he liked grilled mutton kidneys which gave to his palate a fine tang of faintly scented urine.

JAMES JOYCE

For my part I wonder what state of soul or mind the first man [had] who touched his mouth to gore and brought his lips to the flesh of a dead creature, who set forth tables of dead, stale bodies and ventured to call food and nourishment the parts that had a little before bellowed and cried, moved and lived.

PLUTARCH

If asked what we ate for breakfast this morning (much less *yesterday* morning), most of us would have a hard time remembering.[1] Eating, like so many other activities in our fast-paced society, is often done on the run, distractedly and hurriedly. We grab a slice of toast on our way out in the morning and zip into a fast food restaurant at noon. Exhausted after a long day at work, we get take-out on the way home or pop one of those conveniently preprocessed meals into the microwave, often eating while watching television or surfing the internet. Except for holidays or special occasions, we just don't pay that much attention to what we eat. Eating is something that we do so regularly that it doesn't stand out any more than our other routine activities. Familiarity doesn't necessarily breed contempt, but it does encourage taking things for granted. So it's not surprising that the details of what and how we eat tend not to lodge in our memories.

But here's the interesting thing. Although we normally don't pay too much attention to what we eat, we become quite defensive and even angry if our regular diet is challenged by someone else. We don't want to be nagged about filling up on too much fat, too much sugar, or too many carbohydrates. Even if we're willing to concede that our eating habits aren't the healthiest ones in the world, and even if we silently rebuke ourselves as we chomp into fast food for the third time in a week, we don't like it when other people criticize how and what we eat. There are at least two explanations for this. First, we believe that the choice of what to eat is a purely private affair, a matter of individual taste. What we decide to make a meal of is no one's business but our own. Second, we believe that when someone criticizes what we eat, what they're *really* doing is criticizing *us*—negatively judging our character, our values, and our lifestyle. Whether something is actually said or an eyebrow merely lifted, we feel as if anyone who comments on our diet assumes a position of moral superiority. And that burns us up.

In the United States in particular but also in Canada, Australia, England, and many countries in Europe, one of the surest ways to raise hackles is to advocate, or even just embrace, a vegetarian diet. Nonvegetarians often bristle defensively or erupt in outright anger and ridicule when the topic comes up. Sometimes all it takes to set them off is simply sharing a meal with a vegetarian. Most vegetarians have had the experience of being heckled or ridiculed when dining with meat-eaters.[2] Holiday meals can devolve into red-faced shouting matches if a member of the family passes on the turkey or goose and sticks to the vegetable side dishes. Defiant bumper stickers which read "PETA: People Eating Tasty Animals" mock the animal rights organization People for the Ethical Treatment of Animals. Groups such as Vegetarians Are Evil and the Anti-Vegetarian Society of Meat Eaters denounce "Kitchen Police" who go around "telling people what they can and cannot eat" (Anti-Vegetarian Society of Meat Eaters 2009). Stand-up comedians love to use vegetarians as the butts of their jokes, and audiences respond enthusiastically. ("If it's not natural to eat hamburgers, why did God make cows so easy to catch? You don't see anybody eating cheetah-burgers, do ya?" quips comic Kathleen Madigan, to delighted roars of laughter.[3]) And more than one otherwise perfectly reasonable and normally restrained philosopher has been known to see red and write purple when responding to academic defenses of vegetarianism.[4]

Take another look at the epigraphs from Joyce and Plutarch that preface this Introduction. Their intensity suggests that the choice to eat meat or to abstain from it is more than simply a matter of gustatory attraction or revulsion (although it's certainly that, too). Joyce's character Leopold Bloom relishes meat. But the sensual obsessiveness of his attraction gestures at a deeper source than mere dietary preference. Alternatively, Plutarch is clearly repulsed by meat. But his disgust is so visceral that it too suggests a deeper source than aesthetic displeasure. Philosopher Mary Midgley believes that the intensity exhibited by Bloom and Plutarch suggests that the diets of meat-eaters and vegetarians reflect two different ways of thinking about the world and one's place in it. The "symbolism" of the two diets, she says, is "never neutral." "To himself, the meat-eater"— the Leopold Blooms among us—"seems to be eating life." To the vegetarian—the Plutarchs—"he seems to be eating death. There is a kind of gestalt-shift between the two positions which makes it hard to change, and hard to raise questions on the matter at all without becoming embattled" (Midgley 1983, p. 27).

If Midgley is correct, the act of eating is much more significant than we typically give it credit for being. As long as our dietary habits aren't called into question, we typically don't think much about them. But once they're challenged, either overtly or simply by exposure to alternative eating patterns, our hackles rise because such challenges call into question some of the basic beliefs, values, and choices by which we situate ourselves in the world—what Midgley refers to as our "gestalts."

Aspects of the gestalt the meat-eater is likely to bring to the table are assumptions about the naturalness and healthiness of an omnivorous diet, the self-evident superiority of the human species, the inappropriateness of extending moral consideration to non-human animals, and the hands-off privacy of our food choices.[5] These assumptions may be so deeply engrained—they are, after all, conventional wisdom in the West—that the meat-eater never examines nor even, perhaps, articulates them. They simply serve as part of the rather blurry background of his everyday world. But his diet reflects them. As Midgley says, diets are never neutral.

The gestalt the vegetarian brings to the table includes beliefs that meat isn't necessary for human health and well-being, that humans may owe a certain amount of moral consideration to animals, that what we eat has far-reaching consequences on the environment and other people, and that eating is a normatively public rather than a value-neutral private choice. This conviction on the part of many vegetarians that food choice is essentially (although not exclusively) ethical is a characteristic feature of their gestalts. For the most part, it's also foreign to the general culture's way of thinking about eating. "We don't usually think of what we eat as a matter of ethics," note Peter Singer and Jim Mason (2006, p. 3), and because of that "it is quite likely that otherwise good people are making bad choices in this area simply because they have not really focused on it, or do not have access to the information they need to make good choices" (p. 8).

Vegetarians generally work hard at making what they consider to be moral dietary choices. Ideally, their decision to abstain from meat, as philosopher Michael Allen Fox puts it, is "a way of redrawing the mental geography with which we negotiate around our world so that it includes an expanded sense of what has value in and of itself. Above all, it is a path leading to less harm to the planet and more peaceful coexistence with other sentient life-forms" (Fox 1999, p. 111). Of course, different vegetarians have different reasons for their adoption of a meatless diet. Some emphasize the importance of animal welfare, others personal health, and still others the stability of the environment as major factors in their decision. But all of them, by deciding to forgo the food item—meat—which is such a staple in the Western diet, definitely remap the mental and normative geography of their culture. In so doing, whether they intend it or not, they do indeed challenge those who accept the conventional gestalt. After all, as Peter Singer says (2009, p. 162), vegetarianism is a "form of boycott," whether or not individual vegetarians intend it to be. This fact only underscores the likelihood that disagreements between vegetarians and meat-eaters will be heated. Challenges to habits deeply rooted in traditional assumptions, especially when those habits are pleasing, as meat-eating is for omnivores, are always threatening.

Who are vegetarians?

It's not uncommon for people who limit their intake of animal food to fish and/or poultry to refer to themselves as "vegetarians." But they aren't. Vegetarianism allows for a certain amount of flexibility, but that leeway doesn't stretch to allow the eating of meat of any kind. (I use "meat" here and throughout as a conveniently generic even if technically inaccurate term to refer to *all* forms of animal flesh: beef, poultry, mutton, pork, fish, seafood, and so on). People who limit their meat intake to poultry or fish, and who eat sparingly of either, are sometimes called "flexitarians."

The most common type of vegetarianism is known as ovo-lacto (from the Latin *ovum* = egg and *lac* = milk), whose practitioners allow themselves eggs and dairy products. Other vegetarians (ovo) allow themselves eggs but not dairy products; still others (lacto-vegetarians) eat dairy products but not eggs. Vegans are vegetarians who eat neither eggs nor dairy products.[6] (For purposes of convenience again, I use the generic terms "vegetarian" and "vegetarianism" throughout this book.)

Vegetarianism is a minority diet around the world. Because meat-eating is seen as a status symbol in most parts of the world, many people in developing nations whose diets are primarily vegetarian would prefer to eat meat if it was affordable. Even in a nation such as India, where Hinduism and Jainism both discourage meat-eating (we'll explore this in Chapter 8), no more than a third of the people voluntarily abstain from meat. Percentages of vegetarians in European Union countries range from 9 or 10 percent in Germany and Italy to 1 percent or less in Denmark, Poland, and Portugal. Seven to 11 percent of UK inhabitants self-report as vegetarians, as do about 4 percent of Canadians.

A 2008 survey by *Vegetarian Times* magazine revealed some interesting demographics about vegetarians in the United States. A little over seven million Americans, 3.2 percent of the population, self-reported as vegetarian, while an additional 22.8 million, or 10 percent, claimed to follow a "vegetarian-inclined" diet. Fifty-nine percent are female and 41 percent male, with the greatest percentage of them (42%) falling in the 18–34 age range, closely followed by nearly 41 percent between the ages of 35 and 54. When asked why they adopted a vegetarian diet, responses ranged from concern for animal welfare (54%) to weight maintenance (24%). But substantial numbers were also motivated by environmental concerns (47%), food safety concerns (31%), and "natural approaches to wellness" (39%). A different survey conducted six years earlier revealed that less than 10 percent of vegetarians in the United States are motivated by religion (Maurer 2002, p. 13).

The safest conclusion to draw from these data is that most vegetarians choose their diet for a number of reasons. Ethical concerns seem to predominate, with a desire to live a more "natural" life following closely. Some people may be single issue vegetarians, motivated in their choice of diet by an exclusive concern for animals or, alternatively, by worries about the environmental degradation caused by food animal production. But the average vegetarian is motivated by a cumulative cluster of concerns, which only confirms Mary Midgley's suspicion that the choice of what we eat is more gestalt than narrowly gustatory.

In this book, I explore the variety as well as the strength of the vegetarian position. Consequently, I focus on seven different normative arguments for a meatless diet, ranging from animal welfare-centered ones (Chapters 1–5), to environmental ones (Chapter 6), human-centered ones (Chapter 7), and religious ones (Chapter 8). Each chapter examines specific arguments for vegetarianism as well as objections to them. Many of the objections are, predictably, from non-vegetarians. But some are also from vegetarians themselves, reflecting the in-house disagreements that arise between proponents of a meatless diet. Throughout, I strive to offer a balanced account of the pros and cons of vegetarianism.

The literature on vegetarianism is enormous and growing by leaps and bounds. It's impossible within a book of this size and purpose to do justice to it all. So I instead focus on major debates and key players. If the book isn't and can't be exhaustive, it at least can be and is representative.

"An appropriate place to begin"

In the internet-connected world in which we live, the flow of information with which we're continuously bombarded attunes us to current events with a real-time immediacy that can be bewildering.

We regularly hear about famines and droughts in Africa and Asia, destruction of rain forests in Latin America, land, water, and air pollution in every corner of the globe, and poverty and hunger even in the United States, arguably the most affluent nation in history. The problems seem so huge, so systemic, and so urgent that we don't know where to begin, as individuals, to do something about them. But it's also true they can sometimes seem so removed from our tiny, snug corner of the world that their distance allows us to fancy we're not implicated in them in any significant way.

Yet two points ought to be kept in mind. The first, as E. F. Schumacher (1999) and others remind us, is that big problems don't necessarily call for big solutions. The latter, in fact, can sometimes exacerbate rather than remedy the former. The second is that the shrinkage of the world guarantees that problems which seem far away are really much closer to home than we may like to think. As we'll see in Chapters 6 and 7, the everyday food choices we make contribute to poverty and environmental degradation—not to mention animal suffering—across the globe. It's true that I am what I eat. But it's equally true that *others* are what I eat, too.

Vegetarians argue that being mindful of diet is one obvious way in which we can both accept moral responsibility for how our personal habits affect the world and act directly to ameliorate poverty, hunger, cruelty to animals, and environmental destruction. Tom Regan, one of the most eloquent spokespersons for animal rights, endorses this point of view. When it comes to a moral lifestyle, he writes, "I cannot help believe that an appropriate place to begin is with the food on our plates. For here we are faced with a direct personal choice over which we exercise absolute sovereign authority. Such power is not always in our grasp" (Regan 2004a, p. 184). Peter Singer and Jim Mason, equally influential champions of vegetarianism, echo Regan's conviction. "The food you consume three or more times daily is your constant and ultimate connection with the environment and the living world around you. If you reflect your concerns for them in your food habits, you will be healthier in every way" (Mason and Singer 1990, p. 188). At the end of the day, this expansion of our mental and *moral* geography, as Michael Allen Fox might put it, is a most compelling reason for considering vegetarianism as a dietary and lifestyle choice.

CHAPTER ONE

Animals, pain, and factory farms

There is a gulf between the reality of animal production and the perception of animal production in the non-farming American public.

WES JAMISON

The production-line maintenance of animals . . . is without doubt one of the darkest and most shameful chapters in human culture.

KONRAD LORENZ

The in-laws are coming to dinner, and the pressure is on to prepare a meal that lives up to their persnickety standards. Examining the various cuts of meat at your local butcher's, you wonder if they'd prefer a nice side of shmoo, a fricassee of Chicken Little, or a goulash of renew-a-bits. After some consideration, you opt for the shmoo roast. It's not as exciting as the goulash or fricassee, but it *is* a safe choice.

If these three meats are unfamiliar to you, the reader, it's because they don't exist. They're the fantasies of a philosopher and a pair of science fiction novelists. Shmoos, named in honor of one of cartoonist Al Capp's characters, are animals whose only desire in life is to be killed and eaten by humans. Chicken Little, the science fiction creation, is meat grown *in vitro,* absolutely devoid of brain or pain sensors—a mere "blob of inert and insensate flesh awaiting consumption," as one commentator puts it (Fox 1999, p. 165). Renew-a-bits is meat from animals genetically engineered to provide body parts for human consumption without having to be killed. Their limbs can be removed with no distress to the animal, after which they spontaneously regenerate.[1]

The first interesting thing about these fantasy meats is that they seem to eliminate reasons for any moral qualms about eating flesh. Animals don't suffer in providing them. Chicken Little is no more sentient than a finger nail, shmoos positively long to be eaten, and renew-a-bits animals are neither killed nor hurt. In the case of Chicken Little, there's no worry about polluting land and water with excess animal waste. Since no real harm is done to shmoos or renew-a-bits animals when their body parts are harvested, there's little chance of slaughterhouse workers or meat consumers growing callous to pain inflicted on food animals. Additionally, let's stipulate that the same genetic engineering science that gives us these new varieties of meat also makes them cholesterol free, so there's little health risk in consuming them. The only obvious objection that might be raised to eating shmoo, Chicken Little, or renew-a-bits meat is from a perspective that sees all life as somehow sacred. But surely in vitro meat isn't "alive" in any interesting sense of the word, shmoos *want* us to kill and eat them, and regenerative food animals aren't harmed any more than tomato bushes are when their fruit is plucked.[2]

The second interesting thing about this imaginary scenario is that its message appeals to us at a deep level. Most of us have never heard of fictional shmoo, Chicken Little, or renew-a-bits meat. But we're continuously exposed to food advertising that depicts happy, pink, and plump pigs inviting patrons to come into barbeque joints to eat them, smiling chickens who can't wait for you to bite into one of their legs, and cows joyfully leaping out of green pastures and landing on our plates as juicy steaks and hamburgers.[3] This cartoonish kind of marketing is pervasive because it works, and it works because it reinforces what we want to believe: that the animals whose meat we eat aren't any more inconvenienced or harmed than shmoos, Chicken Little, or renew-a-bits critters would be.

But that, of course, is the *real* fantasy. In the world in which we live, we must kill an animal to eat it, and most of the billions of land animals we eat—the favorites being chickens, turkeys, cattle, pigs, and sheep—display unmistakably aversive behavior at slaughterhouses. Moreover, the conditions under which the vast majority of them are raised are unspeakably horrendous. Food animals are warehoused by the tens of thousands in facilities aptly called "factory farms." They live in cramped quarters, are stuffed with hormones to accelerate growth and antibiotics to keep at bay the multitude of illnesses their unsanitary living conditions breed, and often never see the light of day until they're herded into trucks on their way to the slaughterhouse. As one observer notes, "The vast majority of food animals are now raised under methods that are systematically abusive. For them, discomfort is the norm, pain is routine, growth is abnormal, and diet is unnatural. Disease is widespread and stress is almost constant"[4] (Fearnely-Whittingstall 2004, p. 24). To top things off, factory farms pollute the environment and expose humans to a spectrum of health risks ranging from *Escherichia coli* infection to avian flu and mad cow disease. (We'll explore this more fully in Chapter 7.)

The treatment of animals who supply our meat is so inhumane that more than one commentator, as we'll see shortly, has likened factory farms to Nazi death camps. Predictably, the comparison often offends people. But most of those who object to it have little or no idea of what goes on in modern factory farming. That's not surprising, given another marketing deception: bacon, eggs, dairy products, veal, and even hamburger meat are frequently sold in wrappings or cartons that suggest they come from small, family-owned farms. Even though such farms have nearly vanished, replaced by agri-industry that raises food animals on a huge scale, the average American consumer still believes that his hamburger comes from a cow peacefully grazed in green and open meadows, fresh air, and sunshine

Given these realities, moral questions about the propriety of eating meat take on a certain urgency. The most obvious question arising from them is whether humans are justified in a dietary choice that inflicts so much suffering and destruction upon so many animals. Chapters 2–5 will wrestle specifically with this problem. But we need to do a couple of preliminary things. First, we need to examine the claim made by a few philosophers that animals are actually incapable of the suffering that opponents of factory farming techniques claim they endure. Following that, it's important to take a closer look at just what goes on in factory farms. Defenses of vegetarianism today are fueled in great part (but not exclusively) by moral revulsion with factory farming methods. So a better understanding of them is good preparation for examining animal-based arguments for vegetarianism in later chapters.

Animals and pain

The assertion that animals, at least higher order ones like mammals and birds, are incapable of feeling pain strikes most of us as bizarre. But philosophers are in the business of questioning nearly everything, and some have even taken on what most of us see as self-evident: the claim that animals feel pain.

The seventeenth-century philosopher Rene Descartes popularized the notion that animals were painless because they were mindless. Before him, even though most European thinkers denied that animals possessed souls, none of them thought beasts incapable of pain and generally condemned the infliction of needless suffering on them.

Descartes broke with this tradition. As a dualist, he believed that humans were thinking creatures because they were composites of two distinct substances, body and mind. (Exactly how the two managed to interact is a riddle neither he nor any other dualist has persuasively cracked.) But because he found no sign of mind in animals—rationality, for example, or language—he concluded that they possessed but one substance: body. The "greatest of all prejudices," he wrote, "is that of believing that brutes think," an error born "from having observed that many of the[ir] bodily members . . . are not very different from our own in shape and movements, and from the belief that our mind is the principle of the motions which occur in us" (Descartes 1999, p. 263). But animal behavior, unlike human behavior, doesn't come from cogitation. It's simply an automatic series of reflexes, more analogous to the motion of a clock than to the conscious deliberation practiced by humans.

What this means, concluded Descartes, is that animals are incapable of experiencing pain. Pain, after all, is a mental state. Since animals lack the capacity for mental states, they lack the necessary condition for the experience of pain. They may behave in pained ways, shrieking or snarling or running around in circles. But such activity no more entails pain than does the whistling, quivering, or bursting (to make a twentieth-century comparison) of an over-heated car radiator.

Modern-day philosophers Peter Carruthers and Peter Harrison agree with Descartes's denial of animal pain, although not his brand of dualism. As far as Carruthers is concerned, there's no evidence that animals possess enough of an interior life to have conscious experiences at all. Their bodies may react to certain stimuli in biochemically "pained" ways, but the beasts themselves lack con-scious awareness of the pain because they are incapable of "think-ing about their own thinkings" (Carruthers 1994, p. 193). Lacking consciousness, much less the ability to reflect on their experiences (which Carruthers denies they have anyway), their unfelt biochemi-cal "pain" is in no way relevantly similar to human-felt experiences of pain.

Peter Harrison denies animal pain by appealing to a purportedly evolutionary argument. Unlike animals, he says, humans aren't closed instinctual systems. We possess free will, the ability to make choices in the world. Our capacity for pain is an evolutionary attribute that signals the need for us to make a choice when faced with a poten-tially dangerous situation. Animals, by comparison, are simply pro-gramed to flee potentially harmful situations. They have neither the need nor the capacity to make choices. Consequently, ascribing pain to them is unnecessary because they have no evolutionary need for it. They possess no continuous sense of self that would enable them to grasp any experience of pain as their own anyway. Animals, like chronic amnesiacs, always live in the present moment. Even if they had felt pain receptors, they would be unable to recall or, for that matter, anticipate pain (Harrison 1989, 1991, 1993).

Philosopher Jan Narveson takes a less extreme, more common sense approach than either Carruthers or Harrison. He doesn't deny the capacity of certain animals to feel pain, but he questions the propriety of likening either its intensity or its moral weight to human pain.

> Isn't it reasonable to hold that the significance, and thus the quality, and so ultimately the utility, of the sufferings of beings with *sophisticated* capacities is different from that of the sufferings of lesser beings? Suppose one of the lower animals to be suffering quite intensely. Well, what counts as suffering of

like degree in a *sophisticated* animal—one like, say, Beethoven or Kierkegaard, or you, gentle reader? If we are asked to compare the disutility of a pained cow with that of a pained human, or even a somewhat frustrated one, is it so absurd to think that the latter's is greater? (Narveson 1977, p. 166)

Narveson's point is that "sophisticated" human pain typically involves more than just immediate physical discomfort. Implicated in the experience of pain are mental states such as fear, anxiety, dread, frustration, regret, shame, hope, and disappointment. All of them flow from an acute "aware[ness] of the future stretching out before us, and of the past in the other direction" (Narveson 1983, p. 53). Animals lack this temporal sensibility, thus making their experiences of pain profoundly different from humans'.

Two broad assumptions typically underlie many arguments that deny pain capacity to animals. The first is the Cartesian-inspired claim that animals lack *any* kind of mental states—not merely experiences of pain, but also beliefs, language, or the capacity to reason. Denying a creature these qualities is tantamount to saying that it isn't a person, since only persons, from a Cartesian perspective, are capable of mental states. So animals don't experience pain because they're not persons. The second assumption reflects a rather tired epistemological skepticism about the possibility of knowing other minds. I observe only the external behavior of others, not their interior mental states. How, then, can I know with any degree of certainty that the mental states I infer on the basis of their behavior are actual? Perhaps the person under observation is pretending. Or perhaps she's a robot, an automaton programed to behave in certain person-like ways but utterly devoid of mental states. Any mental state I ascribe to her is ascribed, not observed, and inferences based on observation are always liable to error. And if I can't speak with certainty about mental states when it comes to fellow humans, how can I possibly be confident in assuming that animals have them?

There are a couple of responses to the first assumption. To begin with, an argument can be made for the claim that personhood ought not to be limited to humans. If the determining characteristics of what it means to be a person include abilities such as reasoning, believing, or manipulating language, then it's entirely possible that nonhuman mammals such as chimpanzees and gorillas qualify as persons.[5] If that's the case, we have no reason for denying them mental states like pain.

Granted, no one wants to argue that great apes possess the reasoning skills of a normal human adult. But they may well be similar to that of a human toddler or a developmentally disabled adult.[6] And this brings us to the second response to the Cartesian-inspired denial of mental states in animals. We don't doubt for an instant that human persons, even marginal ones, experience pain. When we observe an infant or an adult with the mental capacity of a toddler scream and flinch after touching a hotplate, we immediately infer the presence of pain. Yet neither of them has fully developed reasoning skills. Why then presume that animals with similar cognitive capacities are incapable of experiencing pain? As we'll see in the next chapter, Peter Singer argues that there's no good reason whatsoever to do so, and chalks the presumption up to a prejudice he calls "speciesism."

But what about animals that obviously fail to qualify as non-human persons? This question brings us back to the epistemological skepticism that denies we can know the mental states of other humans, much less animals. From a philosophical perspective, the perplexity is intriguing. But from a practical one, it seems profoundly irrelevant. Doubt about whether other humans have mental states is surely contrived rather than genuine. We may be honestly perplexed about what the exact nature of another person's mental state is, but we don't really doubt its presence simply because we can't offer a rigorous proof for it. Even more, the mental state of pain is correlated with certain behavioral displays that we all recognize. Granted, a person can either fake or hide pain. But in the first case, she mimics the behavioral display that everyone associates with pain, and in the second she inhibits it.[7]

If we observe similar behavioral displays in nonperson animals, we have good reason to presume, by analogy, that they are indeed experiencing pain—without, again, being able to offer a knockdown proof. Peter Singer, for example, notes that "the basis of my belief that animals can feel pain is similar to the basis of my belief that my daughter can feel pain. Animals in pain behave in much the same way humans do, and their behavior is sufficient justification for the belief that they feel pain" (Singer 2008, p. 69). Feminist vegetarian Josephine Donovan agrees. In her opinion, a homologous analogy can be drawn between humans and animals that focuses on displays such as body language, eye movement, facial expression, and tone of voice:

> If that dog is yelping, whining, leaping about, licking an open wound, and since if I had an open wound I know I would similarly be (or feel like) crying and moving about anxiously because of the pain, I therefore conclude that the animal is experiencing the same kind of pain as I would and is expressing distress about it. One imagines, in short, how the animal is feeling based on how one would feel in a similar situation. (Donovan 2007c, p. 363)

But surely, it might be objected, homologous analogy will take us only so far. How can we invoke the same behavioral standards that we use to determine pain in mammals to, for example, cuttlefish and lobsters? Facial expressions and tones of voice obviously won't do at all. Aversive behavior—Donovan's "moving about anxiously"—is fraught with risk too; after all, amoebae and paramecia display aversive behavior when exposed to light. But are they experiencing pain?

To address the analogy difficulty, some animal behaviorists and philosophers (Birke 1994; Dawkins 2006; Rollin 1989) suggest additional criteria for identifying pain. First, careful observation of animals may teach us species-specific signs of distress that signal pain in even hard cases like cuttlefish and lobsters. In addition, we can gauge animal pain by paying attention to physiological changes in hormone levels or the ammonia content of muscles, the presence of pain-inhibiting chemicals such as endorphins and enkephalins, and fluctuation in body temperature, all of which can signal the presence of pain. It may, however, be objected that focusing on physiological signs of pain is still an exercise in homologous inference. And as we've already seen, Peter Carruthers makes a distinction between unfelt biochemical "pain" and felt pain.

Speaking of Carruthers, what about the specific arguments against the possibility of animal pain defended by him, Peter Harrison, and Jan Narveson? Carruthers, it will be recalled, argued in Cartesian fashion that animals lack the capacity for genuine mental states such as pain because they're unable to "think about their own thinkings"—or, in other words, to reflect on the content of their consciousness. But if this self-reflection is a necessary condition for possessing mental states, then we're forced to deny that young human children have them, and such a position is easily refuted by parental experience (Pluhar 1995). Moreover, taking Carruthers seriously may mean we have to deny that human youngsters are even persons.

Harrison's argument, notwithstanding its ingenuity, can be challenged in two ways. In the first place, it seems to violate the very evolutionary approach it wants to take. Harrison argues that humans need pain as a survival skill, while animals don't. But an obvious question to ask is why this parting of the ways between species that otherwise share so much in common. It seems to fly in the face of everything we know about evolutionary homology. As philosopher James Rachels points out,

> we have virtually the same evidence for animal pain that we have for human pain. When humans are tortured, they cry out; so do animals. When humans are faced with painful stimuli, they draw back and try to escape; so do animals. Pain in humans is associated with the operation of a complex nervous system; so it is with animals . . . Darwin stressed that, in an important sense, their nervous systems, their behaviors, their cries, *are* our nervous systems, our behaviors, and our cries, with only a little modification. (Rachels 1990, p. 131)

The second line of objection to Harrison's denial of the possibility of animal pain has to do with his claim that even if animals do experience something like pain, they have no sense of its endurance because their awareness, like an habitual amnesiac's, is always in the present moment. If this is true, though, it would seem more an affirmation of animal suffering than a denial. Since an animal's experience of pain exists only moment by moment, it fills their entire world without the relief offered by memory of past or hope of future painlessness (Rollin 1989). But it's probably not necessary to appeal to this criticism of Harrison's position. Both ordinary experience and animal research suggests that at least in the case of mammals and possibly birds, memory of past pain (and past pleasure) influences behavior (DeGrazia 1996; Masson 2003).

Even if animal awareness doesn't lock an animal in Harrison's eternal now, it's indisputable, as Jan Narveson points out, that animals, whether they're persons or not, are incapable of the "sophisticated" cognitive functions characteristic of humans. Moreover, it's

reasonable to presume that there are declining levels of awareness
as one moves down the animal chain. Cuttlefish and lobsters, not
to mention sponges and protozoa, are less aware than elephants,
chimpanzees, and canines. But as we've just seen in examining
Harrison's position, possession of less-than-human mental capacity doesn't automatically mean that animal pain is somehow less
burdensome than human pain. It's quite true that an animal's distress isn't exacerbated by the existential sense of dread that often
befalls humans in pain. But neither is animal pain ameliorated by
the ability to understand the source of the pain, the opportunity to
seek medical relief, or religious solace. To be trapped in an ever-
present experience of pain, or to endure pain without any hope of
future surcease, is more likely to be characteristic of animal than
human pain. Both seem quite dreadful. And even if animals do suffer pain differently than humans in similar circumstances, this in
no way discounts what they endure. As Stephen R. L. Clark (1977,
p. 42) observes, "a burning cat is as agonized as any burning baby.
Even where we do have reason to impute a lesser pain, yet pain is
painful."

Factory farms: Animals as units

Despite the caveats of a handful of philosophers, most everyone
agrees that many animals, especially the ones humans are most
likely to eat, are capable of pain and suffering. Hunted or domesticated food animals as well as animals used for labor have experienced pain at the hands of humans for centuries. But within the
last couple of generations, the pain that domesticated food animals endure from birth to death has increased exponentially. The
unrelieved misery of their lives and the stunning numbers of them
slaughtered each year—between 20 and 25 billion, with upwards of
11 billion in the United States alone[8] (that's 27 million a day, over a
million an hour)—have prompted several commentators (Bernstein
2004; Coetzee 1999; Derrida 2008; Patterson 2002) to draw comparisons between the plight of animals and those of genocide victims. Jewish author Isaac Bashevis Singer famously insisted that "in
relation to [animals], all people are Nazis; for the animals it is an
eternal Treblinka" (Singer 1983, p. 271). The thinking behind this
judgment isn't just that humans invent and manipulate technology

for the systematic and merciless extermination of animals. It's also that animals, like "nonAryans" under the Nazis, are killed for no other reason than for being what they are. In comparing the slaughter of food animals to Nazi persecution of Jews, ecofeminist Carol Adams (2007b, p. 26) concludes that "animals are killed daily for *being* rather than for *doing*; they may be killed because they are 'just animals.'"

As we saw earlier, the source of the colossal surge in animal suffering is the factory farm (sometimes called a Confined Animal Feeding Operation, or CAFO) system of rearing huge numbers of food animals in cramped, warehoused conditions. The first factory farming of domesticated animals—chickens—really got off the ground during World War II, when huge quantities of poultry were needed to feed troops. The birds were raised in large cramped sheds. Vitamins A and D were added to the feed to compensate for their lack of sunlight and exercise. Shortly after the war, chickens were fed newly developed sulfa drugs to cut down on illness and to accelerate growth. The factory farming of cattle and hogs didn't emerge until the 1960s, and industrial fish farming, although now big business, is a relatively late arrival on the scene.

The bad news for animals is that the relationship between consumer demand and factory farming is one of mutual reenforcement. The factory farming of animals produces huge quantities of product which drive down prices and escalate demand. At the same time, the public's habituation to meat as an easily affordable staple encourages factory farms to proliferate and to increase production. What's certain is that the amount of meat demanded by American, Canadian, and English consumers can't be supplied by small-scale, privately owned farms. So long as meat remains a staple of the standard Western diet, factory farms will be necessary, guaranteeing that the suffering of food animals will continue. As Peter Singer notes, "It is not practically possible to rear animals for food on a large scale without inflicting considerable suffering" (Singer 2009, p. 160). Either we drastically cut back on our meat consumption, or we accept what Isaac Bashevis Singer calls "an eternal Treblinka" for factory-farmed animals.

Factory farms are aptly named. Like industries that produce inanimate commodities, the goal of the factory farm is to churn out as many animals as the market can absorb at the lowest possible cost to the manufacturer. The sheer number of creatures involved in the vast assembly line-like process of rearing, herding, and slaughtering encourages thinking about them in abstract, impersonal terms: "units," "product," "commodities." This unsurprisingly fosters insensitivity to the suffering the process imposes on the animals—they become just so much raw material—and this insensitivity is in turn legitimized by the industry as good business sense. In a widely quoted article from the trade journal *Hog Farm Management*, the author offers advice to pig farmers that parallels advice given in other venues to cattle and chicken farmers: "Forget the pig is an animal. Treat him just like a machine in a factory. Schedule treatments like you would lubrication. Breeding season like the first step in an assembly line. And marketing like the delivery of finished goods"[9] (Gruzalski 2004, p. 127).

Chickens

These days, the hottest commodity manufactured by factory farms is chicken. It's America's favorite meat, and also the one with the cheapest price tag. (As we'll see in Chapter 6, however, the hidden costs to the environment associated with factory farming ratchet up the real cost of chicken into the billions of dollars.) In the United States, eight to ten billion chickens are raised and slaughtered each year (at least 150 million per week) to feed poultry-hungry consumers, and 99 percent of them are factory farmed. To appreciate the enormity of the killing, it's helpful to keep in mind that the earth's entire human population topped seven billion in late 2011. The chickens, or "broilers" as they're called in the trade, have a lifespan of about a month and a half. Brought as chicks to the long sheds in which they'll spend the bulk of their life, their beaks are typically cauterized, a process that involves snipping off and searing the upper part of the beak on arrival. Because the beak of a chicken is its primary point of tactile contact with the world, it's loaded with sensors and nerves that make the cauterization a terribly painful procedure.

Beak cauterization is bad news for chicks, but it makes good business sense if the goal is to maximize unit output. A typical chicken shed or house is long and narrow, around 500 by 50 feet, and holds some 30,000 chicks. As they grow into adult birds, the space becomes so cramped that each bird-unit is confined by the sheer weight of bodies to a space roughly the size of an 8.5 by

11 inch sheet of paper—this for a creature that needs 74 inches just to stand, nearly 200 square inches to turn around, and 133 square inches just to scratch the ground while standing in place. Like most other animals, chickens become testy and aggressive when confined with others in close quarters. Beak-trimming minimizes wounds from the inevitable fighting the cramped conditions encourage.

The crowding of huge numbers of birds into small spaces also creates a suffocating ammonia-filled, dust and dry feces-laden, and oxygen-deficient atmosphere that the chickens breathe day in and day out. The ground on which they stand and sleep likewise becomes toxic with uric acid from their droppings, burning their feet, bottoms, and breasts. This in turn encourages staph infections which factory farmers try to keep under control by loading the chicken feed with antibiotics. The ammonia in the air causes conjunctivitis, an extremely painful malady that blinds many of the birds and makes then easy targets of competitors for food and space.

The diseased and filthy conditions endured by factory-farmed chickens are even harder to endure for today's biologically engineered birds. The American consumer of poultry favors breast meat. So through selective breeding and hefty doses of growth-stimulating hormones, broilers today have chests several times larger than their ancestors of only a few years ago. This artificially induced obesity adds more white meat to the birds, but at a terrible cost to them. Their skeletons and legs simply can't support the added weight. They develop arthritis in their leg and wing joints, or their legs snap from the extra load they're carrying. Even those birds who somehow manage to carry the weight are especially susceptible to infected ulcers because they stand closer to the moist, feces-covered floors. Heart failure and heart attacks induced from the strain of obesity are common.

Egg batteries

Ninety-eight percent of all egg-laying hens in the United States— some 250 million of them—are units in factory farms the industry calls "batteries," a term which is appropriately though unintentionally descriptive. Like broiler sheds, egg batteries hold thousands of birds in a toxic atmosphere of ammonia, dust, and feces. But the conditions endured by the hens are even more severe than those which broilers suffer. Instead of roaming as best they can on an open floor, battery hens are confined in mesh wire cages stacked on top of one another three or four tiers high. The tier system allows for the confinement of huge numbers of birds—sometimes upwards of 80,000—in a single house. Eight or nine hens are crammed into a single cage, giving each of them even less personal space than broilers have. Like broilers, the hens have their upper beaks seared off to cut down on lethal attacks.

If the broiler is seen by factory farmers as simply a meat unit, the battery hen is viewed as nothing more than an egg producer. Her job is to manufacture eggs as rapidly as possible. In a mechanical factory, care is taken not to overwork the machinery because it's expensive to replace. But hens, the machinery of a battery, are plentiful and cheap. So it's in the interest of the factory owner to work them at full throttle until they wear out and then replace them with fresh birds.

Like their broiler cousins, hens are fed massive amounts of antibiotics and hormones, the first to keep them from succumbing too quickly to their horrendous living conditions and the second to stimulate egg production. Artificial lighting floods the batteries, mimicking daylight, to encourage laying. When the hens wear themselves out after about a year, they're starved for a couple of weeks so that they'll molt, tricking their bodies into a new laying cycle. Most birds last less than a year after that, at which point they're slaughtered and generally wind up in domestic pet food as well as in cattle, pork, and even poultry feed. Once it becomes clear that a hen is no longer capable of laying and so fit only for the slaughterhouse, she's no longer fed. The rationale is that there's no sense in wasting food and drink on an animal headed for the knacker's. About 500 million exhausted battery hens are slaughtered annually in the United States.

One of the reasons hens wear out so quickly under a battery's artificially accelerated laying cycle is that calcium rich minerals which otherwise would build up their bone density get diverted to the creation of egg shells. Like broilers, but for different reasons, battery hens are often unable to support their own weight. To exacerbate matters, the wire cages in which they're confined tend to deform their claws, making it painful for them to stand. The legs, wings, and necks of birds get caught in the cage mesh, often preventing them from reaching water or food and making them easy targets for other birds with whom they share the cage.

The filth of a typical hen battery is shocking. Because the cages are stacked, birds in the lower tiers endure the droppings of birds in upper ones. The battery floor is thick with bird manure as well as the corpses of hens who have been removed from their cages and tossed for the sake of convenience into the excrement. The filth as well as the heat (often 80°F) from the close confinement of tens of thousands of birds breeds a rash of infectious ailments. Revealingly, the only one that the public tends to notice is *Salmonella*, which of course poses a risk to the consumer since it's passed on in eggs. The diseases spawned by their foul environment that affect only the hens go largely unpublicized.[10]

Beef cattle

Although beef has been replaced by chicken as America's favorite meat, huge quantities of it—at a cost of 36 to 40 million cattle annually—are still consumed. Nearly all of them are factory farmed.

Beef cattle are generally raised on grazing land with their mothers until they're around 6 months old. As calves, they're branded (often on the face until 1995, when the practice was outlawed), castrated (if male) to reduce aggression and encourage bulk, and dehorned. All three procedures are terrifying and painful for the young animals. Shortly after they're weaned, the calves are sold and shipped to a commercial feed lot where tens of thousands of cattle are housed in a tightly confined area. The sheer number of animals milling about in the limited space guarantees that the ground within the feed lot is grassless and slick with feces and urine. The environment is as unnatural for cattle as broiler and battery sheds are for chickens.

The sole purpose of a feed lot is to fatten up cattle; the more weight per unit, the more profit—but only if the cost of adding the weight can be minimized. So cattle are fed large amounts of corn that quickly adds bulk and marbles their meat with fat, a combination pleasing to the palates of many beef-eaters. Because of generous governmental subsidies to corn growers, heavily lobbied for by the beef industry, corn is grown in abundance and so is an extraordinarily inexpensive feed. Steroids are added to cattle feed to accelerate growth, and a cocktail of antibiotics are mixed in to offset the illnesses bred by the close and filthy quarters.

Corn is an unnatural diet for cattle. Cows are ruminant creatures biologically hardwired to live on grasses. Corn is difficult
for them to digest, resulting in chronic diarrhea, and a diet of
it also encourages the growth of *E. coli* (despite the antibiotics
pumped into them) in the cows' stomachs which a grass diet
largely inhibits. As we'll see in Chapter 7, much of the beef that
consumers purchase in super markets is tainted to one degree or
another by *E. coli*-laced excrement that befouls carcasses during
the slaughter process. And speaking of slaughterhouses, operators of factory farm feed lots, striving for the quickest possible
turnover of their product, often supplement the corn diet with
slaughterhouse leftovers such as beef blood, pork and poultry
parts, fat, and gelatin. An even cheaper bulk builder mixed into
cattle feed is chicken litter, which contains not only bits of dead
birds and ammonia-saturated sawdust, but also huge quantities
of feces. About a million tons of the stuff is fed to cattle each year.
The beef loved by American consumers comes from cows which,
on average, have each eaten nearly 70 pounds of chicken manure
during their miserable lifetimes.

Veal calves and dairy cows

Thanks largely to public outcry, the consumption of veal has
dropped in the United States from nearly three pounds per person
annually in 1975 to barely half a pound a generation later. But
800,000 to 1,000,000 calves are still turned into veal each year
under conditions that, by most people's standards, are unacceptable. Veal calves are always males, taken from their mothers shortly
after birth and raised for the next four months in bare wooden or
plastic crates too narrow for much movement. The recommended
stall dimensions are 2 × 5 feet. Their tiny size is intentional, since
lack of exercise reduces the amount of muscle the calf is able to
grow, thereby keeping its meat tender. His feed is a liquid formula
of dry milk products such as whey heavily laced with sugar, starch,
and antibiotics, a diet intended to induce anemia in the calf so that
his meat has the pale pink shade prized by veal-lovers. The calf
often has neither hay nor straw for his bedding, lest he grazes on it
and coarsens his flesh. Instead, if he's given bedding at all, it's likely
to be something like shredded newspaper. But there's a risk that
he'll eat even that, starved as he is for iron and salts. Veal calves

are systematically deprived of any food which contains iron, lest the mineral reddens their meat. For the same reason, their crates are never made of metal, because the anemic calves, in their iron-hunger, will obsessively lick them.

Most veal calves come from dairy factory farms, which of course have little use for males born to their cow herds. Today's dairy cow has been selectively bred to produce three times more milk than a dairy cow gave a half century ago. But even this hardwired increase of milk output isn't enough for the factory system, so dairy cows are regularly injected with bovine somatotrophin, or BST, an artificial hormone that accelerates milk production. BST is outlawed in Europe and Canada because it encourages mastitis, a painful udder infection. In the United States, 20 percent of factory-farmed dairy cows suffer from it at any given time.

Because the sole purpose of cows on dairy farms is to produce units of milk, and because milk production in a cow declines shortly after she gives birth, dairy cattle are artificially inseminated on a regular basis, with only a two or three month resting period between pregnancies. The unnatural rate of births forced on dairy cows quickly wears them out. The average lifespan of a milk cow should be about 20 years. Factory-farmed dairy cows are lucky to see five before they're packed off to the slaughterhouse.

When most of us think of dairy cows, we have images of green pastures spotted with gently grazing black and white Holsteins or soft brown Guernseys. But the reality is that in the United States, three fourths of today's milk comes from cows that have never grazed in meadowlands and typically spend their entire adult lives in feed lots and milking stalls. Confined enclosures make them easier to feed and milk—and also to douse with antibiotics, BST, and, apparently, insecticides. A 2004 study (Pike) discovered that 13 percent of lactating cows are given daily pesticide coat sprays. Some of those chemicals leach into the creatures' fat, wind up in their milk, and eventually making their way to us and our children.

Pork

Over 100 million hogs are slaughtered each year in the United States. Almost all of them are raised in factory farms, housed in pig sheds that hold thousands of the creatures in cramped and filthy quarters. Pig sheds generally have concrete slatted floors to facilitate hosing feces down between the slats into a collection pit. The procedure not only keeps the pig manure moist and malodorous, but also washes away straw bedding in the stalls, leaving the hogs nothing to lie or walk on but hard and often wet concrete. They regularly develop infected hoofs and skin abrasions, and the thick clouds of ammonia and urea that rise from the pits cause the hogs respiratory distress. Upwards of 70 percent of them suffer from pneumonia by the time they're slaughtered.

From the standpoint of the factory farm operators, the smaller the hog stalls, the better. Small stalls mean that more animals can be crammed into a single pig shed. But just as importantly, their size prohibits the animals from moving around too much. A sedentary hog is more likely to accumulate weight than an active one, and weight is the bottom line when it comes to pork units.

Even more restricted in their ability to move than the hogs that will be butchered for their meat are the breeding sows whose sole purpose is to birth piglets. There are slightly more than one million of them in the hog industry, and 80 percent of them spend most of their lives in quarters so narrow that there's no room for them to turn around. Artificially inseminated over and over, pregnant sows are kept in so-called gestation crates until they're ready to birth. Then they're moved to farrowing crates, which are constructed so narrowly that the sow has no choice but to lie at an angle which constantly exposes her teats to the piglets. She remains in this relatively immobile position until the piglets are taken away from her, at which point she's returned to a gestation crate and artificially inseminated again. The European Union, whose citizens consume twice as much pork as the United States, has banned sow crates.[11] But so far the powerful pork lobby in America has managed to keep them legal and in use.[12]

Fish

A largely overlooked type of factory farm is the burgeoning aquaculture industry. The global consumption of aquatic animals is enormous, accounting for 16 percent of the animal protein humans ingest each year. The annual worldwide kill rate most likely exceeds 100 billion tons, with the United States alone accounting for 17 billion tons. The numbers are truly mind boggling.

The world's gargantuan appetite for seafood has resulted in serious depletion of fishing stocks throughout the world's oceans and seas. Wild Atlantic salmon and cod, for example, have been commercially fished to the point of near extinction. This shortage in turn has inspired the creation of fish farms where domestic salmon, cod, catfish, trout, and other fish species are bred, raised, and harvested. One-third of the fish eaten in the United States now comes from factory farms.

The methods of factory-farming fish are similar to those used in the industrial production of any food animal. The fish are typically confined in places too small for their numbers, either shallow cement troughs or underwater cages and nets in lakes and oceans. The overcrowding encourages aggression on their part as well as parasitic infestations that not only spread quickly throughout the population but also, in the case of cages sunk in oceans and other large bodies of water, migrate to infect wild fish.

One of the reasons fish is so popular in the United States may be the desire of many consumers to eat more compassionately. Fish, they believe, are either incapable of suffering, or at any rate are much less susceptible to pain than mammals. But research has shown that rainbow trout, for example, display "profound behavioral and physiological changes . . . comparable to those observed in higher mammals" when they're exposed to painful stimuli (Singer and Mason 2006, p. 131). Moreover, their pained behavior ceases when they're given morphine. It may be that fish feel pain less acutely than mammals or birds. But there's no good reason to suppose they're impervious to it.

Slaughter

If they survive the horrid conditions in which they spend most of their lives, factory-farmed animals wind up at the same grim destination: the industrial slaughterhouse, which typically kills, dismembers, and dresses thousands of beasts each working day. The intensely frightened, panicked, and pained behavior they display both in transit and upon arrival is further testimony that the animals we eat are all too capable of mental and physical suffering.

Once in the slaughterhouse, cattle and hogs are driven with electric prods along a chute that takes them into a stall known as

the "knocking box." There, the creatures are shot in the forehead
with a compressed air gun that drives a retractable steel bolt into
their brains. The theory is that the shot should kill the animal. But
because of the rapid pace of animals arriving at the knocking box,
the person manipulating the gun—the "knocker"—frequently suc-
ceeds only in stunning them. Consequently, when the fallen animal
is chained and winched by one of its hind legs to dangle headfirst in
midair—the next step on the slaughter assembly line—it frequently
regains consciousness and thrashes and shrieks until a worker
known as a "sticker" cuts its throat. After they bleed out and presumably are dead, cattle, often still twitching, are skinned and evis-
cerated. Hogs go into vats of boiling water to soften their bristles
for scraping. It's not uncommon for them to be thrown into the
water while still alive.

The United States Humane Slaughter Act of 1958 requires that
cattle and hogs be rendered unconscious before they're killed. But
there's no such requirement for poultry, who generally are dis-
patched by being hung upside down on quickly moving overhead
conveyor belts and having their throats cut by mechanical knives
as the birds whisk by. For efficiency's sake, the birds are frequently
stunned by running them through a constant-voltage water bath.
Such baths, particularly the ones used in American slaughterhouses,
have been criticized for not using sufficiently high voltage to effec-
tively stun the birds because doing so would damage their carcasses.
Consequently, many of the chickens regain consciousness before
they reach the killing blade.

The slaughter of fish, which is totally unregulated by legislation,
is even more brutal. Most often, harvested fish are pulled out of
water to be thrown onto piles of ice where they suffocate to death, a
process which, depending on the species, takes up to a quarter of an
hour. Salmon and other large fish are frequently beaten with wooden
bats or cut open and gutted while still alive and flapping.[13]

Bridging the moral gap

There's no shortage of easily accessible descriptions of what goes
on in factory farms and slaughterhouses. (Bernstein 2004; Davis
1996; Eisnitz 1997; Lyman 2001; Marcus 2001; Mason and Finelli
2006; Mason and Singer 1990; Pollan 2007; Rifkin 1992; Robbins

2011; Scully 2002; Singer and Mason, 2006; Walsh 2009, 2011) Yet, as Wes Jamison notes in the epigraph to this chapter, the average consumer's understanding of where his or her meat comes from is pretty spotty. Part of the reason for this, as we've already seen, is clever marketing that keeps the factory farming system out of consumer sight. Part of it is also doubtlessly attributable to the fact that many Americans, especially these days, are working so hard to support their families that they have little time or energy left over to think about their food. Finally, it's also reasonable to presume that part of our ignorance is willful.[14] Many of us are at least vaguely aware of the suffering our gustatory preferences inflict on animals, but choose not to learn more lest we be discommoded in one way or another.

Regardless of the reasons, the animals whom we eat have become largely invisible to us. Their lives are so disconnected from ours that we sense little or no kinship to them. As author Michael Pollan notes,

Except for our pets, real animals—animals living and dying—no longer figure in our everyday lives. Meat comes from the grocery store, where it is cut and packaged to look as little like parts of animals as possible. The disappearance of animals from our lives has opened a space in which there's no reality check, either on the sentiment or the brutality. This is pretty much where we live now, with respect to animals. (Pollan 2002a)

Like Pollan, vegetarians worry that the "disappearance of animals from our lives" encourages a sentimentality which causes us to weep over the fate of Bambi but remain callous to the suffering of real animals (including deer) who eventually wind up on our plates. That animals experience pain is a claim no reasonable person can dismiss, clever philosophical denials notwithstanding. That the current method of meeting consumer demands for meat inflicts untold suffering upon beasts is also indisputable. Vegetarians argue that what's needed to bridge the open space or gap between perception and reality when it comes to our treatment of animals is moral sensitivity to their suffering, a living awareness of our complicity in it, and a firm resolve to do something about it. The next four chapters will explore arguments for vegetarianism that focus squarely on building that bridge.

CHAPTER TWO

The basic argument

*[Sympathy] is just a gracious thing, an act of clemency only more
to our credit because the animals themselves cannot ask for it,
or rebuke us when we transgress against them, or even repay our
kindness.*

MATTHEW SCULLY

*I'm truly sorry Man's dominion
Has broken Nature's social union,
An' justifies that ill opinion,
Which makes thee startle,
At me, thy poor, earth-born companion,
An' fellow-mortal!*

ROBERT BURNS, "TO A MOUSE"

If Michael Pollan is correct, the disappearance of animals from our
lives distances us from awareness of the suffering they endure in
factory farms and slaughterhouses. This physical distancing is conceptually reinforced by the traditional Western view that beasts are
inferior and hence properly subordinate to humans. We saw in the
last chapter that one of the fruits of this way of thinking was the
utterly implausible belief, defended by Descartes and a handful of
contemporary philosophers, that beasts are organic automata incapable of such mental states as pain. Most meat-eaters have probably
never read Descartes. But because fewer and fewer of us have contact with the actual animals we eat, instead buying and consuming

nicely packaged and anonymous slabs of meat, we may be just as prone as he was to think of them as things or objects rather than subjects. An animal, unlike a human, is an "it," and this way of thinking makes the "open space" between us very wide indeed.

But the open space isn't an inevitability. We can become aware of the connection between the meat we eat and the breathing, feeling, and concretely particular animal from which it was taken. When that happens, the gap closes. We can no longer objectify creatures as mere its, thereby distancing ourselves from them, because we have been sensitized—discomfortingly so—to the suffering they endure for the sake of our palates.

For feminist vegetarian Carol Adams, the gap closed when she was still a teenager. A favorite horse of hers had suddenly died, and she was devastated. Sitting down to a hamburger meal the same day, she was suddenly overwhelmed with the realization that the meat before her had once been a cow every bit as vibrantly alive as her beloved horse (Adams 1993a). Author Alice Walker also remembers the moment in her life when the gap closed for her. She and a few friends were passionately discussing "freedom and jus-tice" over a steak dinner. Walker realized with a sudden and deep rush of shame that she was "eating misery," and that the very act of meat-eating was incongruous with her political and ethical ideals (Walker 1988, p. 8). The nineteenth-century French poet Alphonse de Lamartine recalled a similar moment of insight when he was taken as a child to a slaughterhouse. "I saw some men, their arms naked and besmeared with blood, knocking a bull in the head; oth-ers cutting the throats of calves and sheep, and separating their still heaving limbs." The sight of such cruelty instilled in him a "repug-nance . . . to cooked flesh."[1]

Ethicist and vegetarian Tom Regan, who has devoted his adult life to bridging the moral gap between animals and humans, is no stranger to the often cruel ways humans objectify animals and thereby render them invisible. But even he was shocked to the core while watching a documentary which featured a segment about a restaurant in China where patrons select live dogs and cats they wish to eat in the same way that Americans select live lobsters and fish at seafood restaurants. In the documentary, a patron makes her choice, a fluffy white cat, after scrutinizing several caged feline can-didates. The cook, followed by the camera man, takes the animal back to the kitchen.

While the cat claws and screeches, the cook hits her several times with an iron bar. Clawing and screeching more now, she is abruptly submerged in a tub of scalding water for about ten seconds. Once removed, and while still alive, the cook skins her, from head to tail, in one swift pull. He then throws the traumatized animal into a large stone vat [filled with water] where . . . we watch her gulp slowly, with increasing difficulty, her eyes glazed, until—her last breath taken—she drowns. The whole episode, from selection to final breath, takes several minutes. (Regan 2004b, p. 1)

Regan's reaction was intense and predictable. "I have never been more stunned in my life. I was literally speechless . . . Watching the awful shock and suffering of the cat was devastating. I felt a mix of disbelief and anger welling up in my chest. I wanted to shout, 'Stop it!' "[2]

Witnessed instances of cruelty to animals and even second-hand reports—who among us isn't at least a little disturbed by de Lamartine's and Regan's stories?—can shock us into a shift in our awareness of animals. So can "aha!" moments of recognition such as Adams' insight that the meat on her plate was taken from an animal not unlike her beloved pet, or Walker's sudden realization that anger at cruelty to people ought to extend to cruelty to animals as well. These sorts of experiences invite (or compel) us to view animals and our relationship to them from a different perspective. Instead of being relegated to the periphery of our moral awareness as vaguely machine-like anonymities that supply us with hamburgers and chicken nuggets, food animals get seen as concretely particular creatures who, like us, have the capacity to suffer mightily. And with this new awareness comes the realization that contributing to their unnecessary suffering is an act of indecency which properly ought to repulse us. This moral revulsion at needlessly hurting animals is the driving force behind what's been called the "basic argument" for vegetarianism. All ethical defenses of vegetarianism which base their case on animal welfare, regardless of how much they differ from one another, embed and build on it. It's simply that fundamental. It or some variety of it is also what you're most likely to hear if you ask the average vegetarian why he or she abstains from meat. Critics of the argument contend, as we'll see, that it's too simple to be persuasive. But persuasive or not, it *is* pervasive.

The nuts and bolts

The basic argument's most succinct description comes from philosopher James Rachels (2004). He points out that the argument "is not tied to any particular theory about the nature of ethics," but instead rests upon a "simple principle" that "every decent person already accepts." The principle? "[I]t is wrong to cause pain unless there is a good enough reason" for doing so (pp. 71, 70, 71). Not all infliction of pain, Rachels reminds us, is morally illegitimate or indecent. Inoculating a reluctant child or obliging a high school student to study for an exam instead of watching television are examples of actions which may cause immediate pain but carry no moral onus because they're directed towards a good end. But causing pain when there's no good reason for it is condemnable cruelty. Whether the cruelty is born from indifference to the suffering of another or sadistic enjoyment of another's suffering, it's something which every decent person finds morally reprehensible.

As we saw in the last chapter, the meat, eggs, and dairy products most of us in the Western world eat come from factory farms. In Rachels' view, factory-farmed animals not only suffer terribly—mistreatment of them, he says, is "one of the world's great causes of misery" (p. 79)—but they also suffer unnecessarily, because we humans can easily nourish ourselves with vegetable foods. Nor is the gustatory pleasure we derive from eating factory-farmed beasts a strong enough counterweight to morally neutralize the harm we do them. Whenever we eat food animals, we are complicit in the cruelty they endure in factory farms and slaughterhouses. Consequently, concludes Rachels, vegetarianism is a principled stand *for* moral decency and *against* the way food animals are typically treated. Put in its very simplest terms, the argument runs like this:

1 it is indecent to inflict or benefit from cruelty
2 factory-farmed animals are treated cruelly
3 most of our meat comes from factory farms
4 therefore, all things being equal, we ought to adopt a
   vegetarian diet.

Rachels believes that a selling point of the basic argument is its common sense approach. It not only steers wide of philosophical hairsplitting about whether animals are "persons" or capable of feeling pain, but also refrains from making "sweeping prohibitions" against meat-eating that fail to take particular circumstances and contexts into consideration (p. 79). It may be the case, for example, that not all organisms experience pain or feel it equally, suggesting that it might be morally acceptable to eat *some* animals but not others. Or the basic argument may well allow for the consumption of meat from cattle, chickens, and pork raised humanely on old-fashioned family farms (although these are increasingly far and few between). Finally, persons and societies without genuine access to vegetable foods can hardly be condemned for following a meat-based diet. "Becoming a vegetarian need not be regarded as an all-or-nothing proposition," concludes Rachels. "From a practical standpoint, it makes sense to focus first on the things that cause the most misery" (p. 79). And at the top of that list is factory farming. So according to the basic argument, abstention from factory-farmed animals is certainly a necessary, although perhaps not sufficient, moral response to the suffering of food animals. As Rachels (p. 75) says,

> [if] you are opposed to cruelty, you have reason not to participate in social practices that are brutal as they stand. As it stands, meat producers and consumers cooperate to maintain the unnecessary system of pig farms, feedlots, and slaughterhouses. Anyone who finds this system objectionable has reason not to help keep it going. The point would be quickly conceded if the victims were people. If a product—curtains, let's say—were being produced by a process that involved torturing humans, no one would dream of saying: "Of course I oppose using those methods, but that's no reason not to buy the product. After all, the curtains are very nice."

Kinship and sympathy

It's not unreasonable to ask why we should take seriously the basic argument's assertion that cruelty to animals is an act all decent people ought to reject. It won't do to appeal to abstract justifications based on rights and duties, because many people repulsed by cruelty to animals aren't at all convinced, as we'll see in Chapter 4, that animals are the sorts of creatures who properly possess rights. Besides, one of the basic argument's supposed benefits is that it isn't tied down to any specific ethical model. Condemnation of cruelty is a primary response. Ethical analyses that seek to justify it come later.

One way to make sense of our intuitive condemnation of cruelty to animals is the presumption of a kindred or shared bond between us and them. This is the move made by Adams, Walker, de Lamartine, and Regan. We know firsthand what it feels like to suffer; we're personally familiar with the way suffering erodes our well-being by tearing us down physically, emotionally, and psychologically. We infer that an analogue to the distress we feel when we experience pain is shared by at least some animals. So when we see them in distress we feel sympathy or empathetic concern for their plight. (Although there's a technical difference between the two, I follow convention by using "sympathy" and "empathetic concern" interchangeably.)

Most of us have no problem with acknowledging the appropriateness of *intra*-species sympathy. David Hume and other Enlightenment-era philosophers argued that kin sympathy is the foundation of morality. Hume famously asked, "Would any man, who is walking along, tread as willingly on another's gouty toes, whom he has no quarrel with, as on the hard flint and pavement?," and answered his own question by asserting that it's "impossible for such a creature as man to be totally indifferent to the well or ill-being of his fellow-creatures" (Hume 1960, p. 61). Defenders of the basic argument see no reason not to include most food animals in the category of "fellow-creatures" with whose well-being we're naturally concerned. The simple fact is that most of the creatures that we humans like to eat are susceptible to pain and suffering, just as we are. This shared capacity creates a kindred bond between us–not as strong a one as the one between humans, perhaps, but one that nevertheless cries to be taken seriously. If cruelty to humans is indecent because it diminishes well-being, cruelty to animals is indecent for the same reason. If I sympathize with other humans in distress because I recognize a kindred bond between them and me based, minimally, on our shared capacity for suffering, I ought likewise to sympathize with animals in distress for the same reason. If the decent thing to do is to alleviate unnecessary pain in humans, the same goes for animals—especially when we realize that food animals have done absolutely nothing to provoke human cruelty. It's difficult to sympathize with something for which I sense no kinship. I may well regret the destruction of a beautiful painting or the strip-mined devastation of a once majestic mountaintop. I may sincerely grieve for their loss. But if I say that I sympathize with the damaged painting or the mutilated mountain, I'm speaking metaphorically. Paintings and mountains can be harmed. But, unlike me, they can't experience pain and suffering. It's impossible to feel genuine kin sympathy for them, and to claim to do so is to misunderstand the term's meaning.

Food animals are a different story. Unless we've conceptually (and falsely) transformed them into Cartesian automata or physically banished them to unseen and unheard of factory farms, we sense kinship with them and feel sympathy for their pain. Philosopher Brian Luke thinks the biological and social bond between humans and animals is so primal that it haunts human consciousness. Our social and personal efforts to deny it only attest to its existence. "Enormous amounts of social energy are expended to forestall, undermine, and override our sympathies for animals," he observes, "so that vivisection, animal farming, and hunting can continue" (Luke 2007, p. 136). J. Baird Callicott stops short of arguing for a primal connection. But he does believe that domesticated animals and humans are closely bound by an "evolved and unspoken social contract" (Callicott 1989, p. 56).

The notion that humans and animals are kindred and hence morally connected by bonds of sympathy, although a minority opinion in the West, nonetheless has a long pedigree. The ancient philosophers Pythagoras and Empedocles recommended vegetarianism to their followers partly because they advocated simple lifestyles, but also because they believed in the transmigration or reincarnation of souls. To eat an animal, warned Pythagoras, ran the risk of literally devouring the life-force of a dead mother, father, or sibling. For him, kinship between humans and animals wasn't an abstract biological or evolutionary claim. It was intensely personal (Pythagoras 1999).

In the nineteenth century, philosopher Arthur Schopenhauer and composer Richard Wagner (who was heavily influenced by Schopenhauer) each defended the idea of moral sympathy for animals

based on a recognition of inter-species kinship. Schopenhauer condemned any morality that reduced animals to "mere things" good
only for "vivisection, hunting, coursing, bullfights, and horse rac-
ing, [or pulling] heavy carts of stone" (Schopenhauer 1998, p. 96).
A genuine morality, he insisted, must be grounded on kin sympathy with all creatures—including animals—capable of pain and
pleasure. To feel sympathy for another's misfortune is "in some
way [to be] identified with him." Sympathy erodes "the difference
between me and everyone else . . . [T]he very basis of my egoism is
eliminated"[3] (p. 144).

Wagner agreed with Schopenhauer about the ethical importance
of kin sympathy for animals, but took it a step further. He argued
that feeling sympathy for the suffering just of fellow humans, while
good so far as it went, too narrowed the scope of moral concern.
"The more insignificant the being with which I can [sympatheti-
cally] suffer," he declared, "the wider and more embracing is the
circle which suggests itself to my feelings" (Wagner 1999, p. 94).
Wagner even claimed that he found it harder to sympathize with
suffering humans than with suffering animals. "The latter," he
wrote, "are totally denied the capacity to rise above suffering, and
to achieve a state of resignation and deep, divine calm" (p. 95). They
lack human defense mechanisms such as rationalization, repression,
and hope to lighten their burden of suffering.

In our own day, the notion that kin sympathy is a fundamental
motivation to refrain from inflicting cruelty on animals has especially influenced ecofeminist vegetarians, who tend to talk about care
rather than sympathy. We'll explore their arguments in Chapter 5.
For now, mention ought to be made of two contemporary thinkers
who offer defenses of food animals that have similarities to both the
basic argument's kin sympathy and ecofeminist care: the philosopher Jacques Derrida and the novelist J. M. Coetzee.

In a remarkable reflection that was prompted, he tells us, by the
experience of being gazed at by his cat, Derrida concedes that the
exact nature of animal consciousness is a puzzle. In thinking about
how to understand it, "we are not standing on the rock of indubitable certainty" (Derrida 2008, p. 122). But the phenomenon of
animal suffering is different. As opposed to questions about what
animal consciousness might be, "the question 'can they suffer?'
leaves no doubt. In fact, it has never left any room for doubt." Of

course animals suffer, as plainly demonstrated by their behavior. Their suffering is so self-evident, in fact, that it's even too weak to call our knowledge of it "indubitable." "[I]t precedes the indubitable," contends Derrida. "[I]t is older than it." Similarly, and herein lies the common ground between Derrida and the basic argument, there is "no doubt either, then, for the possibility of our giving vent to a surge of compassion, even if it is then misunderstood, repressed, or denied." Our sympathetic response to the sight of animal suffering is as "undeniable" as the suffering itself. The latter elicits the former in a prereflective, first-order way which pushes aside any lingering remnants of the artificial Cartesian divide between humans and beasts. The relationship between humans and animals, says Derrida, is revealed to be at one and the same time "close and abyssal" (p. 124), suggesting that even though there are distinct and insurmountable differences, there is also a kinship that allows for sympathy or "compassion." Derrida's preindubitable response of sympathy or compassion is a necessary condition for the decent treatment of animals.

Coetzee agrees that humans and animals are close in some respects and abyssally different in others. Some philosophers emphasize the differences by choosing to focus on those qualities in animals that make them seem distantly alien to us. For example, animal subjectivity—what it actually *feels* like to be an animal—will likely remain a closed book to us forever. In Thomas Nagel's (1974) memorable phrase, we may never know what it's like to be a bat. But what we *can* connect with in animals is their suffering, and we do so, says Coetzee, through "a faculty, sympathy, that allows us to share at times the being of another. Sympathy has everything to do with the subject and little to do with the object, the 'another'" (Coetzee 1999, pp. 33–4). We can look *at* animals with clinical detachment, seeing them as its, or we can look *into* them as subjects, discerning, through kin sympathy, the suffering they endure. The "sympathetic imagination" which allows us to do the latter, states Coetzee, is boundless. "[T]here is no limit to the extent to which we can think ourselves into the being of another" (p. 35). This probably goes too far. But it doesn't diminish Coetzee's normative conclusion: sympathetically putting oneself in the place of suffering animals, which we're able to do by virtue of our kinship to them, discourages cruelty and encourages decency.

Is the basic argument *too* basic?

The basic argument for vegetarianism is appealingly spartan. It rests on the fundamental principle that the infliction of cruelty is indecent because it diminishes the well-being of the victim by inflicting gratuitous pain and suffering on him or her. Taken by itself, this principle accounts for why I personally might object to being treated cruelly, but not necessarily for why I find cruelty to others, humans as well as animals, repugnant. The notion of kin sympathy, which posits a bond between similar beings that enables them to feel empathic concern for one another's distress, does. If Derrida is correct in claiming that a compassionate response to suffering is prereflective, kin sympathy precedes (and grounds) second-order ethical reflection.

But not everyone is convinced that the basic argument is a good enough justification for vegetarianism, nor that kin sympathy is sufficient or even necessary for the ethical treatment of humans, much less animals. Obviously nonvegetarians disagree with the basic argument. But even many vegetarians who accept its core principle, that cruelty is wrong, believe that the argument, as it stands, leaves too many questions unanswered.

Underdetermined

One criticism of the basic argument is that its case is underdetermined because the mere presence of kinship, whether biological or social, doesn't guarantee sympathy with the suffering of others. Moreover, even if it does, this doesn't guarantee compassionate behavior towards them. Experience demonstrates that it's entirely possible (1) to feel no sympathetic bond with kin, (2) to sympathize with nonkin, (3) to act decently to those for whom we feel no sympathy, and (4) to act indecently to those for whom we do feel sympathy. If this is the case, then kin sympathy is a less-than-firm foundation on which to ground the principle that moral decency entails inflicting no unnecessary suffering. The weak link here could well be that the notion of kinship is too vague, and that the further out one moves from immediate blood ties and intraspecific ones, the more contestable it becomes.

A like-minded objection comes from the same Tom Regan who was so shocked by the video of the torture and killing of a cat. Obviously, Regan feels a great deal of sympathy with the suffering of animals, and would affirm that indifference to their cruel treatment is a sign of moral weakness. But he worries that sympathy isn't enough to guarantee morally decent behavior or to ground a compelling defense of vegetarianism. Kin-based compassion or kindness *is* important in the moral life. But

> there is no guarantee that a kind act is a right act. If I am a generous racist, for example, I will be inclined to act kindly towards members of my own race, favoring their interests above all others. My kindness would be real and, so far as it goes, good. But I trust it is too obvious to require argument that my kind acts may not be above moral reproach—may, in fact, be positively wrong because rooted in injustice. So kindness, notwithstanding its status as a virtue, simply will not carry the weight of a theory of right action. (Regan 1985, p. 18)

As we'll see in Chapter 5, Regan and others level similar criticisms against the care-based vegetarianism defended by ecofeminists.

Anthropocentric

The presumption that underlies the basic argument is that suffering in some animals, especially many of the ones we eat, is like (even if not identical to) the suffering that humans experience. This accounts for the kinship we sense between ourselves and animals as well as our sympathy for their pain. Because we believe their suffering is analogous to ours, we find it just as indecent to inflict unnecessary suffering or cruelty on them as to inflict it on fellow humans.

Feminist vegetarian Carol Adams objects to this move because she believes its appeal to a human standard to measure animal suffering tends to submerge the latter in the former. She fears that the message that comes across, even if unintentionally, is that animal suffering is worthy of our moral attention not in its own right but only because it resembles human suffering. When we compare factory farms and slaughterhouses to Nazi death camps, for example, the same thing happens to animal suffering that happens to women's suffering "when a heroic notion of men's suffering prevails": it disappears. And this, says Adams, "is anthropocentric. Why not talk about the way animals—including us—suffer? Instead of saying, 'animals' suffering is like human's,' relying on metaphors, why not say animal suffering in their body is theirs?" (Adams 2007a, p. 212). Although ecofeminist defenses of vegetarianism share some common features with the basic argument's sympathetic concern for animals, this charge of anthropocentrism puts a good deal of distance between the two. As will become clear in Chapter 5, it's the foundation for the analysis of dualism and hierarchy that distinguishes the ecofeminist from other defenses of vegetarianism.

The gustatory objection

While the charge that the basic argument is underdetermined can be leveled by both vegetarians and nonvegetarians, the criticism from anthropocentricity is likely to be made mostly by vegetarians. But there's another objection based on gustatory grounds made only by nonvegetarians. It's one of the most common objections to all defenses of vegetarianism, but the basic argument is especially susceptible because of its refusal to rule out the possibility of eating animals under certain conditions.

Animal flesh, so the objection runs, tastes good. It brings pleasure to those humans who eat it, and to be deprived of it is a sacrifice that would diminish their well-being. We surely enjoy a closer kinship bond to other humans than we do to animals. Consequently, our empathetic concern for the welfare of humans properly outweighs our sympathy with any animals who suffer for our gustatory pleasure. It would be heartless and wrong to inflict unnecessary pain on them; the basic argument is right about that. The best of all possible worlds is one in which food animals live pleasant lives and then are slaughtered without causing them mental or physical pain. But given the huge demand for meat, this just isn't possible. Factory farms and industrial slaughterhouses are necessities, and so the suffering they inflict is also necessary. Consequently, there's nothing indecent about eating animals, even though one wishes there were less inhumane ways to go about it, because the suffering imposed by factory farms is necessary, not gratuitous.

Several responses to this objection may be made. The first is that it's strangely inconsistent to feel sympathy for the suffering of animals yet continue to contribute to it by eating them, especially if we don't need their meat to survive. The poet Oliver Goldsmith nicely expressed the unsettling nature of this position by writing of meat-eaters that "they pity, and they eat the objects of their compassion!" (Goldsmith 1999, p. 62). It should be noticed, however, that while Goldsmith's objection oughtn't to be ignored, it's not necessarily a fatal blow. As we've seen, a defender of the gustatory argument can respond that sympathy for humans (including their gustatory preferences) properly outweighs sympathy for animals (including their loss of life).

There are, however, stronger responses. As philosopher Mark Rowlands (2009, p. 82) points out, "no one has a right to eat something just because they happen to find it tasty. If I happen to find [human] babies good to eat, it does not mean that I have the right to eat them."[4] This is because what's at stake, the suffering and death of a living creature, surely carries more moral weight than the mere satisfaction of a dietary preference. Other tasty foods that don't involve the sacrifice of well-being or life, even though the well-being and life in question belongs to "only" an animal, can be found to please the palate.

But what if they can't? What if some or perhaps even all meat-eating humans simply can't find adequate meat substitutes and as a result experience real gustatory distress? Even then, it may be argued, it's not necessary to subject animals to suffering. Meat-craving palates are perfectly free to eat the flesh of road-kill or animals who have died naturally. Stephen R. L. Clark (1999, p. 205) offers an additional suggestion. "It would seem a simple solution both to our flesh-craving and to the increasing storage problem to cook the [human] victims of automobile accidents"—a different kind of road-kill, as it were. Traditionally religion-based objections to utilizing human corpses as sources of transplantable organs or in scientific research have softened. So why should we object to using dead humans as food, especially since their flesh, by the time it wound up in a supermarket, would be as anonymously and unoffensively packaged as animal flesh? It seems a reasonable enough way to address the meat-eater's craving.

Clark's suggestion is only partly tongue-in-cheek. His recommendation of human flesh as a substitute for animal flesh gestures at a larger and crucial point. A defender of the gustatory objection to vegetarianism is likely to contend that the basic argument only prohibits the infliction of "unnecessary" suffering upon animals, but that his meat-craving is such a strong and permanent part of who he is that the suffering animals endure to satisfy it is very necessary indeed. Consequently, as we've seen, although their pain may be unfortunate, it can't really be considered cruel.

Clark's response is that "necessary" and "unnecessary" are conveniently moveable categories for the meat-eater. Much like Carol Adams's claim that animal suffering is too often taken seriously only because it resembles human suffering, Clark argues that the parameters of "necessary" suffering when it comes to animals are nearly always calibrated to favor humans. But, he says (p. 205), "[i]t is of little use claiming that it is wrong to inflict unnecessary suffering if anything at all will do as a context for calculating necessity." If meat-eaters are unwilling to eat human corpses, a move that would render the suffering of food animals completely unnecessary, then they are merely "pay[ing] lip service to the thesis that it is wrong to cause unnecessary suffering to an animal" (p. 204).

Killing animals allows them to live

The basic argument leaves open the possibility that eating animals raised on small farms is morally permissible, although some vegetarians may still object that taking the life of a cow, pig, sheep, or even chicken, howsoever "humanely," trespasses against the principle which forbids the infliction of unnecessary harm. Michael Pollan, not himself a vegetarian but someone who takes the basic argument's decency principle seriously, argues that if there *is* something like kin sympathy between humans and animals, it's the result of centuries of domestication (an opinion shared, as we've seen, by J. Baird Callicott). To his mind, the "characteristic form of life" for food animals has evolved into a relationship of "mutualism" or "bargain" with humans: we care for them and they in turn feed us with their eggs, milk, and flesh. Domesticated animals have fared much better as a result of this relationship than animals in the wild. So "from their point of view," Pollan concludes, "the bargain with humanity has been a great success"—or at least it was, he concedes, until the advent of factory farming (Pollan 2002a). Chef Hugh

Fearnley-Whittingstall agrees. Farm animals have evolved to be dependent on humans and we on them. They rely on us for their health, contentment, and well-being, and we rely on them for food—which of course means their death, if the food we're talking about is their flesh. But their "short, domesticated lives," Fearnley-Whittingstall contends, "are, on balance, better than no lives at all" (Fearnley-Whittingstall 2004, p. 12).

Pollan and Fearnley-Whittingstall agree that food animals should be treated as humanely as possible, and neither of them believe that factory farming allows for that. But there are other critics of the basic argument who are much less bothered about the quality or duration of a food animal's life. They point out that domesticated food animals would not be alive in the first place except for the human practice of eating them. So continuing to raise them for food is actually a kindness to them. When the eighteenth-century English man of letters Samuel Johnson remarked that the misery of animals is recompensed by their existence, he had the same intuition (Boswell 2008, p. 545). So did Leslie Stephen, the father of novelist Virginia Woolf, but he voiced it in less genteel terms than Johnson's. "Of all the arguments for vegetarianism," he wrote, "none is so weak as the argument from humanity [that is, humane treatment of animals]. The pig has a stronger interest than anyone in the demand for bacon. If all the world were Jewish, there would be no pigs at all" (Singer and Mason 2006, p. 251). Modern-day pig farmer James Cargile is of the same opinion. Although the animals he raises are destined for slaughter, he insists that "short lives are better than no life at all" (Cargile 1983, p. 249).

Others have endorsed this position with varying degrees of subtlety. Roger Crisp (2009) turns the basic argument on its head by affirming that a refusal to eat meat is actually a morally indecent violation of kin sympathy because a vegetarian diet deprives thousands of food animals the opportunity to live. Philosopher Roger Scruton (2004) offers a refreshingly thoughtful variety of the argument. When looked at from a moral perspective, he says, it can't be denied that "a great number of animals owe their lives to our intention to eat them. If we value animal life, therefore, we should endorse our carnivorous habits," provided that the animals we eat are raised humanely outside of factory farms. But Scruton goes on to say that there's another way, "from the point of view of religion," of approaching the issue which "poses a challenge" to the moral claim. "It is asking the burger-stuffer to come clean; to show just why it is that his greed should be indulged in this way, and just where he fits into the scheme of things, that he can presume to kill again and again for the sake of a solitary pleasure that creates and sustains no moral ties." Scruton's implied condemnation of putting the solitary pleasure of meat-eating over and above acts that "sustain no moral ties" sounds very much like the basic argument's appeal to decency and kin sympathy. What he calls a "religious" point of view could easily be seen as an expression of the principle not to inflict unnecessary suffering, especially if the suffering is imposed merely for gustatory pleasure. (We'll return to Scruton's argument in Chapter 7.)

There are several responses to the position that eating domesticated food animals is morally permissible or even obligatory on the grounds that it's a necessary condition for their very existence. Peter Singer and Jim Mason, for example, object to Pollan's use of contractual language to describe the relationship between food animals and humans. The ability to enter into a contract—that is, to enter into a mutually beneficial relationship with eyes wide open—is surely beyond the ability of animals. A chicken or a cow can't consciously strike a bargain with humans to "trade her eggs or milk, or even his or her flesh, for a year or two's food and protection from predators" (Singer and Mason 2006, p. 250). But the language of bargaining suggests that animals willingly contract with humans to be slain and eaten. It may take the edge off the guilt that comes from violating the primal bond that Brian Luke claims exists between humans and animals, but it does so only by an especially misleading anthropomorphism.

Another response is that there's something metaphysically strange about the claim that "offering" existence to an as yet unborn creature, human or animal, benefits the creature. There is, after all, no creature around to be benefited—or harmed, for that matter—until it actually comes into existence. So the argument that we do a service to food animals by bringing them into existence so that we can eat them needs a lot more unraveling before it can be taken seriously.

Even if we overlook this problem, it's not clear that the benefit of bringing food animals into existence, even when they're raised humanely, outweighs the trauma of the inevitable slaughter that awaits them. Bart Gruzalski argues that the killing of even nonfactory-farmed animals is a brutal interruption of natural lifespan.

[A]nimals raised on family farms are violently and unexpectedly killed in the prime of their lives. For example, the lifespan of a pig is between ten and twenty years, yet pigs killed for food are often slaughtered at six months of age and almost always before two years of age. Broiler chickens, which are always female, are killed at about seven weeks, although the lifespan of a chicken is about seven years. What happens to the baby male chicks? Because males are considered less tasty, the baby male chicks are killed within days of hatching. (Gruzalski 2004, p. 128)

Gruzalski's point is that it's morally indecent to deprive food animals of a full lifespan because doing so robs them of future enjoyment. Frederike Kaldewaij (2008) argues along similar lines, contending that killing animals prematurely deprives them of the goods that their future lives could provide. But these arguments can easily backfire. In the first place, it's no clearer how the absence of life harms a dead creature than a not-yet-born one. Second, if life is such a benefit that cutting it short is a misfortune, why not take seriously Pollan's and Cargile's assertion that some life for food animals is better than no life? Finally, it's not clear that killing an animal, if we can do so quickly and humanely (admittedly, a big "if"), is as distressful as inflicting it with protracted suffering. When humans face a premature death, a great deal of the turmoil they experience is their realization of lost future opportunities. But it's not at all obvious that food animals have a similar sort of ability to look toward the future and regret opportunities that will never come to fruition because of their premature deaths. If the only distress that an animal experiences at its death is fear of an unfamiliar event, depriving it of future opportunities means nothing to it.

A final response to the position that the killing and eating of animals is justifiable on the grounds that they receive a short period of life as recompense is to ask why mightn't the same "bargain" be struck with human infants and perhaps even toddlers? Why not breed and raise a certain percentage of humans for the explicit purpose of eating them while they're still too young to be aware of what's going on? It's arguable that an infant has even less self-awareness than a chicken, or that toddlers, at least up to a certain age, are more or less on the cognitive level of a cow or pig. If we raise them for food, treat them well while they live, and slaughter them humanely, we give them the gift of existence in exchange for their flesh. This seems perfectly analogous to the arguments offered by commentators like Stephens and Crisp. Most of us nevertheless blanch at the mere suggestion. But as we'll see Peter Singer maintain in the next chapter, to draw a distinction between how we treat animals and how we treat humans in similar cases like this is a form of arbitrary prejudice. If we value consistency, we should be just as willing to breed and eat infants as we are cows, pigs, and chickens.

Fellow creatures

In an influential article entitled "Eating Meat and Eating People," Cora Diamond (1978) argues that ethical models which seek to bestow ethically laden interests or rights upon animals—models which we'll explore in the next two chapters—aren't ultimately what persuade people to become vegetarians. Such models may be philosophically interesting, but at the end of the day their appeal rests in large part upon whether or not animals are looked upon as fellow creatures. Seeing them in this way means relating to them as kindred subjects rather than alien objects, and once that shift of perspective kicks in to bridge Pollan's open space between them and us, it's impossible to see a food animal as "simply a stage (the self-moving stage) in the production of a meat product" (Diamond 1978, p. 475). For me to view another living being as a fellow creature is to acknowledge, even if only implicitly, bonds of sympathy between him or her and myself. Without this sense of kin sympathy, so nicely expressed by Robert Burns' referring to himself as a mouse's "poor, earth-born companion, An' fellow-mortal!," abstract philosophical defenses of vegetarianism probably won't do much to reduce meat-eating and animal suffering.

Both Diamond and defenders of the basic argument who agree with her may be on to something. When it comes to trying to persuade others that the meat diet they enjoy is morally wobbly, abstract arguments alone aren't likely to do the trick. Habituation is too strong and our talent for defensive rationalization too clever.

So a more fruitful strategy might well be to help them appreciate that the food animals they're most likely to eat are properly looked upon as *fellow* creatures, rather than as only *creatures*. This kind of moral suasion expands humanity's "compassionate footstep" (Bekoff 2010), a move that benefits both animals and humans. (In Chapter 7, we'll explore arguments for the claim that sympathetic treatment of animals improves human character.)

But while this sense of empathetic connection seems to be a psychologically necessary condition for taking animal suffering seriously, it may not be sufficient. Kin sympathy alone doesn't help us in the hard work of navigating those choppy waters where our concern for animal suffering legitimately clashes with concern for human interests, or when the welfare of one animal is in conflict with the welfare of another. Ethical reasoning may be second-order in comparison to the prereflective kin sympathy that condemns cruelty, but it's crucial in helping us figure out how to act on the sympathy in the best possible way. In Chapter 3, utilitarians such as Peter Singer will argue that evaluation based on a comparison of animal and human interests or preferences is the necessary calculus. In Chapter 4, Tom Regan and others will argue for a navigational tool based on the postulation of animal rights. Both models go beyond the basic argument. But its fundamental insight, that unnecessary harm to animals is indecent, remains intact.

CHAPTER THREE

The argument from interests

*The question is not, Can [animals] reason? nor Can they talk? but,
Can they suffer?*

JEREMY BENTHAM

*The principle of equal consideration of interests acts like a pair of
scales, weighing interests impartially.*

PETER SINGER

We would be hard pressed to find anyone who didn't consider cruelty, or deliberately inflicted and unnecessary suffering, to be indecent. Disagreement arises in determining just what actions *are* cruel. Some might argue that while it's cruel to slap and tease a child simply out of pique, it's not cruel to torture a prisoner of war who has information that could save hundreds of lives. The situational difference, they conclude, makes a significant moral difference. Similarly, some might argue that species differences justify different standards of cruelty for humans and animals. Confining humans in overcrowded quarters before slaughtering them en masse is cruel. Rearing food animals in factory farms and killing them in industrial slaughterhouses isn't, while tossing a live puppy into a microwave oven would be. Factory farming is a necessity, given the consumer demand for meat. Gratuitously hurting animals isn't. The bottom line: People are people, animals are animals, and the species differences between them carry significant moral weight. We can do things—although not *anything*—to animals that we simply ought not to do to people.

The basic argument for vegetarianism uses kin sympathy to bridge the moral gap between humans and animals. There is enough similarity between humans and at least some food animals to create a compassionate connection to the suffering they endure in factory farms. This sympathy in turn awakens the conviction that it's indecent to sustain their suffering by contributing to consumer demands for their flesh, especially when their flesh isn't necessary to sustain human life.

But as we saw in the preceding chapter, many people think that the basic argument is a good place to start but not to end in defending vegetarianism. They argue that its fundamental principle, the indecency of cruelty, requires supplementation, precisely because of the common belief that species differences allow for the redefining of what counts as cruelty when it comes to animals. A stronger bridge between humans and animals than kin sympathy is needed, one that extends the injunction against cruelty to food animals in a more rigorous way.

One of the most influential efforts to strengthen the basic argument's principle that inflicting needless suffering on animals is wrong is the Australian-born Peter Singer's appeal to utilitarianism, the ethical position which maintains that behavior is properly evaluated in terms of how much aggregate interest or preference satisfaction ensues from it. Singer's isn't the only utilitarian defense of vegetarianism, but it *is* the most influential. In this chapter we'll explore his argument as well as some of the objections that have been leveled against it.

Equal consideration and interest satisfaction

Imagine two creatures who are members of different species. They share roughly the same cognitive and physical abilities. Both are capable of feeling pleasure and pain, although neither is able to do much in the way of forming a self-concept or anticipating the future.

Now, imagine also that these two creatures are in roughly equal amounts of pain. Both of them, let's say, are suffering from the symptoms of food poisoning: stomach cramping, vomiting, dizziness, fever, and so on. They're each clearly in a bad way.

Finally, imagine that one of the creatures is a pig, and the other is a developmentally challenged human.

If upon learning this you suddenly shift from a more or less equal distribution of concern for the two creatures to a greater or even near-exclusive concern for the human, Peter Singer argues that you do so only because you've chosen to privilege your own species. But there's no justification for doing so. Pain is pain, and intense or enduring pain diminishes well-being, regardless of whether the victim is a pig or a human. "If a being suffers," says Singer, it's in its interests, "[n]o matter what the nature of [its] being," not to suffer. If I grant moral concern to the developmentally challenged human, there's no good reason not to grant it to the pig as well. "[T]here can be no moral justification for refusing to take [its] suffering into [equal] consideration" (Singer 2008, p. 57). "Our concern for others and our readiness to consider their interests ought not to depend on what they are like or on what abilities they may possess" (Singer 2009, p. 5).

The problem is that we humans do, of course, tend to count our pain as more important and worthier of moral concern than animal pain. The presumption is that the possession of sophisticated cognitive apparatus naturally makes a creature more sensitive to pain. Typically hidden within this is the claim that only "persons," the supposed pinnacle of cognitive sophistication, deserve full moral consideration when they suffer—with personhood, of course, belonging exclusively to humans. But as we saw in Chapter 1, personhood is a slippery label. Depending on the cognitive capacities we associate with it, some humans are clearly persons but others, those severely mentally disabled or in a vegetative comatose state, seem not to be. Moreover, some animals such as chimpanzees may possess just enough of the pertinent cognitive capacities to qualify as persons. So intelligence level and degrees of personhood don't seem particularly useful moral barometers in deciding who deserves moral consideration. Because of the fluidity of personhood, "no objective assessment can support the view that it is always worse to kill members of our species who are not persons than members of other species who are" (Singer 2008, p. 117). Sentience, the capacity for pain and pleasure, is a much better gauge of who belongs in the moral community.[1] The crucial test for membership in it, as Jeremy Bentham noted in the early nineteenth century, is whether the creature in question can suffer. And as far as Singer is concerned, "pains of the same intensity and duration are equally bad, whether felt by humans or animals" (p. 61).

Following Bentham, Singer posits what he considers to be a fundamental moral truth, or what he calls the "basic principle of equality": that the suffering of any being "be counted equally with the like suffering—insofar as rough comparisons can be made—of any other being" (Singer 2009, p. 8). As we've already seen, he believes the refusal to do so is a form of species chauvinism. Using the British psychologist Richard Ryder's 1970 coinage, Singer calls this prejudice "speciesism": a "bias in favor of the interests of members of one's own species and against those of members of other species" (p. 6). Speciesism, he famously claims, is cut from the same cloth as other oppressive biases such as sexism, racism, and ageism and calls for a similar response. "[W]e would be on shaky ground if we were to demand equality for blacks, women, and other groups of oppressed humans while denying equal consideration to nonhumans" (p. 3).

Critics have objected strongly to Singer's empirical claim that rough comparisons can be made between animal and human suffering and his normative one that privileging humans at the expense of animals is prejudicial. He acknowledges that determining like suffering in members of different species isn't an exact science. But common sense and a judicious appraisal of all pertinent variables are reliable guides in most situations. Common sense tells me, for example, that a thick-hided horse can more easily absorb a slap than a human infant can. Horses and infants alike experience pain, but not necessarily in the same way (Singer 2008, p. 59; 2009, p. 15). On the other hand, if I throw a live cat into a pot of boiling water, it's reasonable to infer that it will feel agony very much like a scalded human would. I don't need exact measurements in order to come to either of these conclusions. When in doubt about the extent to which an animal may suffer, Singer suggests it's best to err on the side of generosity (Singer 2009, p. 175). We don't know for sure whether lobsters suffer when they're boiled alive. But if they do, they must suffer awfully.

Predictably, the charge of speciesism has generated more heat than Singer's claim of parallels between human and animal pain. Although many applaud it—such as Mary Spiegel (1997), who points out similarities between the treatment of food animals and human slaves—others reject it as a trivialization of human victimization. Leslie Francis and Richard Norman (1978) contend that speciesism can't be analogous to human oppression because humans, unlike animals, are able to express why they are aggrieved and to struggle in their own interests. Carl Cohen argues that the comparison between speciesism and racism or sexism is "worse than unsound; it is atrocious. It draws an offensive moral conclusion from a deliberately devised verbal parallelism that is utterly specious" (Cohen 1986, p. 867). But one wonders whether such objections really hit the mark. It's surely possible for a person to be oppressed by structural racism, for example, without having a clear awareness of the causes of her oppression. Victimhood requires neither an expression of grievance nor a protest. Moreover, it may be argued that the notion of speciesism is offensive only if humans are indeed worthier of moral consideration than animals. But in order to establish that, Singer's argument, and not his use of the word "speciesism," must be addressed. Ultimately, even if one concludes that speciesism is too loaded a term, it is wise to keep in mind, as Les Brown (1988) argues, that we frequently do privilege ourselves at the expense of animals for no apparently good reason.

Singer's principle of equality establishes to his satisfaction the inclusion of animals in the moral community. Just as I can't conclude that my personal interests matter more than yours just because they're mine, so humans can't automatically assume that their interests matter more than animals' just because they're human. All claims based upon a sentient creature's fundamental interest in avoiding suffering and maximizing interest or preference satisfaction deserve equal moral consideration.

But what about equal *treatment*? Do all claims carry the same weight? Singer's answer is no.

The extension of the basic principle of equality from one group to another does not imply that we must treat both groups in exactly the same way, or grant exactly the same rights to both groups. Whether we should do so will depend on the nature of the members of the two groups. The basic principle of equality does not require equal or identical treatment; it requires equal consideration. Equal consideration for different beings may lead to different treatment and different rights. (Singer 2009, p. 2)

One reason for inequality in treatment is that there is a sliding scale of sentience-based interests in the animal kingdom. The demarcation of sentience levels isn't a precise science. But we can say with some assurance that mammals and birds are more capable of sentience than, say, mussels and clams. Consequently, in a clash between the fundamental interests of a cow and a clam, although their interests carry equal weight when it comes to moral consideration, the higher level of the cow's sentience would, all things being equal, tilt the treatment scale in her favor.

Additionally, Singer has never denied that the life of a "self-aware being, capable of abstract thought, of planning for the future, of complex acts of communication, and so on, is more valuable than the life of a being without these capacities" (Singer 2008, p. 61). In a clash of fundamental interests between a human and a cow, the treatment scale properly swings, all things being equal, humanward.

But Singer is well aware that moral clashes rarely involve only two parties. Individual interests are typically interconnected in such a way as to form vast and complex networks. If moral consideration is based on taking interests or preferences into equal consideration, appropriate ethical behavior is based on acting in such a way that the greatest aggregate of interests or preferences is satisfied or protected. So after equal moral consideration of the interests of all involved parties, the right thing to do is to choose the course of action that is most useful, or has the greatest utility, in promoting the interest of as many involved parties as possible. As Singer (2008, p. 22) puts it, "The principle of equal consideration of interests acts like a pair of scales, weighing interests impartially. True scales favor the side where the interest is stronger or where several interests combine to outweigh a smaller number of similar interests; but they take no account of what interests they are weighing."

As Singer's scale metaphor suggests, comparing and evaluating interests is a complex task that goes far beyond a mechanical toting up of the number of bodies on either side of a conflict. Interests must be weighed not only in terms of how many creatures share them but also according to the interests' intensity and relative weight. An excruciating degree of pain in one individual might, for example, outweigh what's merely a mild irritation in ten others, such that morality obliges us to come to the aid of the one before the ten. But as Gaverick Matheny (2006, p. 18) points out, things can go the other way too. "[T]he sum of a larger number of interests of lesser intensity (such as 100,000 people's interests in $1 each) can still outweigh the sum of a smaller number of interests of greater intensity (such as my interest in $100,000)." The relative weight of clashing interests is important as well. I have an interest in playing my stereo at full volume into the wee hours. You have an interest in getting a good night's sleep so that you can go to your job in the morning and be a productive citizen. The consequences of you performing your job efficiently may well carry more weight than the satisfaction I receive from blaring my stereo at full throttle, even if my own satisfaction in doing so is intense. Similarly, as we'll see shortly, the pleasure I derive from eating steak may not at all balance out, much less override, the suffering endured by a factory-farmed cow from whom the steak is taken. In evaluating interests, these are the sorts of variables that need to be considered.

Singer's defense of animal welfare, in sum, is based on an egalitarian vision of justice—everyone's interests ought to count equally—and a utilitarian measuring rod which strives for the best possible overall balance between satisfaction and frustration of interests or preferences for all parties involved. Even though he occasionally uses the language of rights, as we've already seen in some of the quoted passages, Singer rejects a rights model of morality, deeming it both conceptually confused and normatively unnecessary. All that's required to ground morality is the presence of interests in sentient creatures.

Eating animals

From Singer's way of seeing things, a vegetarian diet would greatly reduce "the total sum of suffering in the universe" (Singer 2008, p. 61) because it would safeguard the interests of many more sentient creatures than would be discommoded by it. The interests of food animals in not suffering and dying are simply weightier in both sheer numbers and relative importance than the gustatory preferences of the humans who eat them (p. 64). It's one thing if animal flesh is needed for human survival. As creatures that are capable of long-term plans, our interest in surviving qualitatively outweighs the interests of animals who lack the ability to hope for and anticipate the future. But for the most part, people in (at least) Europe and North America have abundant sources of alternative foods that are both nourishing and tasty. And even if they didn't, the horrific suffering factory-farmed animals endure, as well as the manner in which they're slaughtered, would raise serious questions about the propriety of eating them.

Philosopher Bart Gruzalski, invoking utilitarianism's practice of weighing opposing interests, demonstrates how difficult it is to justify a meat diet if one takes the egalitarian principle seriously.

> In order that eating meat be justified, the pain caused to animals by this practice must not only be *outweighed* by the omnivore's pleasure, but *there can be no alternative act that would foreseeably result in a better balance of pleasure over pain.* Since eating plants is one alternative, and since this alternative produces pleasures of taste, soundness of health, and no unnecessary suffering for animals, it follows that, if a person is trying not to contribute to unnecessary suffering in the world, then that person would not eat animals raised and slaughtered for food. (Gruzalski 2004, p. 125)

Actually, it might be argued that Gruzalski has understated his case. It's not only the meat-eater's pleasure in meat that must outweigh the food animal's pain, but his pleasure in meat *minus* the pleasure he could experience from an alternative vegetarian diet that must outweigh the pain of the food animal. Measured in these terms, the possibility of the meat-eater's interest in gustatory pleasure outweighing the food animal's interest in not suffering and being slaughtered diminishes to the vanishing point. As we'll see in Chapter 7, even this calculation is incomplete, leaving out as it does considerations such as the interests of developing-world peoples not to go hungry because of the enormous waste of grain protein fed to food animals.

But does this rule out eating *any* animals? Probably not. Jeremy Bentham, whose insistence on the moral relevance of animal sentience inspires Singer, refused to deny the moral acceptability of killing them for food. In eating animals, he argued, humans "are the better for it," while beasts "are never the worse." In fact, our slaughter of them is speedier and therefore less painful than their "natural" deaths from protracted diseases would be (Singer 2009, p. 210). Even Singer concedes (2008, p. 64) that it might be morally permissible to eat animals provided that they're raised and slaughtered in a way compatible with equal consideration of interests. Minimally, however, this would entail a complete break with the factory farm assembly line production of food animals and the replacement of it with small farms in which animals can live in natural habitats under conditions most conducive to their well-being.

Even then there are difficulties, some practical and some normative. Is it possible to kill food animals in such a way as to minimize the assault on their interest in not suffering? What would that entail? Surely something along the lines of Bentham's speedy and less painful death. But would that mean killing food animals when they're asleep, or in some other surreptitious way so that they experience no fear and only an instant (if that) of pain?

Aside from these practical perplexities about how to kill humanely (leaving aside the question of whether the expression "humane killing" makes sense in the first place), normative ones arise. What about the effects, for example, the death of a slaughtered animal has on its mate and members of its herd or social group? Shouldn't the confusion and discomfort caused them by the abrupt disappearance of one of their own be taken into consideration when weighing the killing's overall consequences? After all, as involved parties, their interests ought to count too.

Another normative difficulty, introduced in the previous chapter (and considered at greater length in the next), is also pertinent. Recall Frederike Kaldewaij's (2008) argument against killing animals: even if the slaughter is done so humanely that the victim experiences neither pain nor fear, its interests have still been harmed if the killing deprives the animal of the goods that continued life would have brought it. If a sentient creature's lifespan is cut short because it is slaughtered for its meat, and if a continuation of the creature's life would've brought it more pleasurable than painful experiences—a reasonable assumption in the context of a small family owned farm—then, in the absence of overriding contrary interests, it has been treated unethically.

J. M. Coetzee makes a similar case against the killing of even family-farmed animals. According to him, food animals (but not only them, of course), like humans, display a will to live. They may not be able to anticipate the future or make long-term plans that are annihilated by premature death, but they possess a visceral, hardwired desire to remain alive that Coetzee claims is apparent to anyone who's ever witnessed their slaughter. Put another way, animals have an interest in living. "Anyone who says that life matters less to animals than it does to us," says Elizabeth Costello, one of Coetzee's fictional characters who speaks for him, "has not held in his hands an animal fighting for its life. The whole of the being of the animal is thrown into that fight, without reserve" (Coetzee 1999, p. 65).

These reservations about the propriety of killing food animals seem especially pertinent when speaking about specific beasts. But things might change if instead of focusing on individuals we think globally, or in terms of what Singer calls the "total" view. From Singer's perspective, neither animals nor humans possess inherent value. This is one of the reasons he rejects ethical models based upon rights. The only carriers of value are experiences. Pleasant experiences that satisfy my preferences or interests have value for me. Experiences that satisfy the preferences or interests of a great number of people have even more value. The goal of the moral life is to maximize the number of preference-satisfying experiences across the board, or at least to ensure that the ratio of satisfying to frustrating experiences stays in the black.

What this suggests, as Singer admits, is that "sentient beings [are] valuable only in so far as they make possible the existence of intrinsically valuable experiences like pleasure. It is as if sentient beings are receptacles of something valuable" (Singer 2008, p. 121). Obviously, receptacles are disposable. What's of value is the stuff they hold—in the case of sentient beings, pleasurable experiences which express their preferences. All one need do if a receptacle cracks is to replace it with another one equally able to hold experiences.[2]

How does all this relate to food animals? If what's valuable about them is their pleasurable experiences, then it's possible, given certain conditions, to replace them with other sentient creatures without in any way disrupting the sum total of pleasant experiences. In other words, "the loss meat-eaters inflict on one animal is thus balanced, on the total view, by the benefit they confer on the next" (Singer 2008, p. 121). This is known as the "replaceability" argument.

What are the "certain conditions" that must apply? Philosopher Evelyn Pluhar (1995) spells them out nicely. The animals in question must exist only because they've been deliberately bred for food, and they must have led pleasurable lives. The second of these stipulations rules out the possibility of factory farms. Next, the creatures' deaths must be free of pain and fear—an empirically problematic condition, as we've already seen—and their mates and mothers must not be distressed by their disappearance. Finally, the slaughtered beasts must be replaced by other beasts that will live and die under the same conditions.

The replaceability argument may not speak to the perplexing question of how to kill humanely, but it does address the objection that food animals have a desire to stay alive and will lose future opportunities for preference satisfaction if prematurely slaughtered. In the first place, food animals can't really "desire" more life because they're unable to conceive of themselves as creatures with a future. They are, suggests Singer, "impersonal," and therefore killing them apparently "does them no personal wrong" (Singer 2008, p. 125). What killing them *does* do, of course, is diminish the overall quantity of preference satisfaction in the world, but that's easily remedied by replacing them with other food animals. Second, future opportunities for satisfaction of preferences really *aren't* lost from an objective point of view, because slain animals are replaced with placeholders for those opportunities. The loss of opportunities for satisfaction is "counter-balanced by bringing into existence similar beings who will lead equally happy lives" (p. 125).

But the replaceability argument isn't without its critics. Even Singer is ambivalent about it, admitting that there's an "air of peculiarity" to the claim that the death of one creature can be compensated by the birth of another, especially if the slain creature is "capable of having desires for the future" (Singer 2009, pp. 228–9). But something far less than the capacity of future-directed sensibility may also lend peculiarity to the argument. Coetzee's point, that when the time comes to slaughter them, most food animals behave as if they desperately want to live, surely ought to carry some weight. Singer himself notes that if the overall normative goal is to create as much interest or preference satisfaction as possible, then it makes sense to put as many well treated, sentient creatures on the planet as it can hold rather than keeping the sum total of satisfaction at steady state through replacement (Singer 2008, pp. 121–2).

Stephen R. L. Clark is also skeptical about the replaceability argument. His intuition is similar to Coetzee's: death, regardless of how physically painless it might be, is still a hurtful and undesirable event that robs living creatures of what they long for. To suppose otherwise, he says, is rationalization of the most transparent kind. "It is surely extremely paradoxical that death should not be recognized as the greatest of single hurts, the final pain for fear of which all other pains are intensified. If death is no hurt, what ill is done by those who have their cats 'put down' for not matching the new decorations?" (Clark 1977, p. 76).

Evelyn Pluhar (1995) suggests another difficulty with the argument. Suppose we deliberately breed a special group of humans for food and rear them in the same humane conditions that she spelled out for food animals. We make sure that they're treated well, enjoy pleasurable lives, and are slaughtered without distress to them or their companions. After slaughtering them, we make sure to replace them with other specially bred humans so that no preference-satisfaction opportunities are lost. Surely, Pluhar suggests, the cold-blooded arithmetical calculation that goes into this way of thinking would be morally chilling enough to raise serious doubts about the replaceability thesis.

It's not clear, though, if Pluhar's arrow hits the mark. Humans are complex beings with the capacity, as Singer points out, for self-awareness, forward thinking, meaningful relations with others, and so on. As a consequence, it may be inappropriate to compare them with animals lacking these qualities, thus taking the punch out of her analogy. After all, as Singer (2008, p. 126) says, "beings who are conscious, but not self-conscious, more nearly approximate the picture of receptacles for experiences of pleasure and pain." When we kill an animal, we kill a rather self-enclosed organism. But when we kill a human, to invoke an old rabbinic saying, we kill an entire universe.

For Singer, given that it isn't "practically possible to rear animals for food on a large scale without inflicting considerable suffering" on them, the "absolute minimum" for anyone "with the capacity to look beyond considerations of narrow self-interest" is to abstain from factory-farmed meat as a form of moral boycott (Singer 2009, pp. 160, 170). But as we've seen, Singer is also uncomfortable with the replaceability argument's defense of killing family-farmed food animals. Although the argument is perfectly consistent with his utilitarianism, its peculiar depersonalization of animals suggests a disconcerting coarsening of regard for life (a danger we'll explore further in Chapter 7). Mention has already been made of Singer's advice to err on the side of cautious generosity when it comes to killing animals for food, and this recommendation, although made in part for the benefit of animals, is also a safeguard against the empathetic coarsening of humans. As Singer says (2008, p. 134), "at the level of practical moral principles, it would be better to reject altogether the killing of animals for food, unless one must do so to survive. Killing animals for food makes us think of them as objects that we can use as we please. Their lives then count for little when weighed against our mere wants."[3]

Singer's critics

Singer's utilitarian defense of animal interests has had immense influence, and is rightfully credited with inspiring the many activist organizations and movements endorsing "animal liberation." But his claim that sentient animals deserve equal moral consideration has also been criticized for a number of reasons. Some object that utilitarianism is a flawed ethical model incapable of offering animals (or humans, for that matter) the protection Singer thinks it can. Many ecofeminists reject it for what they see as its patriarchal overreliance on abstract norms. (We'll examine this criticism at some length in Chapter 5.) At least one environmental philosopher argues that Singer's utilitarian defense of animals, if pushed, leads to absurd conclusions, and at least one utilitarian critic argues that Singer is confused about what animal interests really are. Still other dissenters contend that the differences between humans and animals so outweigh the similarities that Singer's principle of equal consideration is inappropriate.

Inadequacy of utilitarianism

Tom Regan and Mark Rowlands, who defend two different varieties of the rights argument that we'll examine in the next chapter,
both contend that utilitarianism raises more ethical problems than
it addresses. Regan, for example, while graciously acknowledging
"an enormous debt" to Singer (Regan 1983, p. 220) and granting that the "great appeal" of utilitarianism stems from its uncom-
promising insistence that "everyone's interests count and count as
much as the like interests of everyone else," argues that the model's
fatal blind spot is its lack of concern for "the equal moral rights of
different individuals" (Regan 1985, p. 19). Taking Singer's receptacle simile seriously—that it's satisfied *experiences,* not the satisfied *experiencer,* that have value—Regan worries that the integrity
of individuals, at least some of whom he believes (as we'll see in
Chapter 4) are inherently valuable, is disregarded. This is especially
likely given utilitarianism's claim that ethical choices should be
based upon the aggregative satisfaction of interests. If we're obliged
to "choose that option which is most likely to bring about the best
balance of totaled satisfactions over totaled frustrations" (p. 20),
it's entirely possible that circumstances could justify sacrificing perfectly innocent individuals for the sake of satisfying the interests of
the group.

   As an example of the way utilitarianism can justify stepping on
individuals for the sake of the greater good, Regan asks us to consider a Raskolnikov-like scenario in which a nephew murders his
"old, inactive, cranky, sour" aunt who also happens to be wealthy.
He plans the murder so carefully that he won't be caught. After the
inquest, he inherits her fortune. In order to get a tax write-off, he
donates a good chunk of it to a children's hospital, and his gift benefits many sick children as well as their parents, relatives, and friends.
The nephew, suffering no pangs of conscience over his deed, and
never being suspected by the law, has enough of the fortune left over
to enjoy "more than sufficient comfort—as [he] lie[s] on the beach
at Acapulco—in contemplating the joy and health [he has] brought
to so many others" (Regan 1985, p. 20). Regan's point is obvious. A
utilitarian would have to conclude that the aunt's murder is morally
justifiable because of the greater number of satisfied interests that
her death brings to her nephew, the sick children, and their relatives

and friends. But according to Regan, this violates a rock bottom ethical principle: a good end doesn't justify a wicked means.

When it comes to protecting animals and justifying vegetarianism, Regan believes that utilitarianism again falls short. After all, he contends, it's not the actual animals that are Singer's focus, but whether or not the frustration of their interests outweighs the contrary interests of humans who wish to eat them. The fundamental moral wrong, as Regan sees it, isn't the system of factory farming or even the suffering that it inflicts upon animals. Rather, it's the fact that animals are looked upon and treated as renewable resources that lack inherent value. Singer's model does little to chip away at that attitude, even though, as we saw earlier, he worries that eating animals risks so coarsening us that we subordinate animal lives to our gustatory desires. The aggregative principle contributes to that insensitivity, leaving open the possibility as it does that the factory farming of food animals could indeed, under certain circumstances, bring about the greatest interest satisfaction and hence be morally justifiable (Regan 1983, p. 228).

Rowlands agrees that utilitarianism is deficient, taking on both its principle of equal consideration and its focus on aggregation. The former he strongly rejects as "crucially deficient" because both "intuitively" implausible and coercive (Rowlands 2009, pp. 32, 47). Its implausibility lies in the fact that no distinction is made between morally legitimate and illegitimate interests or preferences. According to the utilitarian, each must be considered equally, and their relative value determined only after the sum total of satisfied interests has been tabulated. But Rowlands believes this puts the cart before the horse. Some interests are morally unacceptable regardless of the numbers involved and ought not to be given any moral consideration at all, much less *equal* consideration. "My interest in watching unwilling gladiators fight to the death for my entertainment would be—if I had it—an illegitimate interest. So too would be my interest in ensuring that I and members of my own racial group get an advantageous distribution of goods, commodities, and freedoms" (p. 47). Toting up the percentages of satisfied and frustrated interests in cases like this is not only unnecessary. It's disingenuous.

To make matters even worse, Rowlands contends that the principle of aggregation plainly clashes with the principle of equal consideration. Majority interests outweigh minority ones, even if the former are illegitimate, and what that means is that the determination of how far the minority's interests ought to be satisfied is decided by the majority. Take Rowlands' gladiator example. If a majority of people—the spectators—want the minority—the gladiators—to fight, even if the gladiators themselves are unwilling to do so, then the fate of the gladiators is determined by the role the majority has forced on them. This makes an equal consideration of their competing interests a sham from the very start.

A utilitarian defender of animals might not be especially bothered by this last criticism. After all, the number of food animals that are reared and slaughtered each year far outweighs the number of human meat-eaters in the world. Consequently, questions of legitimate and illegitimate interests to one side, simple aggregation of interests might be enough to protect animals. However, Rowlands points out that things are more complicated than that. It's not a question simply of weighing the interests of humans in eating animals against the interests of animals in not being eaten. "[T]here are more human preferences involved than those of the merely gustatory sort," (p. 54) because the food industry is immense, exerting direct or indirect influence on an international scale. Most immediately implicated in it are the people who raise food animals. However, there are also "the feed producers and retailers; cage manufacturers and designers; producers of growth stimulants and other chemicals; those who butcher, package and ship the produce" (p. 54). Veterinarians, meat inspectors, county extension agents, and supermarket personnel are also involved, and along with all these must be counted their families and dependents. And of course there are also all the consumers who have a gustatory interest in meat-eating. Finally, to complicate matters even more, a staggering number of complex calculations, such as the "short- and long-term global economic consequences of a sudden or gradual transition to vegetarianism," (p. 55) must be made in order to arrive at an accurate weighing of interests or preferences.

Rowlands ultimately concludes that this vast nexus of human interests, which extends far beyond mere gustatory considerations, probably doesn't outweigh the suffering food animals endure, simply by virtue of their sheer numbers. But this assessment may be overly optimistic because, as we've already seen, aggregated interests aren't measured solely numerically, but also in terms of intensity and weight. Surely a case can be made for the claim that the weight of the multiple interests at stake in the economic and social well-being of humans is, in the final analysis, more significant than the suffering of animals, intense as it may be. And in fact we'll examine such an argument in some detail shortly.

Arbitrariness

One of the more ingenious arguments against Singer's utilitarian advocacy of vegetarianism has been made by environmental ethicist Mark Sagoff (1984). Anyone who seriously believes that reduction of the world's total aggregate of preference frustration is a moral imperative, he argues, must be ready to safeguard wild animals at the cost of interfering with the integrity of the ecosystems in which they dwell. In the wild, animal species reproduce in excess because the mortality rate of youngsters is so high. This seemingly wasteful system is actually natural selection's way of ensuring that the fittest live long enough to reproduce. It is essential to the health of both species and the ecosystems within which they flourish.

Moreover, the prospect for most wild animals of escaping an early and painful death is generally dismal. If they don't die savagely under the fangs and claws of predators, they're likely to die of starvation, exposure, or lingering disease. Death and suffering in the wild, in other words, is colossal, both in numbers and intensity—much worse than the cruelty of factory farms and industrial slaughterhouses. So if Singer wants to champion the amelioration of the one, says Sagoff, consistency demands that he also argue for the amelioration of the other. Adopting vegetarianism is a strategy especially aimed at reducing the suffering endured by factory-farmed domesticated animals. Regularly scattering food laced with contraceptives throughout wilderness areas, converting national parks into supervised preserves, and constructing heated winter shelters for cold mammals and birds would all help to mitigate the suffering endured by wildlife. But the cost of such mitigation is to do violence to the ecosystem, whose integrity depends not upon the flourishing of individual members of species but upon the system's symbiotic equilibrium, regardless of how much suffering the maintenance of the equilibrium imposes on individuals. Besides, if the ecosystem crumbles, the individuals within it suffer even more than they do when the ecosystem flourishes. Therefore, seeking to alleviate the suffering of wildlife by morally misguided interference only risks increasing it.

Sagoff's argument most immediately suggests that Singer's utilitarian defense of vegetarianism unaccountably privileges some animals—those that are factory farmed to feed humans—but not others—those who live and die in the wild. Such a distinction hardly honors the principles of equal consideration and aggregation, although in regards to the latter Singer might respond that the flourishing of the ecosystem in fact represents the interests of the animals within it better than strategies like contraception-laced food or heated shelters would. Sagoff's point isn't simply that a utilitarian concern about animal suffering seems not to have environmental value. More importantly, his argument suggests that a case for the moral consideration of animals which arbitrarily and inconsistently excludes a huge class of them is suspect.

Confusion

Nonutilitarians aren't the only critics of an interests-based defense of vegetarianism. At least one utilitarian, philosopher R. G. Frey, has also taken Singer on, arguing that he fundamentally misunderstands what it means for an animal to have an interest.

Frey argues that we need to make a distinction between interests as psychological desires or preferences and interests as needs. The former are tied to sentience, but the latter can be ascribed to anything, sentient or not, "having a good or well-being which can be harmed or benefited" (Frey 1980, p. 79; see also Frey 2008). An automobile, for example, has an interest, or need, to be serviced regularly. But it obviously feels no pain or distress if it runs out of oil and its motor freezes. My lawn has an interest, or need, in getting watered and mowed, because both actions are conducive to a lawn looking like it's supposed to look (or at least living up to what American suburbia demands of it). But it feels no preference frustration if I neglect it. Consequently, it is absurd to say that my car or lawn deserves moral consideration from me. A need isn't the same thing as a preference.

Now if one turns to animals, one quickly discovers, argues Frey, that they've more in common with cars and lawns than humans. Animals lack desires, because desires rest upon beliefs, and beliefs in turn require the ability to distinguish between truth and falsity.[4] But such distinctions can only be made through language—which animals lack. Certain actions may be *in* their objective interests— whatever actions that enable them to flourish as animals—but they cannot be said to have psychological desires or preferences that can be thwarted. Frey won't grant even "simple desires" to animals because he believes that they too are ultimately based on beliefs such as "This is good for me" or "This is bad for me," of which animals are incapable. The upshot is that it may be good to treat beasts well in the sense that doing so is in their best interests, just as changing the oil regularly is in my car's best interest. But, like my car, they fall outside of the moral community because they have no preferences or desires.

Frey's argument is clever, and reminiscent of the ones offered by Peter Carruthers and Peter Harrison in Chapter 1 in the debate over whether animals are capable of pain. But, like theirs, it flies in the face of ordinary experience. It also raises perplexing questions about marginal humans. Does a human infant, as yet incapable of forming beliefs, really not suffer pain? And if not, is she outside the moral community? It might be argued that for human infants as well as (at least) mammals and birds, that which is in their best interests coincides with preference satisfaction—that is, one of the factors contributing to their well-being is precisely not being pained. Consequently, drawing the sharp distinction between needs and desires that Frey does fits well with cars and lawns, but not so well with (at least some) organisms.

But if Frey's denial that animals deserve moral consideration because they lack the necessary condition for it—genuine interests or preferences—is rejected, he offers another argument against utilitarian defenses of vegetarianism. Singer contends that choosing a vegetarian diet is more than "merely a symbolic gesture" or a self-centered search for moral purity. Instead, it's "a highly practical and effective step . . . toward ending both the killing of non-human animals and the infliction of suffering upon them" (Singer 2009, p. 161). Frey, however, accuses Singer of naïveté. "No one really believes," he says, "that the expected consequence of anyone's abstaining, or of the acts of all those who abstain added together, is that the meat industry will be brought to its knees" (Frey 2004, p. 122). In fact, matters are probably worse for food animals now, a generation after Peter Singer began advocating vegetarianism, than when he began. True, the number of vegetarians in the United States has grown. But the number of commercially farmed animals has skyrocketed in the same amount of time, indicating that moral objections to vegetarianism do next to nothing towards persuading consumers not to eat meat. And it's a sorry ethical model, especially if it's a utilitarian one that does nothing to rectify the abuses it condemns.

Tom Regan goes even further than Frey in calling into question the effectiveness of utilitarian defenses of vegetarian. According to him, a major stumbling block is what he calls "Singer's Paradox."

> What it comes to is that in being a vegetarian I am doing what I ought to do *only if* it happens to be true that enough other people happen also to be vegetarians so that, when the effects of their boycotting meat are joined with the effects of my boycott, it happens to be the case that some number of chickens that would have been raised on a factory farm are spared that fate. If, on the other hand, the effects of our collective boycott happen not to make any difference . . . then, in being vegetarians, we are not doing what we ought to do, not because of any failing on our part . . ., but because of the effects of the decisions of others (i.e., nonvegetarians), whose demand for meat more than offsets the effect of our boycott. But to make the rightness of what vegetarians do contingent upon the decisions of those very persons who are doing what vegetarians deplore . . . is paradoxical at best. (Regan 1983, p. 225)

Regan's objection, somewhat similar to the one made earlier by Rowlands, does more than support Frey's contention that utilitarianism is an ineffective tool against animal suffering. It aims to show that there's a weakness at the very heart of utilitarianism's understanding of value.

Human specialness

One objection to Singer's utilitarian model can actually be applied to most defenses of vegetarianism: that there's something special about being human, a quality or qualities that animals lack, which puts us inside and them outside the moral community. This special status isn't merely physical ability, since many animals are swifter, stronger, or more agile than humans. Instead, the difference is often expressed by ascribing to humans a soul, language, rationality, or the capacity to have moral obligations. (More of this last characteristic is in the next chapter.) Whatever the distinctive quality is reckoned to be, it bestows a status upon humans that makes them worthy recipients of moral concern. Animals, not possessing it, may share some qualities with humans, but none of the ones that are morally telling. Therefore, what Singer calls "speciesism" in fact isn't an arbitrary decision to privilege humans at the expense of animals. As Carl Cohen argued earlier, drawing moral boundaries between humans and animals is a reasonable move because humans and animals don't have like interests. Trying to apply standards of justice across species by appealing to common interests (or kin sympathy, as we saw in the last chapter, or shared rights, as we'll see in the next) is simply a smokescreen.

This objection is widely endorsed because it's so intuitively plausible (although Singer would probably say that it only seems so because species chauvinism is deeply engrained in our culture).[5] It may be pointed out, as we've already seen Singer do, that some of us seem not to display the special quality that sets humans apart from other species, while some animals come close to displaying it. But at the end of the day, very few want to deny a uniqueness to the human species which bestows upon it a certain moral status not enjoyed by animals. Surely few if any vegetarians (including Singer) want to say that an animal's life is just as valuable as a human's (all things considered), or that when there's a life or death conflict of interests between the two, the human life shouldn't be privileged.

But even if we grant a specialness to humans that makes their preferences more worthy of moral attention than animals', this doesn't necessarily mean that we're entitled to eat animals. Philosopher Elizabeth Telfer makes this point with an insightful analogy. Suppose, she says, that there's cultural agreement that children are more important than husbands. This in no way entails an obligation on the part of wives/mothers to "always do exactly what suits the children, whatever the cost to the husband. At most it means that, in cases where the children's and husband's interests are similar and in conflict, the children's interests should take precedence. In every other case the question is what degree of additional importance justifies what degree of privilege." So it is with humans and animals. Even if we conclude that we're more important than animals, "all that follows is that we are entitled to put our preferences first in similar cases." But when it comes to eating animals, the interests are dissimilar. One is "a mere preference," and the other is "fundamental," and this outweighs the privilege our special status gives us (Telfer 1996, p. 74).

"Commandment number 7: All animals are equal"

Readers of George Orwell's fable *Animal Farm* (2003) will recognize this "commandment," adopted by the animals shortly after their revolt against Mr Jones of Manor Farm. It is, of course, a principle embraced by Peter Singer—he even uses it as the title of the first chapter in *Animal Liberation*, his best known defense of vegetarianism—provided that we qualify it with the capacity for preference or interest satisfaction or frustration. All *sentient* animals are equal. As we've seen, Singer doesn't mean that all animals have equal abilities or natures or even deserve equal treatment. Instead, what he has in mind is that any creature capable of preferences or interests deserves moral consideration equal to the consideration given other creatures with like interests. The egalitarianism advocated by Singer is crucial to his utilitarianism. If the proper ethical goal is to minimize preference or interest frustration on a global scale, and if billions of sentient creatures suffer each year because their preferences are in conflict with human ones, then it's wrongheaded not to take them into consideration.

In the next chapter, we'll examine a defense of vegetarianism based not on a consideration of animal interests but instead on arguments that ascribe moral rights to most if not all food animals. Like the utilitarian argument from interests, the argument from rights is inspired by the basic principle that it's indecent to treat beings cruelly. But whereas utilitarians justify this by focusing on the quality of experiences rather than their holders—Singer's "receptacles"—rights theorists argue that moral focus is properly on holders, not their experiences.

The argument from rights

What sort of dinner is not costly for which a living creature loses its life? Do we hold a life cheap?

PLUTARCH

It is not an act of kindness to treat animals respectfully. It is an act of justice.

TOM REGAN

In his book *Dominion: The Power of Man, the Suffering of Animals, and the Call to Mercy,* Matthew Scully expresses a viewpoint held by many vegetarians and even some omnivorous animal lovers.

> Turning to the question of animal rights, I confess that I could hardly care less whether any formal doctrine or theory can be adduced for these creatures. There are moments when you do not need doctrines, when even rights become irrelevant, when life demands some basic response of fellow-feeling and mercy and love.[1]

Although he's done his share of abstract theorizing about animal rights, philosopher Stephen R. L. Clark is not unsympathetic with Scully's impatience. Attending to the ways in which animals enrich our lives, he believes, is often more revealing than philosophical investigations into whether animals are rights holders. "[T]he cats who share my household have no 'right,' in the abstract, to my special care and attention, but once received into the household and contributing their particular value to it, they do have such a right" (Clark 1987, p. 130). When it comes to questions about animal rights, so far as Clark is concerned, it's more than appropriate to think of them as acquired through caring relationships with humans rather than something which animals innately possess.

Philosopher Tom Regan, who with Peter Singer is the most influential defender of ethical vegetarianism, never loses sight of the importance of compassionate fellow-feeling for animals. But he worries that stronger medicine is needed. Animal activists, he warns, are too often caricatured by critics as sentimentalists who lead with their emotions instead of their reason. To debunk this disdainful stereotype, Regan believes it's important for vegetarians to make "a concerted effort not to indulge [their] emotions or parade [their] sentiments" (Regan 1983, p. xii) but instead to offer closely argued philosophical justifications for their position.[2]

Singer's utilitarian model won't do. As we'll see in more detail shortly, Regan thinks its exclusive focus on interests has too many holes through which animals can fall. If the ultimate goal is to maximize preference or interest satisfaction for all concerned parties, there's no necessary reason why utilitarian calculations can't continue to place food animals at the short end of the stick, at least in regard to the "painless" slaying of them. As we saw in the last chapter, even Singer acknowledges that the replaceability argument, although peculiar, could justify killing food animals just so long as the overall level of preference satisfaction remained acceptable and constant.

In Regan's opinion, what's needed to clinch moral standing for animals is a model that grants them actual rights based on the claim that, far from being mere experience-receptacles with no value in and of themselves, they possess inherent value. In the eyes of many, this is a hard row to hoe. Utilitarians like Singer deny that either humans or animals have inherent value, while most defenders of rights, whether they think of them as inherent or social constructs, hold that only humans possess them. But for Regan, the rights view is the most rationally satisfying theory of morality. Proper treatment of both humans and animals isn't a matter of kindness, as he says in the passage that serves as one of this chapter's epigraphs. It's a matter of justice, based on a recognition of and respect for rights. Needless to say, this perspective is controversial.

Subjects-of-a-life, inherent value, and rights

Whatever else a right may be, it's minimally a valid claim, as philosopher Joel Feinberg (1974, pp. 43–4) puts it, "*to* something and *against* someone, the recognition of which is called for by legal rules or, in the case of moral rights, by the principles of an enlightened conscience." The claim "*to* something" establishes an entitlement of some kind, while the claim "*against* someone" establishes that others have a duty to respect my entitlement. Rights and duties are complementary notions. If I have a right to something, there is a corresponding duty on the part of (at least some) others to respect and perhaps even defend that right. Likewise, I'm obliged to respect and possibly defend theirs.

It's obvious that many rights are the products of social convention or legislation. I have a legal right in the United States, for example, to purchase and drink alcohol after my twenty-first birthday. But no one wants to say that this right is somehow "naturally" mine simply by virtue of my being human. Instead, it is contextual and alienable, or controvertible. It's a legally defined entitlement that may or may not be a part of the legal codes of other countries, and American legislators can change the drinking age and have done so in the past. Moreover, it's a right that can be lost. Prisoners over the age of 21, for example, have no right to drink alcohol.

But in addition to socially constructed rights, some argue that there are natural rights, universal and inalienable entitlements that belong to all humans simply on the basis of our natural attributes. Unlike socially constructed rights, these cannot properly be overruled by culture or legislation. Natural rights theory has a long tradition in the West, tracing its roots at least back to Aristotle (Tuck 1982). Both the American Declaration of Independence and Constitution presume the existence of natural rights, with the former document asserting that life, liberty, and happiness are three of them. But there have been many critics of the theory, especially since the eighteenth-century Enlightenment. The utilitarian Jeremy Bentham, whom we met in the last chapter, dismissed the very idea as "mischievous nonsense" and memorably sneered at talk about natural rights as mere "nonsense upon stilts" (Bentham 1823, p. 501).

If we take seriously the possibility that natural rights exist, three consequences follow. The first is that, all things being equal, others are not morally free to violate our rights or to interfere with our pursuit of them. Legislated rights, as we've seen, are provisional. They can always be changed, or even suspended in moments of crisis. But natural rights are fundamental and inalienable. The second is that natural rights are the same for all who hold them, regardless of specific differences between the holders. If you have a right to life, for example, you have a full right, not a partial one, and you hold the right regardless of your gender, intelligence level, or physical capabilities. The third is that moral agency, or the capacity to behave morally, isn't a necessary condition for possessing natural rights. Moral "patients," subjects unable to behave morally, have the same natural rights as moral "agents." Were it not so, we would be forced to conclude that infants lack them. An infant may certainly be without certain legislated entitlements, such as the right to read whatever she wishes, simply because she's developmentally incapable of doing so. But if natural rights exist, the infant possesses them as fully as an adult does. Moral patients have no duties. They can't be expected to reciprocate our respect for their rights. But they are still entitled to it.

The standard assumption—so standard that for the most part it goes unspoken—is that if natural rights exist, only humans possess them. But during the last two centuries, this assumption, although still the majority opinion, has not gone unchallenged. Lewis Gompertz, who founded the Society for the Prevention of Cruelty to Animals in 1824, argued that beasts have a fundamental right to the free use of their bodies that trumps humans' desire to slaughter and eat them (Gompertz 1997). Towards the end of the nineteenth century, Henry Salt elaborated on Gompertz's contention. "Animals," he wrote, "have rights [that] consist in the 'restricted freedom' to live a natural life—a life, that is, which permits of individual development" (Salt 1980, p. 28). Salt contentiously argued that food animals, similar to humans, possess self-aware qualities such as "individuality, character, [and] reason." Consistency demands that if we assume humans possess natural rights on the basis of characteristics such as these, we must conclude that animals likewise possess them. Justice demands that we respect the natural rights of all holders, regardless of their species. To deny animals natural rights or to refuse to treat them accordingly is a "purely arbitrary" decision (p. 10)—or, as Peter Singer would say, is speciesist.

Tom Regan's contemporary defense of the natural rights of animal has similarities to both Gompertz's claim that animals have a right to the free use of their bodies and Salt's that animals have a right to live a natural life. He grounds his analysis of natural rights in the twin notions of subject-of-a-life and inherent value.

Like Singer, Regan takes humans as his starting point. Singer believes that the capacity for interest or preference satisfaction or frustration is the bottom line standard for determining appropriate moral treatment of humans, and his principle of equal consideration posits that *any* creature with the same capacity belongs in the moral community. Regan, as we've seen, is critical of Singer's interests-based model, worrying that its utilitarian orientation bestows value on experience but not on individuals. We ought not, he insists, "determine the inherent value of individual moral agents by totaling the intrinsic values of their experiences" (Regan 1983, p. 235). Otherwise, we risk concluding that unhappy people lead less valuable lives than happy ones. Similarly, he worries that the utilitarian calculus endorsed by Singer justifies moral decision making which inflicts harm on individuals "merely on the grounds of its producing the best consequences for all affected by the outcome" (p. 239). To avoid these difficulties, Regan assumes that individual humans, and not their experiences, are fundamentally valuable, and that their value in turn confers fundamental rights upon them.

But what accounts for the value of the individual? Or, to put it in the language of natural rights, what is there about the nature of humans that bestows fundamental rights upon them? Regan is uncomfortable with many of the traditional answers. Soul is too nebulous, personhood too fluid (Regan agrees with Singer that not all humans are persons and not all persons are human), language or intelligence too exclusive, the mere presence of life too inclusive. Instead, what accounts for the value of individual humans, and what therefore grounds rights, is the capacity to be mattered-to: a subject's awareness of the world, of what happens to him in the world, and an interest or preference about what happens to him in the world. Humans have value and rights because, to use Regan's term, they are "subjects-of-a-life." More precisely, subjects-of-a-life

> have beliefs and desires; perception, memory, and a sense of the future, including their own future; an emotional life together with feelings of pleasure and pain; preference- and welfare-interests; the ability to initiate action in pursuit of their desires and goals; a psychophysical identity over time; and an individual welfare in the sense that their experiential life fares well or ill for them, logically independent of their utility for others and logically independent of their being the object of anyone else's interests. (Regan 1983, p. 243)

So far as Regan is concerned, any human who is also a subject-of-a-life (because, as he's defined it, not all humans necessarily are; humans in irreversible vegetative states, for example, lack the requisite awareness to be subjects-of-a-life) possesses inherent, not instrumental or utilitarian, value. The capacity to be mattered-to in and of itself is owed respect by moral agents. Interfering with it is an illegitimate violation of the subject-of-a-life's well-being. Moreover, because inherent value is a quality of individuals rather than their experiences, all who possess it do so equally, regardless of whether their lives are happy or unhappy, successful or unsuccessful.

But Regan argues that humans aren't the only creatures with the capacity to be mattered-to. Some animals—certainly mammals, probably birds, and perhaps reptiles and amphibians—display all the characteristics necessary to qualify as subjects-of-a-life. Consistency demands, then, that we recognize them as likewise possessing inherent value. This, of course, is a radical break with the normal way of viewing animals. Typically, if they're granted any value at all, it's of an instrumental kind. As Regan notes, our culture encourages us "to view animals as our resources . . . Since animals exist for us, to benefit us in one way or another, what harms them doesn't really matter" (Regan 1985, p. 14). But just as Singer believes creatures displaying sentience are owed equal moral consideration, Regan argues that any creature which displays qualities characteristic of a subject-of-a-life has inherent value. And what that means, of course, is that any creature which is a subject-of-a-life also possesses natural rights. "Since what illuminates why we [humans] have the equal rights we do is our equality as subjects-of-a-life, and since other animals are like us in being subjects-of-a-life, . . . these animals have rights too" (Regan 2004b, p. 59).

Arguing that animals have rights the same as humans do doesn't mean, of course, that they have identical ones. They obviously lack nonbasic legislated rights such as entitlements to education or workplace fairness, because these rights are only relevant to (most) humans. The equality resides in equal inherent value and the equally shared right to be treated in ways, negative as well as positive, that respect their inherent value—a formulation that Regan calls, appropriately, the "respect principle"—even when not being treated with respect builds aggregate (utilitarian) benefit. Moreover, they have a prima facie right not to be harmed—the "harm principle." For Regan, this means not only the termination of factory farms, but the cessation of any activity such as scientific or commercial experimentation that manipulates, much less kills, animals. Singer is open to the possibility that the painless killing of animals is morally permissible, and his utilitarianism necessarily leaves the door open for killing animals if doing so increases rather than diminishes total preference satisfaction. But Regan agrees with Henry Salt's claim that "humane slaughtering" is a "contradiction in terms" (Salt 1999, p. 120). For him, killing animals merely to boost preference satisfaction is a violation of the respect and harm principles. Nor does he buy the replaceability argument that Singer half-heartedly accepts. Individual subjects-of-a-life are unique individuals who possess inherent value. They can't be discarded and replaced by substitutes as if they were inanimate and anonymous cogs in a machine.

But subjects-of-a-life sometimes come into potential or actual conflict with one another. Many conflicts can be adjudicated easily enough because one side is obviously in the wrong through its violation of the respect or harm principle. Yet genuine conflicts can arise even when the two principles are honored. As Regan admits, there are situations in which, "provided that all those involved are treated with respect . . . any innocent individual has the right to act to avoid being made worse-off even if doing so harms other individuals" (Regan 1983, p. 331). This rule, which Regan calls the "liberty principle," acknowledges both the inevitability of tension between subjects-of-a-life competing for the same interests and the prima facie nature of the harm principle.

To anticipate and forestall some conflicts or to help resolve them when they do occur, Regan suggests two additional rules, the miniride and the worse-off principles, which seek to contain damage as much as possible. The first, he argues, is consistent with the respect principle; the second is distinct from it. The miniride or (minimize overriding) principle states that in a situation where all parties are likely to suffer comparable harm, the best course of action is the one that minimizes the number of individuals actually harmed. The worse-off principle on the other hand stipulates that in a conflict situation where the harm suffered by involved parties *isn't* comparable, the best decision is one that harms the individual or individuals with the least to lose and spares those who would be made worse off (Regan 1983, pp. 305–12). Although a casual reading of these two rules might suggest that they're utilitarian in spirit, Regan explicitly denies that they are. The point isn't to aggregate satisfied preferences and minimize frustrated ones. Instead, the goal is to respect the inherent value of each and every individual involved and to do as little harm as possible.

Both the miniride and the worse-off principle are applicable to the clash of interests between human and food animal subjects-of-a-life. The miniride suggests, for example, that if animals *must* be killed for food, the killing be kept to a minimum. The worse-off principle implies that in a clash between the economic interests of a poultry farmer and the lives of tens of thousands of broilers, the individual with the least to lose is the farmer. The chickens, who stand to lose life itself, would be worse off (Regan 1983, pp. 338–47). At the same time, though, the worse-off principle would also legitimize the taking of an animal's life if doing so was necessary to save a human's. Because of our ability to make future plans as well as our relatively long span of life, humans lose more than animals do from a premature death (pp. 351–3).

In grounding his defense of vegetarianism upon what he thinks is the bedrock of inherent value, Regan believes he's offered a strong alternative to both the basic argument's appeal to kin sympathy and Singer's appeal to utilitarian interests. Even if we do feel an empathetic connection with animals—and experience tells us that not everyone does—there's no compelling reason outside of personal choice to treat them decently. But on Regan's model, there is. Justice mandates decent treatment of animals because they possess inherent value as subjects-of-a-life. Similarly, utilitarian defenses of vegetarianism, although well-meaning, in fact tend to minimize actual concern for animals by focusing on the quality of their experiences instead of on them. Moreover, the standard of adjudication utilitarians invoke can, under the right circumstances, actually justify using animals as means, thereby ignoring what Regan takes to be their inherent value.

Regan also thinks that his rights argument has another advantage over arguments from interests. Recall his "Singer's Paradox" criticism of utilitarian models examined in the last chapter. According to it, the moral rightness of what vegetarians do is measured not by the actions they actually perform, but by how many people agree with them and by the response of meat-eaters. But Regan thinks that making the rightness of an action contingent on how many people act similarly, much less on the reaction of opponents, is cock-eyed. If we have a duty to respect the inherent value of animal subjects-of-a-life, we shouldn't depend "on how many others act similarly" nor be deterred "because of the many who continue to support the animal industry" (Regan 1983, p. 350).

Alternative rights arguments

Although Regan's rights argument is recognized as one of the two most influential defenses of vegetarianism (Singer's being the other), it's not without its critics. They generally fall into two camps: those who are sympathetic with ascribing rights to animals but disagree with Regan about how to do so, and those who dispute the claim that animals are the sorts of beings who can have rights. As we saw in the last chapter, Singer's accusation of speciesism is a flashpoint for some nonvegetarians. For many others, Regan's claim that at least some animals possess inherent value is equally incendiary. We'll examine their objections shortly. In this section, we'll take a look at some of the animal rights models that compete with Regan's.

A defense of animal rights that may come closer than any other to Regan's is offered by Paola Cavaliere. She argues that intentionality is the necessary condition for having rights, and defines an intentional being as one "that cares about its goals and wants to achieve them. All the beings that fulfill the requisite of intentionality are characterized by the capacity to enjoy freedom and welfare, as well as life which is a precondition for them, both directly and as prerequisites for action; and, for all these beings, the intrinsic value of their enjoyment is the same" (Cavaliere 2008, p. 33). For Cavaliere, it makes no difference whether the being under consideration is human or nonhuman. What counts is the presence of intentionality, not the specific type of creature possessing it, and whoever has it also has a natural right to respect. Just as we codify laws to honor this natural right in humans, concludes Cavaliere, so we ought to legislate protection of it in animals. Cavaliere's intentionality is similar to Regan's subject-of-a-life category, as is her assumption that it's a necessary condition for the possession of rights.

James Rachels (1976) agrees that it makes sense to say that animals have rights, but sees no reason to found them upon foundations as problematic (as we'll see a bit later) as subject-of-a-life or inherent value. According to him, any creature capable of interests has a prima facie right to not have its interests needlessly harmed. To discern just what rights animals capable of interests possess, we can invoke human analogies. The Universal Declaration of Human Rights stipulates, for example, that humans have a right to liberty and a right not to be tortured. There's no good reason, argues Rachels, not to grant these two rights to animals, because their well-being is clearly diminished when they're fettered in some way or physically and emotionally abused. On the other hand, it makes no sense to endow animals with other rights—the right of religious expression, for example—guaranteed in the Universal Declaration. In other words, consistency demands that we grant interest-capable animals the same rights we grant interest-capable humans, just so long as the interests that are protected aren't exclusive to humans.

Another defense of animal rights based on similarity to humans is proposed by Gary Francione. As he sees it, animals are "for all intents and purposes, the slaves of humans . . . [V]irtually every aspect of our lives is involved in some way or another with the institutionalized exploitation of some animal or another" (Francione 1996, p. 152). But the foundation of any legitimate ethics, Francione argues, is equal consideration of like cases, or fairness. So if some animals have an interest in not being enslaved or exploited that's analogous to the human one, and if we bestow rights upon humans in order to protect that interest, simple fairness dictates that we bestow a similar right upon the animals in question (Francione 2000). Francione sees Regan's postulation of inherent value in animals as another way of making the same point he wants to defend: that animals capable of having interests oughtn't to be treated merely as means to human satisfaction. But, like Rachels, he doesn't think it's necessary.

Philosopher Mary Anne Warren agrees. She's willing to grant rights to animals, but doesn't see the need for any other foundation than sentience. The ability to feel pain and pleasure, and to be interested in the avoidance of the first and the pursuit of the second, is a sufficient condition for the bestowal of rights upon humans and animals. But Warren balks at the notion of *equal* rights, defending instead a sliding scale. The qualities which determine location on the scale are levels of sensitivity and mental ability, such that human interests trump animal ones, and higher order animal interests trump lower order animal ones. Otherwise, she worries, "[w]e are forced to say that either a spider has the same right to life as you and I do, or it has no right to life whatever— and that only the gods know which of these alternatives is true" (Warren 1987, p. 166). Warren calls her model the "weak animal rights" position, in contrast to Regan's "strong" one.

Warren may be correct in her claim that sentience is a sufficient condition for the bestowal of rights, but her interpretation of Regan's equality of rights argument surely pushes it further than he himself wishes to go. Although Regan admits that he intends his subject-of-a-life criterion to be a sufficient rather than a necessary condition for inherent value, thus leaving the door open for granting rights to "lower order" animals, he's also clear that the further down the animal chain one goes, the more difficult it is to establish animal rights. As a consequence, Warren's spider example might be accused of manhandling rather than addressing Regan's point. Equality of rights applies specifically to subjects-of-a-life, not to *any* living thing.

At this point it should be apparent that one common link between all the alternative arguments from rights, with the likely exception of Cavaliere's, is their by-passing of Regan's ascription of inherent rights to animals based on his subject-of-a-life category. (We'll shortly examine some specific reasons why it gives critics pause.) Philosopher Evelyn Pluhar evidently shares their wariness, because her defense of animal rights rests instead on an analysis of basic needs and consistency.

According to her, most but not all humans are agents, or beings capable of acting to achieve goals. At the deepest level, those goals are determined by basic needs such as life, health, and general well-being, in whose fulfillment we're interested. Because these needs are so basic, and because we naturally desire them, we believe that others ought not to interfere with our pursuit of them. Pluhar thinks that this "is tantamount to one's claiming the right to non-interference in these regards" (Pluhar 2004, p. 94). But consistency requires that when we encounter others to whom these needs are likewise basic, we not interfere with *their* pursuit of them. So any being which is a moral agent has the positive right to pursue basic needs and the negative right not to have that pursuit impeded.

But there are some creatures that, although also physically and psychologically dependent on basic needs, are incapable of pursuing them. These nonagent but sentient beings include "[b]abies, children, many accident victims, and the severely mentally disabled" on the human side, but also "some very young and relatively simple nonhuman animals" (p. 95). Consistency again requires that they be treated by moral agents in respectful ways, because their basic needs, even if they can't act in pursuit of them, nonetheless grant them rights to the fulfillment of those needs. Moreover, the right that they have against moral agents is not noninterference so much as assistance. What follows, says Pluhar, is that "other things being equal, moral agents should not regard any of them"—babies, children, accident victims, the mentally disabled, or animals—"as entrees or side dishes" (p. 95).

A version of the argument from rights that has some similarity to Pluhar's is defended by philosopher Bernard E. Rollin. It's inspired in part by the Aristotelian notion of telos: everything which exists has a kind of flourishing appropriate to it by virtue of its nature.[3] The telos of an acorn is to become an oak. When it does so, it flourishes and its telos is fulfilled. Similarly, says Rollin, every creature has a telos, and it's in the interests of that creature to live in the way that best enhances its opportunities for telic flourishing. These interests serve, somewhat along the lines of Pluhar's basic needs, as the foundation for rights. As Rollins puts it, "any animal has a right to the kind of life that its nature dictates." Furthermore, "it has the right to have the unique interests that characterize it morally considered in our treatment of it" (Rollin 2006, p. 118).

Rollin puts the case even stronger when he argues that "any living thing with interests is an end in itself and should never be looked at simply as a means" (p. 117). At times, circumstances may indeed require us to use animals as means. But even while doing so, we should keep in mind that they have intrinsic value and that their ends, "life and interests," are "objects of moral concern" (p. 116).

One of the more interesting aspects of Rollin's argument is his suggestion, in response to the contractarian position that only moral agents properly possess rights (more of this shortly), that at least some animals display behavior which "bespeaks" something akin to moral agency.

> Canids, including the domesticated dog, do not attack when a vanquished combatant bares its throat, showing a sign of submission. Animals typically do not prey upon members of their own species. Pack carnivores share kills according to "fair" rules. Elephants and porpoises will and do feed injured members of their species. Porpoises will help humans, even at risk to themselves. Some animals will adopt young of other species. (Such cross-species "morality" would certainly not be explainable by simple appeal to mechanical evolution, since it is of no advantage whatever to one's own species.) Dogs will act "guilty" when they break a rule such as stealing food from a table and will, for the most part, learn not to take it (pp. 54–5).

Rollins admits that one way to interpret these sorts of animal behavior is to say that they're hardwired. But he points out that a great deal of analogous human behavior might be also, and that in neither case is the practical morality of the behavior thereby diminished. The line between what's "natural" and what's "conventional" is "fuzzy," preventing us from saying with rock bottom assurance that all animals are incapable of moral agency. And if this is the case, treating them as ends rather than means seems the better route to take.

Objections to the argument from rights

Objections to the argument from rights, both Regan's version and the alternative models, range from an outright denial that it makes sense to ascribe rights to nonhumans to the charge, generally leveled by ecofeminist vegetarians, that the rights argument, like the utilitarian interests one, is overly formalistic. We'll examine the feminist rebuttal in the next chapter. Here we'll focus on the criticism that assigning rights to animals is a mistake.

A contrived fit

Peter Singer is one of Regan's more generous critics. In an article in which he compares his utilitarian argument with Regan's rights-based one, Singer (1987) is willing to accept the claim that it's wrong to treat subjects-of-a-life as mere raw resources. But he contends that dragging in rights is an unnecessary complication, because concern for their interests is more than adequate to protect them from harm. Somewhat surprisingly, Singer also implies that Regan has taken Singer's receptacle-filled-with-experiences metaphor too literally. It's impossible to make a clear-cut distinction between a sentient creature and its experiences of preference or interest satisfaction and frustration. An animal isn't the same thing as an empty vessel which then gets filled with experience. So Regan's criticism that Singer disregards the animal by focusing overmuch on the value of its experiences is too strong, once again suggesting that Regan's corrective bestowal of rights on animals isn't necessary.

Some critics aren't as willing to say that Regan's ascription of rights to animals is benignly unnecessary. They argue that the foundation on which he bases it, the claim that subjects-of-a-life possess inherent value, is unjustified. Some of them (Rowlands 2009; Warren 1987) reject it as mysterious or arbitrary. One response to their criticism is that Regan intends inherent value as a hypothetical explanation which best accounts for the moral status of subjects-of-a-life: given that we sense moral obligations to animals, how best to account for it? But Michael Leahy points out that even if we grant that the hypothesis of inherent value is "rationally preferable" to utilitarianism's focus on interests, Regan is still open to the charge that he "has simply invented a quality and invested it with significance" (Leahy 1994, p. 74).

Others argue that even if a connection can be established between the possession of a subject-of-a-life consciousness and value, this isn't enough to warrant a claim of *equal* moral status between animals and humans. In the same vein as Mary Ann Warren's argument for "weak" animal rights, Rem Edwards (Edwards 1993) contends that the qualities which make up a subject-of-a-life are on a sliding scale as one moves from species to species, and that any nonhuman subject-of-a-life has less sophistication, and hence less value, than a human subject-of-a-life.[4] One critic (Petrinovich 1999) suggests that Regan's willingness to privilege a human over an animal life in the situation of a one-to-one standoff shows that he thinks so too.

A shell game

Some critics of Regan's argument from rights who suspect that Regan's inherent value is little more than a *deus ex machina* are much harsher and even intemperate in their remarks. Carl Cohen is one of the most strenuous of them, accusing Regan not simply of being mistaken in his claim that animals possess rights, but of actually running a philosophical "shell game"[5] (Cohen and Regan 2001, p. 247).

Cohen's charge is based on the claim that Regan confuses two senses of "inherent value." Every living creature, insofar as it is unique and irreplaceable (the utilitarian irreplaceability argument to one side, of course), possesses inherent value. But Regan jumps from this minimalist ascription of value in animals to the preposterous claim that animals have "the entirely different sense of inherent value that . . . ground[s] human rights," and does so on no stronger basis than the presence in them of the "crudest subjective experiences" (Cohen and Regan 2001, pp. 246, 250). Inherent value in this second sense comes only from the "special dignity of those who have a moral will" which in turn "entitles them to be treated as ends, and never as means only" (p. 247). Because animals lack a moral will—that is, aren't moral agents, despite anecdotal evidence such as the kind Rollin provides—they aren't entitled to be treated as ends. They, unlike humans, simply aren't the sorts of beings capable of possessing rights, and to treat them as if they are is to try to pull off a slight of hand, or shell game.[6]

The claim that animals lack rights, and that this is a crucial moral distinction between them and humans, is one that Cohen thinks intuitively evident. Our responses are different when we see a predator attacking an animal and a predator attacking a human, and we have no hesitation while driving in choosing between the life of a child and the life of a squirrel (Cohen 2004, p. 157). What muddies the water, however, is the "widespread fear" promulgated by animal rights activists that anyone who denies rights to animals "is likely to be thought callous or even cruel." Consequently, there is a "general reluctance to express the moral truth that everyone grasps intuitively": only humans have moral rights (p. 152).

Despite his scorn for philosophers and activists who ascribe rights to animals, Cohen doesn't go so far as to argue that humans have no moral obligations to beasts. It's good to refrain from gratuitously harming them. This isn't a right that animals have against us, however. Instead, it's just an application to animals of the general codes of decency that prescribe our treatment of those humans who likewise have no formal right against us because their mental or developmental states rob them of moral will. But it's clear from Cohen's analysis that mistreatment of animals, while indecent, violates no moral obligation because animals have no valid claim to our moral consideration. Humane treatment of them becomes merely supererogatory rather than obligatory.

An equally fierce critic of Regan's position is philosopher Tibor Machan. Agreeing with Cohen's insistence that the assignation of rights to animals is mistaken, Machan argues that "[t]he concept of rights simply cannot be appropriated as a rationale for the humane treatment of animals without corrupting it and rendering it untenable for human use" (Machan 2004, p. 21). What Cohen refers to as "moral will," Machan calls "moral nature": "a capacity for discerning between right and wrong and [freely] choosing between alternatives" (p. xv). Humans, or at least most humans, have this capacity; no animal does. True, both beasts and humans "have interests or can feel pain." But the necessary and sufficient condition for moral nature is the capacity to make free choices and to accept responsibility for one's behavior, not the possession of interests or preferences.

Also like Cohen, Machan argues that it's appropriate to treat animals with a certain amount of concern, even though they lack rights. But he insists that decent treatment of "moral patients"—that is, beings lacking a moral nature—if it's bestowed, is done for *our* sake. An animal, Machan says, can be compared with a Rembrandt painting. We "ought to be careful with it. But not because the painting has any rights but rather because of its great value for us as a work of art and also because of the wider respect for culture that informs our actions generally as civilized human beings" (p. 17). So we can have "moral responsibilities" when it comes to animals, although we don't have moral responsibilities *to* them. If we mistreat animals, our actions are condemnable because they violate the norms of civilized culture. But we commit no moral wrong to the animals themselves.

Regan's response to Cohen's and Machan's claim that we have no moral obligations to animals focuses on what he sees as the proper normative relationship between moral agents and moral patients. If a necessary condition for the possession of rights is the possession of a working "moral will" or "moral nature," then we're forced to conclude that so-called marginal humans—persons in vegetative states, developmentally disabled and brain-damaged children and adults, and certainly infants and toddlers—either have no rights or have fewer rights than "normal" adults. Yet even though they're incapable of moral agency, we still grant them basic rights to life and care. It's true that we don't allow them the very same set of rights as normal adults; we don't think they're entitled, for example, to drive vehicles. But this doesn't mean that we strip them of fundamental rights.

In a similar way, says Regan, animals need not be automatically denied rights just because they lack moral agency. If, like most marginal humans, they are subjects-of-a-life, they are entitled to basic rights, although obviously not to *all* of the rights appropriate to normal adult humans. But of course the same thing can be said about the allocation of rights to humans. "Clearly," argues Regan, "human beings do not have to have *every* right in order to have *any* right" (Regan 2004b, p. 65). And neither do animals.

The Benjamin Franklin objection

One objection to the argument from rights that's particularly popular is named after an episode that Benjamin Franklin recounts in his *Autobiography*. It seems that as a youth, Franklin decided to adopt a vegetarian diet. He found it hard going, especially as he was inordinately fond of fish. But his conscience kept him from breaking his new regimen because he considered "the taking [of] every fish as a kind of unprovoked murder, since none of them had or ever could do us any injury that might justify the slaughter." His resolve collapsed one day when he came across some fishermen who were grilling cod over an open fire. The aroma tickled Franklin's nostrils and made his mouth water. "I balanced some time between principle and inclination, till I recollected, that when the fish were opened, I saw smaller fish taken out of their stomachs. Then, thought I, if you eat one another, I don't see why we mayn't eat you. So I dined upon cod very heartily" (Franklin 2009, p. 36).

The salient point of Franklin's reminiscence is his implied argument that even if animals possess rights, humans are under no obligation to honor them because animals don't honor one another's rights. In its crudest form, the argument is a *tu quoque*.[7] In its more sophisticated form, the argument rests on one of two assumptions: either the fact that animals eat other animals *entitles* us (gives us the right to) eat them in turn, or animals *deserve* to be eaten because they eat other animals. But philosopher Elizabeth Telfer makes short shrift of both these assumptions. In regards to the first, no one wants to posit as a moral rule the claim that "we're entitled to do to people everything that they do to others" (Telfer 1996, p. 78). Why, then, would we be entitled to do it to animals? As for the second assumption, the most that it would allow us to do is to eat carnivorous animals, and this includes nearly none of the animals that now make up the bulk of our meat diet. It's also worth considering that the 20 percent or so of animals in the world who are carnivorous *must* eat meat to survive. As we'll see more fully in Chapter 7, humans don't.

Still, the Ben Franklin objection gestures at a criticism of the argument from rights that isn't as easily dismissed. It focuses on the proper relationship of humans to wild rather than domesticated animals. If animal subjects-of-a-life deserves our respect and protection, do we owe an obligation to ones in nature who risk being hunted and killed by predators or harmed by disease, starvation, and exposure? As D. G. Ritchie posed the question at the end of the nineteenth century,

> Well, then, in our exercise of our power and in our guardianship of the rights of animals, must we not protect the weak among them against the strong? Must we not put to death blackbirds and thrushes because they feed on worms, or (if capital punishment offends our humanitarianism) starve them slowly by permanent captivity and vegetarian diet? [Must we] prevent the cat's nocturnal wanderings, lest she should wickedly slay a mouse? (Ritchie 1894, p. 109)

The same Mark Sagoff (1984) who objected on environmental grounds to Singer's argument from interests also takes on Regan.

One of the implications of Ritchie's argument is that individuals count for little from the standpoint of nature. Birds eat worms and cats slay mice. Sagoff agrees, but puts the point in terms of eco-systems analysis. From an environmental view, what's important is the integrity of the ecosystem and the flourishing of the species that coexist in it. But collectivities, he argues, aren't the sorts of things that properly can be said to have rights. Only individuals possess rights. So anyone concerned with the environment can't indeed, shouldn't—allow concern for individual animal suffering to step on a concern for the health of the ecosystem. Regan's concern for the rights of animals would either be impossible to enforce in the wild or, if enforced, would shatter the integrity of ecosystems and thus inflict damage upon the animals within it. So at best, Regan's model applies only to domesticated animals—which seems oddly inconsistent, since Regan argues that any subject-of-a-life, domesticated or wild, possesses rights that ought to be respected. Environmental philosopher Daniel Callicott (Callicott 1989, 1993) agrees with Sagoff. If Regan's argument from rights were applied to wildlife, at the least it would require a systematic campaign to either contain or kill predators, and this would have dire environmental consequences.

Regan's response to those who argue that his rights approach would be disastrous to the environment is less than convincing, and it doesn't help that at one point he accuses them of "environmental fascism" (Regan 1983, p. 362), or valuing individuals only because of their connection with the wider biotic collective or community. More temperately, Regan tries to sidestep the environmental criticism by denying that his rights model requires intervention to protect wild animals. He says that we respect the rights of wild animals when we refuse to interfere with the natural course of their lives by hunting them or exploiting their natural habitats. His reasoning—and it's shared by Stephen R. L. Clark (Clark 1997), who takes on Ritchie's specific example of cat and mouse predation—is that respecting a subject-of-a-life's right to life doesn't entail an obligation to rescue it from nonmoral, or natural, sources of harm and causes of death. Otherwise, presumably, we would be forced to morally condemn a physician whenever she loses a patient.

But this response is problematic. Obviously moral agents can't be held responsible for "natural deaths" except perhaps indirectly and incompletely (if, for example, we encourage someone to smoke cigarettes). If a physician treats patients expertly and conscientiously, she certainly ought not to be held morally accountable every time one of them dies. But on the other hand, it *does* seem reasonable to hold a moral agent responsible when she can prevent death or harm and doesn't, even when the cause of the death or harm is natural. If I see a rock climber about to grasp an unsafe ledge, I surely have a moral obligation, short of causing myself harm, to do *something*, be it to yell at him or even physically intervene. Why wouldn't I likewise have an obligation to do something when I see a lion about to pounce on a gazelle?

Stephen Davis offers a slightly different twist on the tension between Regan's argument from rights and environmentalism. In an ingenious argument (Davis 2003), he contends that truly honoring Regan's harm principle, which urges us to minimize harm to subjects-of-a-life, would oblige us to eat large ruminants rather than cutting them out of our diet. His reasoning is that huge numbers of indigenous mammals and birds (not to mention millions of insects, although they almost certainly aren't subjects-of-a-life) are slaughtered each year by the industrial harvesting of crops such as corn, beans, and rice which humans directly eat. The least total harm would be inflicted on life, therefore, if we transformed vegetable-producing fields into forage pastures for cattle and ate beef instead of vegetables. As an added bonus, the forage pastures would provide habitat for hundreds of species of animals and insects who don't thrive in vegetable fields. It's not entirely clear if Davis intends his suggestion of transforming vegetable fields into pasture to be taken seriously, or if he's instead offering a *reductio ad absurdum* intended to show that Regan's harm principle, when pushed, leads to the conclusion that we should actually eat instead of abstain from animals. But in either case, Davis seems to share the suspicion of critics like Sagoff and Callicott that Regan's model is unduly slanted towards domesticated animals.

Contractarianism

The final objection to Regan's rights argument to be considered here acknowledges the reality of rights, but denies that they're natural. Instead, defenders of this position argue that rights—and, indeed, morality—arise from quid quo pro agreements or contracts between rational, self-interested agents. If I have a right to something and you have an obligation to honor my right, it's only because we have entered, explicitly or implicitly, into a contract that spells out that right and obligation. This is known as a "contractarian" model of rights.

Under a contractarian understanding of rights, only the actual framers of the contract have direct rights which must be respected by one another. But this doesn't mean that they're the only holders of rights. The children of the framers, for example, have indirect rights. They're not moral agents themselves. But as Jan Narveson (Narveson 1983) argues, because they're associated with framers of the contract they're indirectly covered by many of the rights spelled out in the contract. Moreover, it's in the self-interest of the contractors to extend benefits to one another's children, because not caring for them risks their growing up to be maladjusted and dangerous adults.

What about animals? Contractarians deny, over the objections of some philosophers (Melden 1988; Rollin 2006; Watson 1979), that animals have the necessary attributes to qualify as even minimal moral agents capable of entering into quid pro quo arrangements with humans, and consequently have no direct rights.[8] But, like human children, they may be indirectly protected if it's in the interests of the framers of the contract to do so. As contractarian Peter Carruthers says, we may accord animals "indirect moral significance . . . under the rules dealing with private property"—pets or livestock—"or by treating them as a matter of legitimate public interest"—zoo animals, for example (Carruthers 1994, p. 105). But because animals have no direct rights whatsoever, humans have no direct moral obligations to them. Therefore, it's meaningless to talk about weighing animal versus human rights, concludes Carruthers (p. 102), because in the case of animals there's "nothing *to* be weighed." If we treat animals decently, it's always for the sake of something other than themselves. Their suffering is relevant only to the extent that it affects humans. So, for example, both Carruthers (1994) and Narveson (1977, 1983) argue that cruelty to animals is morally dangerous, but only because it risks habituating humans to cruelty, which in turn poses a danger to other humans.

At the same time, though, contractarians argue that when it comes to standards of appropriate normative behavior to humans and animals, clear lines need to be drawn. Carruthers argues that in a world of massive human suffering, it's morally corrupt to be overly concerned about animal welfare, especially when it comes to questions of diet. Louis Pojman (Pojman 1995) agrees, even going so far as to contend that a failure to draw normative distinctions between animals and humans leads to moral nihilism.

Regan objects to the contractarian position for several reasons, not the least of which is to question the assumption, as we've already seen him do, that moral agency is the only source of moral significance. Additionally, he believes that the contractarian position obliges its defenders to two propositions which are impossible to defend: (1) animals don't feel pain or, if they do, (2) their pain isn't morally relevant. The first claim is both counter-intuitive and contrary to ordinary experience. If the second is endorsed, an explanation is required for why the pain of some moral patients (human infants and children) is morally significant, but the pain of others (animals) isn't.

But Regan's most telling reservation about contractarianism is broader than the issue of animal rights. There is nothing in its understanding of rights, he asserts (Regan 1985, p. 17), "that guarantees or requires that everyone will have a chance to participate equally in framing the rules of morality." So contractarianism "could sanction the most blatant forms of social, economic, moral and political injustice," not only to animals but to humans as well. This worry is shared by at least one contractarian, Mark Rowlands (2009), who invokes John Rawls' veil of ignorance thought experiment (Rawls 1971) to grant animals moral significance. In the experiment, Rawls famously asks us to consider what principles of fairness self-interested parties ignorant of the specifics of their own situation would think essential to a just society. Rawls contends that principles which maximize individual liberty and level out accident-of-birth inequalities would be strong contenders. But Rowlands contends that species membership and rationality are accidents of birth, and that for the veil of ignorance experiment to be taken seriously, players must also suspend their knowledge of who is human and who animal. Rowlands' conclusion is that contractual fairness entails that standards of justice apply to sentient nonhumans.

"A matter of strict justice"

From first to last, the conviction that fuels Regan's argument from rights defense of vegetarianism is that any consideration of the moral significance of animals has to be based squarely on objective standards that are consistently applied. If being the subject-of-a-life is a condition for having inherent value, it must be true that *all* subjects-of-a-life, across the board, have equal inherent value. Likewise, it must be true that creatures with inherent value have across-the-board basic moral rights, "including in particular the fundamental right to be treated with the respect that . . . they are due as a matter of strict justice" (Regan 1983, p. 328). Finally, if there arose situations in which fairness requires that some subjects-of-a-right be treated differently than others, clearly defined principles, such as the miniride, worse-off, and liberty ones, must be appealed to.

The rights argument, whether defended by Regan or others, offers a defense of vegetarianism, then, that rests on objective, rational, and universally applicable criteria—or, as Regan says, a "sustained commitment to rational inquiry" (Regan 1983, p. xii). None of the objections to the argument we've examined in this chapter have objected to those standards so much as to the propriety of manipulating them to defend animal rights. But an entire school of vegetarianism, defended largely by ecofeminists, calls into question the very method of Regan's argument from rights—and, for that matter, Singer's argument from interests as well. Ecofeminists agree that animals ought not to be raised and slaughtered for the sake of human consumption. But they believe that the "sustained commitment to rational inquiry" endorsed by both Regan and Singer reflect the very worldview assumptions that legitimize the exploitation of animals in the first place. It's to their argument that we now turn.

CHAPTER FIVE

The ecofeminist argument

There are important connections—historical, experiential, symbolic, theoretical—between the domination of women and the domination of nature.

KAREN WARREN

Caring does not make people more fragile or annihilate them. In fact, through caring, individuals not only acquire new experiences and skills that accompany these experiences, but also discover that they are part of a network that can sustain them even when caring evolves into grief for what is happening.

CAROL ADAMS

Strange as it may sound, the three models we've examined thus far—the basic argument, the argument from interests, and the argument from rights—are both countercultural *and* traditional. They're countercultural in their defense of a diet that goes against the meat-eating grain of most of the developed world's inhabitants, a defense inspired by the equally countercultural conviction that a wide range of animals—not just pampered house pets—deserves moral consideration. But they're very traditional in their philosophical justifications for vegetarianism. All three of them, for example, use humans as the default normative standard: animals deserve moral consideration to the extent that they share certain human characteristics or capacities. Two of them, the interests and rights arguments, appeal to ethical models that emphasize equality and consistency. The same two arguments also place a high premium on the sufficiency of rationality when it comes to ethical decision making.

In recent years, a school of vegetarianism that embraces ecofeminism has emerged as an alternative to the basic, interests, and rights models. Ecofeminist vegetarians argue that the traditional stress on equality and consistency valued by ethicists such as Peter Singer and Tom Regan in fact reflects patriarchal assumptions which have historically oppressed animals and the environment as well as women. They offer instead a defense of vegetarianism grounded in sensitivity to embodiment and an ethic based more on contextual care than abstract principles of fairness.

In addition to breaking with a philosophical tradition that they consider patriarchal and oppressive, ecofeminist vegetarians claim to be wholly rather than partially countercultural in that they locate meat-eating in a moral landscape that connects it with political, ecological, and feminist concerns. While ecofeminist vegetarians see the basic argument's emphasis on sympathy as a refreshing alternative to the interests-and rights-based models, they worry that defenders of the basic argument are more concerned with alleviating immediate animal suffering than with exploring and eliminating its root causes. Similarly, ecofeminists charge that the rights model defended by Regan and others focuses on clashes between rights-holding subjects-of-a-life without considering the social and political contexts in which those clashes originate and take shape. And even Singer's utilitarian model, which is generally credited with launching the animal liberation movement, comes in for criticism. Ecofeminists consider its examination of the mechanisms of social oppression too conventional. Appealing to preference satisfaction and frustration without a prior exploration of the worldview assumptions that define preferences in the first place is a legitimization of the status quo, not a challenge to it.

As we'll see, not all feminists are vegetarians. Some even argue that the ecofeminists' linkage of animal oppression and patriarchy trivializes the struggle for women's liberation. But ecofeminists respond that a genuinely feminist understanding of oppressive structures necessarily connects the two, and that concern for the welfare of animals is of a piece with the struggle to end oppression in any of its manifestations. Vegetarianism is thus more than just the abandonment of a meat-based diet. It's also a radical deconstruction of patriarchal society.

The ecofeminist context

Ecofeminism takes as its starting point the claim that the foundation of Western society's identity is a patriarchal ideology which justifies domination and exploitation by appealing to a falsely dualistic and hierarchical interpretation of reality. This ideology contrives dyads of superiority and inferiority that classify and thus "make sense" of the world, and this classification in turn grounds social and political relationships that privilege the few at the expense of the many. In doing so, they exhibit a distinct bias that contrasts dominant categories such as "man," "human," "white," "mind," and "reason" with subordinate ones like "woman," "animal," "colored," "body," and "emotion." In the qualitative hierarchy established by this scheme, women and animals wind up being inferior to men and humans, and reason and mind superior to emotions and body. This hierarchy not only emphasizes the differences between humans on the one hand and animals and nature on the other by drawing "fierce boundaries" between the two but also "differentiate[s] men from women [and] whites from people of color" (Adams 2007a, p. 203).

The dualism that assigns greater value to humans, reason, and men than to animals, emotions, and women creates a "logic of domination" that justifies power relations in which members of the "inferior" dyads are subordinated to "rational white men" (Gruen 2004, pp. 286–7). Moreover, the "inferior" characteristics attributed to women and people of color—emotionality, less-than-full rationality, a grounding in body rather than mind—are also ascribed to animals. Women, marginalized peoples, and animals all become subhuman.

Not surprisingly, human culture is viewed by patriarchal systems as superior to the natural world. The latter is mindless and possesses value only insofar as it materially benefits humans. Feminist historian Carolyn Merchant (1990) points out that the modern era's use of terms to justify the exploitation of nature is frequently used to describe women. In the seventeenth century, for example,

Francis Bacon likened the "conquest" of nature to the "conquest" of a coquettish woman, comparing the expropriation of raw resources from the former with the wresting of sexual favors from the latter. The logic of domination inherent in patriarchal ideologies thus extends even to the inanimate world of nature.

The obvious conclusion to be drawn, say ecofeminists, is that all forms of exploitation, sharing as they do a common source, are necessarily interconnected with one another. Patriarchal dualism exploits women and peoples of color in ways similar to its exploitation of animals and nature. Sexism is cut from the same cloth as racism, speciesism, and nature-chauvinism. They are all "interdependent oppressions" (Adams 2007a, p. 201).

This is troublesome enough. But the dualism condemned by ecofeminists also infects the very way in which ethics traditionally has been done in the West. Consequently, mainstream ethicists unwittingly mirror and perpetuate the very injustices that their models aim to rectify. Ethical behavior, according to the tradition, must be grounded in the autonomous individual's capacity for rationally examining moral choices and choosing appropriately. Emotions diminish autonomy, enslaving the individual to his desires and interfering with the judicious exercise of reason. This way of thinking, defended in one form by another by most mainstream Western philosophers, is both a reflection and reinforcement of the dominant patriarchal ideology which valorizes masculinity, autonomy, and reason over femininity, relationship, and emotion. It's not surprising, say ecofeminists, that animals, the environment, and women and children have historically been ignored by ethicists. The default exemplar of moral behavior is the rational and autonomous male.

Moreover, ecofeminists argue that because two essential patriarchal norms are individualism and autonomy, the ethical models arising from them are predictably adversarial in spirit. Moral agents are seen as competing with one another for available resources and privileges. What keeps their behavior within acceptable boundaries is the postulation of abstract standards of justice that apply equally across the board to all moral agents. Justice, in fact, is the set of predetermined principles that codify fair and equal entitlements and fair and equal expectations.

Ecofeminists argue that the dyadic worldview of domination and subordination characteristic of patriarchy is both descriptively and normatively false. It doesn't adequately capture human nature or social relationships, and the standards of ethical behavior it defends are unacceptably biased. By way of contrast, they defend a more holistic way of viewing reality which entails "a shift from a conception of ethics as primarily a matter of rights, rules, or principles predetermined and applied in specific cases to entities viewed as competitors in the contest of moral standing" to an ethics that "makes a central place for values of care, love, friendship, trust, and appropriate reciprocity—values that presuppose that our relationships to others are central to our understanding of who we are"[1] (Curtin 2007, p. 88). In positing this alternative way of thinking about ethics, ecofeminists take their cue from Carol Gilligan's (1982) influential distinction between moralities based on autonomy, individualism, and abstract principles of rights and duties, which she suggests are male-oriented models, and ones based on particular relationships and caring responsiveness to needs, which are more female oriented.[2] Care as a normative response is central to the ecofeminist defense of vegetarianism.

Vegetarianism and care

In keeping with ecofeminism's criticism of traditional patriarchal ways of thinking about ethics, ecofeminist vegetarians argue that the models defended by Singer and Regan, while intending in good faith to alleviate animal distress, actually perpetuate it. Josephine Donovan accuses their arguments of an "inherent bias" toward "rationalism," a bitter irony since it's precisely rationalism "in the form of Cartesian objectivism that established a major theoretical justification for animal abuse" in the first place (Donovan 2007a, p. 59). Cathryn Bailey goes a step further by accusing Singer and Regan of so "valorizing reason" that it almost seems as if they're more interested in defending it than animals (Bailey 2007, p. 344). Deane Curtin criticizes them for presuming "that the project of morality is a project of reason to the exclusion of sentiment or emotion" (Curtin 2004, p. 275). Carol Adams agrees, claiming that ignoring the role of emotions in moral decision-making is a "patriarchal disavowal"[3] (Adams 2007a, p. 201).

It would be a mistake to think that ecofeminist vegetarians are irrationalists. None of them believe that theory or abstract categories are useless. It's not a question of choosing reason over emotion or emotion over reason—this kind of dualism is characteristic of patriarchy's domination system—but rather of acknowledging the continuity between them. In the absence of such a recognition, "rationalistic" approaches to vegetarianism, such as ecofeminists believe Singer and Regan defend, leave no room for contextual thinking or an interplay between emotion and reason.

The heart of the ecofeminist model is the claim that vegetarianism is properly grounded on insights that come when caring relationships with animals are cultivated. These relationships are built from personal contact with unique individuals rather than on abstract models of justice.[4] Most relationships aren't voluntarily chosen—circumstances throw them our way more often than not—and they're rarely (if ever) between individuals who are equal in power or ability. So when one moves from thinking about individuals in terms of rights or interests to thinking about them in terms of relationships, a certain messiness is inevitable. To the ethicist who wishes to subsume the particular safely under the universal, the messiness is intolerable. But for the ecofeminist, it's a necessary feature of genuine relationship.

One of the consequences of focusing on concrete care rather than supposedly universal standards of right or wrong is that context becomes important. Ecofeminist Marti Kheel (2004, p. 337) defends what she calls "invitational vegetarianism," a position based not on the prescription of an inflexible moral duty to refrain from animal food but instead on a patient and caring invitation to consider a meatless diet. Moreover, the "invitation" to vegetarianism is always extended with an eye to the material circumstances of those to whom it's offered. Dean Curtin similarly asserts the primacy of the concrete and the particular, arguing that ecofeminist vegetarianism is contextual because it "takes relationships among beings as central, rather than the 'rights' of isolated individuals" (Curtin 2004, p. 273). But Curtin points out this doesn't mean it's relativistic. Ecofeminist vegetarianism condemns power structures and policies based on patriarchal domination, and the speciesist assumption that animals are little more than raw material for human consumption is part and parcel of that domination.

The care which ecofeminists offer as a foundation for vegetarianism has been described as an "attentive love" (Donovan 2007b, pp. 190–1) or "a form of moral attention" which engages at both an intellectual and emotional level with the "circumstances of the other" (Gruen 2004, p. 290). Approaching animals in this way rather than keeping a "comfortable distance" (p. 290) from them creates an empathetic opportunity in which we make ourselves available to the animal in a way that acknowledges and respects its particular being rather than trying to judge it by human categories. As Cathyrn Bailey puts it,

> The animal becomes, not the object of study [the Cartesian objectivism Josephine Donovan criticized earlier], but a kind of interlocutor. Animal discourse so conceived would demand not so much a deduction of the "correct" moral principles, but an opening of self to what is there and that we be present to that being on its own terms instead of through the distancing lens of a very narrowly conceived reason. (Bailey 2007, p. 356)

Bailey's expression "animal discourse" gestures at an essential claim ecofeminist vegetarians make: when we enter into caring relationships with animals, we become more sensitive to them as "speaking subjects[,] rather than merely objects of our speaking" (p. 363). We begin to learn their dialect, as it were, and in doing so we find ourselves more attuned to their capacities for suffering and pleasure. We begin thinking of them not as objects to be observed but as subjects to be listened to—or, better, lovingly attended to.

The notion of "animal discourse" makes less sense to proponents of basic, interests, and rights models of vegetarianism. So far as the ecofeminist is concerned, all of them share the androcentric assumption that animals are inscrutably dense "aliens" inevitably reduced to second class status because they aren't capable of "higher order" thought. Even proponents of the basic argument, despite their defense of kin sympathy with animals, still think of beasts as mute creatures that can be understood only by discerning in them qualities and interests analogous to human ones. The alleged kinship, in other words, is always human- rather than animal-oriented, and this inevitably means that animals are seen by comparison as inferior and subordinate.[5]

The loving attention of care, on the other hand, allows us, in the words of J. M. Coetzee, to "think ourselves into the being of another," with "think" here clearly meaning something broader and deeper than "rationally cogitate." It's more like a deeply empathetic sense of connectedness with the very embodiedness of an animal, and it's an utterly different approach from a Cartesian-inspired emphasis on clear and distinct ideas. As Coetzee has one of his fictional characters, a woman who embodies the ecofeminist sensibility, say:

> To thinking, cogitation, I oppose fullness, embodiedness, the sensation of being—not a consciousness of yourself as a kind of ghostly reasoning machine thinking thoughts, but on the contrary the sensation—a heavily affective sensation—of being a body with limits that have extension in space, of being alive to the world. This fullness contrasts starkly with Descartes's key state, which has an empty feel to it: the feel of a pea rattling around in a shell. (Coetzee 1999, p. 33)

This "heavily affective" heeding of an animal's being is the key to caring for it. Caring for animals is too often thought of solely in terms of the sentimental pampering practiced by some pet owners. But ecofeminist care is more essentially a kind of "listening to animals, paying emotional attention, taking seriously—caring about—what they are telling us" (Donovan 2007c, p. 360). It's the sort of heeding that creates, according to Lori Gruen (2004, pp. 288–9), "interspecies relationships and friendships," thereby enabling the ecofeminist to empathize with and respond to the suffering of animals in a deeper way than the basic argument's kin sympathy. Concern for the animal's suffering comes not merely from a sense of shared sentience but also, and more fundamentally, from care for the animal in and of itself. This care for the very being of a creature naturally serves as an incentive both to come to its immediate rescue and to challenge the social and cultural institutions that legitimate its suffering in the first place.

As we've already seen, ecofeminist vegetarians argue that the exploitation of animals is cut from the same patriarchal cloth as the exploitation of women, people of color, and the natural environment. Ecofeminist Carol Adams even contends that "all forms of oppression can be traced to the treatment of animals by humans. Domestication became the pattern for social subordination" (Adams 2007b, p. 28). Whether this is historically accurate can be debated. But what is compelling is Adams' argument that the objectification and oppression of women and animals follow similar trajectories.

According to Adams, patriarchal modes of domination cultur-
ally rob victims of oppression of their uniqueness, specificity, individuality, or particularity. They become anonymous units, facelessly
piled into a great collective in which no one individual stands out.
This "massification" of individuals, which robs them of any feature which might elicit sympathy or care, allows more readily for
their exploitation. It also invites ethical models which focus on
abstract rules universally applicable to anonymous and contextless
individuals.

The massification of individuals goes hand-in-hand with a process that Adams calls "absent referencing," in which animals and
women are referred to by progressively abstract labels until finally
any hint of their particularity or uniqueness vanishes. So, for example, a living, sentient, individual steer becomes "cattle," which
then becomes "beef," which finally ends up as anonymous "meat."
Coming into contact with the actual creature risks the possibility
of caring for it. So it's literally as well as symbolically ground up
beyond recognition into generic "meat." Similarly, argues Adams,
individual women are sexually absent-referenced into body parts
("ass," "rump," "breasts," "thighs"), thereby erasing their specific
identities and making them ready-to-use generic objects, a maneu-
ver easily seen in pornography as well as much advertising. In both
cases, the words that refer to animals and women obscure the fact
that what has now become "meat" and "ass" were once unique and
valuable individuals[6] (Adams 1995b).

Adams also points out that in many cultures, both meat-eating
and sexual conquest are symbols of male dominance. They "measure
individual and societal virility" (Adams 1995b, p. 26). The thicker
the steak and the more numerous the notches on the bedpost, the
more masculine—and privileged—the man. Moreover, the meat
that's associated with masculinity carries connotations of energy,
high performance, and assertiveness, as in "to beef up" or to behave
"like a red-blooded man." Vegetables, on the other hand, are associated with passivity—"to vegetate" or to be "soft as a peach"—
and are typically associated with women. (In fact, as Adams points
out, many popular cookbooks gear their outdoor barbecue sections
to male readers, even when the rest of the recipes are written for
women.) Finally, just as animals are viewed as nothing more than
meat to be appropriated and consumed by men, so women are basi-
cally sexual objects of male consumption.[7]

It's not surprising, then, that Adams sees vegetarianism as much more than a personal lifestyle choice or even concern for animal welfare. Adopting a meatless diet is, of course, both of those. But it's also a profoundly political act, because it strikes at the heart of one of the most potently masculine behaviors bred by patriarchy. Since meat is "a symbol and celebration of male dominance," a challenge to meat-eating threatens "the structure of the larger patriarchal culture" (Adams 1995b, pp. 34, 37). Thus vegetarianism is part of a larger resistance to domination patterns, and to chip away at it directly is to chip away at the rest of them indirectly. Although speaking about ecofeminist environmentalism as a whole, Huey-li Li's description of the connections between different forms of oppression is perfectly agreeable to ecofeminist vegetarians:

> Ecofeminists' ethical concerns regarding environmental issues are extended to any indication of brokenness and disharmony in the web of life. War, class exploitation, poverty, and animal experimentation are not regarded as peripheral to other urgent ecological issues, such as air and water pollution, oil spills, and the extinction of wilderness and wildlife. (Li 1993, pp. 290–1)

Dissenting voices

Feminist caveats

As mentioned earlier, not all feminists are vegetarians, and even those who are sometimes worry about the implications of tying women's oppression to animals'. One of the most common objections is that there's no real parallelism between the situations of women and animals. As Beth Dixon says, "animals do not share with women the cognitive capacities and the social and cultural context that would allow them to benefit from equal treatment" (Dixon 1996, p. 187), and contriving similarities harms women's causes without benefiting animals. Feminist and animal activist Lori Gruen, who in fact *does* think there are many important parallels between the treatment of women and animals, shares this concern. She warns that overstressing similarities and downplaying dissimilarities "obscures morally salient differences" (Gruen 2004, p. 287).

Comparing the oppression of women with the mistreatment of animals or Nazi death camps with factory farms risks trivializing, or at least underestimating, the evil of the former.[8]

Other feminists (Card 1990; Cocks 1989) worry that advocacy of a meatless diet conflicts with feminism's embrace of normative and cultural pluralism. Diet, they contend, oughtn't to be morally prescribed, but instead seen as a personal choice dependent on what it takes to maintain good health and well-being. They fear that the ecofeminist defense of vegetarianism risks creating a disguised domination structure that, like patriarchy, seeks to impose values and behavioral norms upon women. This worry is reinforced by recent debates within the ecofeminist community itself as to whether ecofeminists should embrace veganism (Adams 1993). Other feminists, especially women of color, are concerned that ecofeminist advocacy of vegetarianism leans toward elitism and racism. And some feminists, who view vegetarianism as a restriction on diet, contend that advocacy of it only encourages eating disorders in a culture already glorifying thin body types at the expense of girls' and women's health (George 2000; Gruen 2004).

In response to these objections, ecofeminist vegetarians are quick to point out that forms of oppression are linked by their patriarchal origins, and that focusing on one needn't at all mean the exclusion of others from consideration. As Marjorie Spiegel notes, "[a]ny oppression helps to prop up other forms of oppression. This is why it is vital to link oppressions in our minds, to look for the common shared aspects and fight against them as one, rather than prioritizing victims' suffering" (Spiegel 1997, p. 30). Jane Meyerding agrees. "I think concern for the lives of all beings is a vital, empowering part of feminist analysis," she writes. "I don't think we can strengthen our feminist struggle against one aspect of patriarchy by ignoring or accepting other aspects" (Meyerding 1982, pp. 22–3).

Additionally, comparisons of the cruelty perpetrated on women and animals aren't meant to imply that women and animals are oppressed in the same way. Comparisons between factory farms and Nazi death camps are intended as analogies, not identities. Ecofeminists argue, as we've seen, that what's important in caring for animals isn't drawing parallels between them and humans so much as opening oneself to their embodied suffering and responding directly to their needs. The point is not to posit similarities between women and animal oppression that risk trivializing the suffering of one or the other group, but instead to underscore the fact that their exploitation has a common origin in patriarchal domination structures.[9]

Feminist objections that ecofeminist vegetarianism is a disguised form of normative hegemony ignore Deane Curtin's insistence that vegetarianism is contextual, although not relativistic, and Marti Kheel's analysis of vegetarianism as "invitational" rather than imposed or unyieldingly prescriptive. Carol Adams offers a particularly interesting response to the feminist charge that ecofeminist vegetarianism illegitimately imposes dietary constraints upon women. She's sensitive to the charge, acknowledging both that women too often have had values thrust upon them by a masculine culture and that restrictions on what's permissible to eat and what's not can aggravate tendencies to eating disorders. But she argues that normative pluralism doesn't mean that there are no theoretical or practical constraints upon behavior. At the least, pluralism should display the consistency of similar responses to similar situations. And according to Adams, the question that needs to be taken seriously is "[w]hat if the values and beliefs imbedded in the choice to eat animals are antithetical to feminism?" Feminists object, and rightly so, to sex trafficking, because it reduces women to the status of exploitable and disposable physical bodies. But what if eating animals supports an analogous "traffic in animals"? (Adams 1993, p. 195). Surely the pluralism celebrated by feminism shouldn't stretch so far that it turns a blind eye to very real suffering in animals that patriarchy ignores.

One of the most hotly debated recent challenges to ecofeminist vegetarianism as well as the models defended by Singer, Regan, and proponents of the basic argument, comes from feminist philosopher Kathryn Paxton George. Her criticism is especially interesting because it combines many of the feminist objections to vegetarianism already mentioned. According to George, vegetarianism assumes that the male body is the normal *human* body, and thereby universalizes the nutritional requirements of the average male across age, sex, place, and culture. But this assumption imposes greater burdens on women, children, and the elderly than it does males, because the first three groups are more dependent on meat protein and dairy products than white men in the developed world. Consequently, she concludes, vegetarianism, far from being a form of resistance to oppression, actually encourages ageism, sexism, and classism (George 1994, 2000, 2004).

But the troublesome consequences of vegetarianism don't end there. George acknowledges that most advocates of a meatless diet allow for exceptional cases. Persons who are physically unable to be vegetarians may eat meat with impunity. Even Regan's strong argument from rights allows for this possibility. But George argues that what appears to be a concession in fact creates a "moral underclass." As she puts it, "if women, and infants, and children, and the elderly, and those who live almost everywhere else besides Western societies are *routinely* excused for doing what would normally be considered wrong, in practice, this relegates them to a *moral underclass* of beings who, because of their natures or cultures, are not capable of being fully moral" (George 2000, p. 106). So in effect, defenses of vegetarianism, including the ecofeminist one, tend to promote the "weak women" image that feminism wishes to refute. At the end of the day, then, "we have no basis to admire the vegetarian on moral grounds." Indeed, doing so could well be "pernicious to equality and human rights due to the inherent bias that lies within the assumption of the adult male norm" (George 2004, p. 279). In other words, feminist defenses of vegetarianism, just like nonfeminist ones, reflect patriarchal dominance.

Responses to George's challenge have been prolific and sometimes disproportionately angry (Adams 1995a; Donovan 1995; Gaard and Gruen 1995; Gruen 2004; Pluhar 1992, 1993). One of the most common ones, which ecofeminists, to their credit, have been quick to point out, is that she misrepresents the positions of Singer and Regan. Singer's utilitarianism, it will be recalled from Chapter 2, doesn't prohibit the killing of food animals, but only the painful slaughter of them. If animals are raised under conditions conducive to their preference or interest satisfaction, and if they're killed without causing them distress, and if there are hungry people whose plight would be alleviated by their slaughter, then Singer sees no moral objection to eating meat. (Granted, the first two conditions for moral meat-eating are unlikely in a culture that depends upon factory farms to satisfy its huge appetite for meat.) Regan's much stronger prohibition against meat-eating is based on his conviction that it is a violation of the fundamental right to life possessed by any subject-of-a-life. But even he, as George recognizes, allows for the moral acceptability of meat-eating if human life is at stake. There's no suggestion in his writings that people who eat meat to prevent harm to themselves are members of a moral underclass, any more than he implies in a well-known thought experiment (Regan 1983, pp. 285–6) that choosing to throw a dog rather than a human off a crowded lifeboat displays moral failing on the part of the boat's human passengers.

Other objections to George's argument focus on her claim that women have different dietary needs than men and consequently would be nutritionally damaged by adopting a vegetarian diet. The criticism is that George has posited abstract universals—the "ideal" woman's body and the "ideal" male's body—to ground her point, and that doing so ignores the very contextuality and particularity that George is intent on protecting. Critics can agree with George that the medical community needs to pay more attention to women's biology while still maintaining that wholesale categorizations such as the one George makes are dubious.

Singer and Regan respond

As we've seen, one of the characteristic claims of feminism in general and ecofeminist vegetarianism in particular is that ethical models focused on universal and abstract rules of conduct, individual autonomy, and autonomous, rational individuals both reflect and reinforce patriarchal patterns of domination. Singer's interests model as well as Regan's rights one are viewed as complicit in this masculine-oriented way of thinking about ethics. Alternatively, ethical models based on a framework of care that emphasize the importance of relationships, responsiveness to contextual needs, and appreciation of others as they are in and of themselves, are better able to respond morally to human and animal suffering as well as to disrupt patriarchal hegemony.

Both Singer and Regan have responded vigorously to the ecofeminist criticisms, arguing that they're overstated, sometimes to the point of caricature. They have no problem, the two men say, with caring or emotional reactions per se to the suffering of animals. Nor, they contend, is it fair to accuse them of supporting, even if unwittingly, patriarchal structures of oppression. Singer has explicitly tied the oppression of animals—speciesism—to the oppression of women, peoples of color, the elderly, and so on. In fact, he is a pioneer in tracing forms of oppression to a common cause. Regan has spent his entire career bucking the conventional view that animals have no rights and may be used for whatever purposes humans wish. Surely, they argue, whatever else may be said about their defenses of vegetarianism, it's unfair to accuse them of promoting domination systems.

What Singer and Regan both claim in their defense is that an ethics of care, much less an exclusively emotional response to the suffering of animals (or humans, for that matter), is an insufficient foundation for ethical concern. This of course is similar to their objections to hanging animal welfare on the kin sympathy that lies at the heart of the basic argument. Singer worries that care is simply too subjective to serve as the foundation of moral behavior. "Ethics," he contends, "requires us to go beyond 'I' and 'you' to the universal law, the universalizable judgment, the standpoint of the impartial spectator or ideal observer or whatever we choose to call it" (Singer 2008, p. 12). Regan agrees with Singer's concern, arguing that care for animals simply doesn't come naturally to most people.

> What are the resources within the ethic of care that can move people to consider the ethics of their dealings with individuals who stand outside the existing circle of their valued interpersonal relationships? . . . [M]ost people do not care very much about what happens to [animals] . . . [T]heir care seems to be . . . limited to "pet" animals . . . What, then, becomes of the animals toward whom people are indifferent, given the ethic of care?[10] (Regan 1991, pp. 95, 96)

Ecofeminists in turn sometimes charge that Singer and Regan misrepresent them as irrationalists, when in fact ecofeminist vegetarians have never denied the importance of reason and theory. Adams acknowledges that she has been influenced by the rights position, and Donovan asserts that "feminist theory must be informed by animal rights theory if we are to avoid the hypocrisies and inconsistencies of the tea-ladies condemned by Singer"—that is, of the crowd that loves pets but eats animals (Donovan 2007a, p. 86). In short, ecofeminist vegetarians such as Adams and Donovan argue that care ethics is intended to complement and refine, not entirely replace, more traditional models like Singer's and Regan's.[11] In all fairness to Singer and Regan, it's not clear that they in fact do accuse ecofeminists of irrationalism. The charge is often based on an unfortunate (and isolated) accusation by Regan, leveled when he was feeling especially beleaguered by feminist criticisms, that "ethic-of-care feminists" were guilty of "abjur[ing] reason" (Regan 1991, p. 142).

A different sort of ecofeminist response to Singer and Regan is offered by Brian Luke, who argues that their contention that care for animals doesn't come naturally to most people and so offers but a weak foundation for vegetarianism is "an oversimplistic understanding of the limitations of people's sympathies." On the contrary, claims Luke, care for animals is deeply rooted in the human psyche: "the disposition to care for animals is . . . the normal state of humans generally" (Luke 2007, p. 134). His evidence for this claim is twofold: the urgency of the stories we tell ourselves to legitimize mistreatment of animals—that animals are inferior to humans, that they don't suffer to the extent humans do, that humans need meat to survive—and the ways in which our affection for animals constantly seeps through our cultural defenses, manifested in the affectionate care we give our pets or the lengths we go to rescue animals in distress such as beached whales. If we really felt nothing for animals, we wouldn't need the first and wouldn't do the second. Luke's implication is that a caring connection with animals, central to ecofeminist vegetarianism, is more than sufficient to ground moral regard for them, and certainly exerts a stronger claim on our conscience than abstract considerations of justice or equality.

No reciprocity

A particularly galling criticism from the perspective of ecofeminist vegetarians has been leveled by feminist philosopher Nel Noddings, a staunch and even pioneering advocate of an ethics of care, but a skeptic when it comes to the possibility of entering into genuinely caring relationships with animals.

According to Noddings, one fundamental condition must be met before we can speak of the fullest expression of care, much less moral obligation, in a relationship. The subject that's cared for must possess, either actually or potentially, the capacity for growth in relation to the carer, and the growth must involve an intellectual or spiritual dimension that matches the carer's own. Simple affection, such as a pet might have for its owner, won't do. In other words, what's necessary is proportionate "responsiveness or reciprocity on the part of the cared-for" (Noddings 1984, p. 150). Genuine care in any relationship is in direct proportion to the likelihood of reciprocity.

Noddings believes that humans have a natural propensity to care for other humans—a kind of intra-species affinity. But care for animals varies, depending on temperament and biography, from person to person. I may be utterly indifferent to all animals, or I may have deep affection for cats (to use one of Noddings' own examples), but am repulsed by rats. Accordingly, I will behave differently in relation to each of them. When my cat purrs and arches its back, inviting me to cuddle or stroke it, I will gladly do so. But if I open my front door to discover a rat perched on the stoop, "I feel no relation to it. I would not torture it, and I hesitate to use poisons on it for that reason, but I would shoot it cleanly if the opportunity arose" (Noddings 1984, p. 57). Contrary to Brian Luke, Noddings discerns no natural inclination on our part to care for animals, precisely because we sense that they aren't subjects and hence lack the ability to grow from our care and to nurture us in return. Simple decency obliges us not to inflict unnecessary suffering on them if they're sentient. A sense of decency might also prod us to try to alleviate their suffering when we can. But we're under no moral obligation to care for them. Even stronger, we *can't* and in fact *shouldn't* care for them in the way we care for humans.

But if that's the case, why *do* we feel affectionate care for some animals—cats, perhaps—and not others—rats or, even more obviously, shellfish or scorpions? It goes back to temperament and biography. If I have pleasant memories of past associations with certain kinds of animals, I'm more inclined to respond to them affectionately than to other sorts of animals. Cultural contexts and custom are doubtlessly influential as well: some family cultures favor dogs, for example, while others prefer cats.

Moreover, the ability of a creature to display even rudimentary affection in response to my overtures is important—one reason why not too many people prefer scorpions or shellfish over mammals as household pets.

But perhaps the most obvious reason to care for some animals and not others is the presence or absence of some kind of relationship. Once I enter into a relationship with an animal, I incur an obligation to it forged by its dependence on me for sustenance and by my affection for it. (This position, it will be recalled from Chapter 1, is not unlike Stephen R. L. Clark's.) But once again, my obligation to the animal is quite different from the ones I owe humans. It's limited only to the particular animal and it's forged by a concrete relationship rather than a natural affinity. Nor can it be reciprocated in the way that care between humans is.

The upshot is that Noddings denies that an ethic of caring obliges us to be vegetarians. We simply cannot have a *genuinely* caring relationship with animals, and are thus under no moral obligation to them in general, even though we may voluntarily take on obligations to particular animals.

There are two ways in which Noddings' argument can be challenged. The first, by now familiar to us from previous discussions, is the objection from marginal cases. If Noddings wants to contend that we have no genuine moral obligations to animals in general because they aren't subjects and consequently can't reciprocate our care, then we may find ourselves in the undesirable position of likewise denying moral obligations to marginal humans likewise unable to reciprocate (Taylor 2003). We may, of course freely take on obligations to this or that specific marginal human, just as we may take on obligations to this or that particular animal. But marginal humans as a whole would fall through the ethical safety net.

Perhaps a more immediate challenge to Noddings focuses on her insistence that reciprocity is a necessary condition for genuinely caring relationships. Deane Curtin for one argues that Noddings has over-generalized. It may be true that some caring relationships only get off the moral ground if there is reciprocity between the person caring and the person cared for—Curtin concedes that educating students, Noddings' primary concern, is one of these—but that generalizing from these "special cases" becomes "dangerous to feminist moral interests." This is because "many of the contexts of caring for that an ecofeminist might be especially interested in are precisely those in which reciprocity cannot be expected" (Curtin 2007, p. 95). Caring for the good of peoples who live far away in the third world and whom one will never meet, for example, would lose moral capital under Noddings' model. As we've already seen, so would care for marginal persons. And, obviously, care for animals would as well. But these sorts of distinctions, argues Josephine Donovan, are arbitrary, and she attributes Noddings disregard for animals to "an unexamined speciesism" (Donovan 2007a, p. 86).

Broadening the circle

The four arguments for vegetarianism we've examined thus far have focused on animal welfare. The basic argument built its case on kin sympathy for animal suffering, the argument from interests on equal moral consideration for all sentient creatures, the argument from rights on the claim that justice requires that every subject-of-a-life deserves certain entitlements, and the ecofeminist argument on the insistence that care is a needed supplement to rights and interests based models, and that animal welfare is inextricably bound up with the welfare of oppressed peoples and the natural environment.

The moral concern of all four arguments, although especially concerned with animals, stretches beyond them as well. Defenders of the basic argument and Tom Regan also believe that cruelty to animals habituates humans in cruelty. Peter Singer and ecofeminist vegetarians worry that meat-eating contributes to the oppression of certain human groups and the degradation of the environment. As we saw in the Introduction, reasons vegetarians have for adopting a meatless diet tend to be multi-faceted rather than simple.

Still, most vegetarians prioritize their reasons, and one usually takes priority over others. For some, the reason that stands out from the rest is dismay at cruelty to animals. For others, the tipping point is concern about what the factory farming of beasts does to the natural environment. Some endorse vegetarianism primarily because they believe that a meatless diet is physically and psychologically healthier than an omnivorous one. Others give up meat because they conclude that the eating of animals exacerbates rather than alleviates the problem of world hunger. And a few, taking an approach different from both animal-oriented and environment or human-oriented models, see vegetarianism as a religious duty. In the chapters that follow, we'll explore all of these perspectives that broaden the circle of reasons to embrace vegetarianism.

CHAPTER SIX

The environmental argument

Raising cattle in huge feedlots, consolidating dairy farms into confinement units with 1,000–10,000 cows, consolidating swine and poultry production into huge confinement units, [is] a frontal assault on the environment, with massive groundwater and air pollution problems.

PETER CHEEKE

If healthy ecosystems are of value . . ., one has a moral reason to avoid needlessly impairing the health of any ecosystem.

PETER S. WENZ

North Carolina's Onslow County is home to Camp Lejeune, the largest Marine Corps base in the eastern United States. The nearly 250 square mile facility is the Atlantic seaboard county's single largest source of income. Cash crops like tobacco bring in another $18 million to the county each year, but the largest revenue generator other than Camp Lejeune is a thriving factory farm industry. Onslow is dotted with dozens of huge chicken and turkey sheds, cattle feedlots, and hog farms, all of which earn nearly $85 million annually. Its hog production is ranked eighth in a state which has hundreds of hog farmers (Onslow County 2010).

In June 1995, Oceanview Farms, one of the county's largest hog producers, housed over 10,000 beasts in 11 giant sheds. The urine and feces excreted by the animals were trapped in an eight acre waste "lagoon," a term to which many environmentalists object. "A lagoon is something a beautiful girl swims in on Fantasy Island, [not a] cesspool," observes one of them (*New York Times* 1995). The artificial lagoon, bounded on all sides by earthen dykes, held 25 million gallons of putrefying liquid excrement pooled 12 feet deep and exuding a nauseating stench smelled for miles.

It started raining in Onslow County on Sunday, June 18. By Wednesday, over 3 inches had fallen, flooding creeks and tributaries. The steady downpour weakened the walls containing Oceanview Farms' cesspool, and on June 21, a 30-feet segment of it crumbled away, releasing a flood of "knee-deep, red soupy" filth that emptied the entire reservoir, drowned tobacco and soybean fields, woodlands, and roads, and eventually flowed into two tributaries of the New River. As one farmer whose crops were destroyed by the flood remarked, "It came through the woods. You could see the dark stuff. It made me sick. I thought, 'Oh, there goes our crops' " (*New York Times* 1995).

Engineers scrambled to repair the dyke, but the damage had already been done. In addition to the destruction of crops and the health risks posed by the 25 million gallons of bacteria-laden muck that coated hundreds of acres, the nitrogen-rich hog waste started suffocating fish in the New River as soon as it hit the water.[1] All told, upwards of 15 million fish perished, the breeding areas of half of all mid-East Coast fish species were decimated, and over 300,000 acres of coastal wetlands were contaminated. Shellfish remained toxic for years afterward (Robbins 2011, p. 242).

North Carolina's hog farms house 7 million animals at any given time. By way of comparison, the state's human population is only 6.5 million. The hogs produce four times as much waste as the state's people. All of it is pooled in open reservoirs, and has a pathogen count that is 10–100 times greater than human sewage (National Resources Defense Council 1998). Even short of disastrous spills like Oceanview's, the waste produced by factory-farmed hogs in North Carolina is an environmental hazard. Add to it the total waste produced by the billions of farm animals raised and slaughtered each year in the United States alone, and the potential risk and actual harm done to the environment is staggering. Moreover, the thousands of tons of animal manure produced each day is only one of several environmental hazards posed by consumer demand for meat. Land integrity, wildlife and forests, cleanliness and availability of water, and even weather patterns are all affected by the factory-farmed production of food animals.

One of the arguments for vegetarianism focuses on the environmental consequences of meat-eating. Its central claim is that the natural resources damaged by factory farming ought to be valued by us, either for themselves or for the sake of their importance to human well-being, and that consequently the adoption of a meatless diet, given the way in which meat is currently produced, is at least a prudential and perhaps even a moral obligation. In this chapter, we'll examine the various ways in which this argument is defended by environmental vegetarians.

Meat-eating and environmental degradation

The ecological disaster caused by the sewage flood at Oceanview Farms spotlights an especially troublesome environmental cost of meat-eating: the hundreds of millions of tons of manure and urine excreted each year by factory-farmed animals. It builds up much faster than it can possibly be used as fertilizer, which was the traditional way of handling manure before the advent of factory farms. Given the high concentrations of bacteria such as *E. coli* in much of it—despite the huge doses of antibiotics regularly given to food animals—it's not especially desirable to use any of it as fertilizer anyway. So much of it, like the pig waste at Oceanview, gets "lagooned."

To appreciate the sheer bulk of waste produced by food animals in the United States alone, something which the average consumer rarely thinks about, just recall from Chapter 1 the huge numbers of animals we eat each year. We devour eight to ten billion chickens. That's more than the human population of the entire world. We eat 300 million turkeys, just a smidgeon under the country's human population. We also eat 100 million hogs and upwards of 40 million beef cattle.

All of these animals are generously fed so that they'll bulk up quickly, and they excrete proportionately. An average 1,100 pound steer produces 47 pounds of manure every 24 hours. Worldwide, beef and dairy cattle produce one billion tons of manure annually. A 60,000-hen egg battery, not an untypical size, produces 82 tons of manure in a single week. In the Delmarva Peninsula, a thumb of land bordered on the west by the Chesapeake Bay and on the east by the Delaware River, Delaware Bay, and Atlantic Ocean, 600 million chickens are raised annually, producing more manure than a city of four million people does (Singer and Mason 2006, pp. 29–30). In a mere seven days, two thousand pigs drop 27 tons of manure and 32 tons of urine. (Recall that there were five times that many beasts at Oceanview.) All told, food animals excrete slightly over 2 billion tons of hard and wet manure each year, equivalent to ten times the amount of human waste produced in the same period. That's four times the combined weight of the world's human population, or 20 tons of manure for every household in America. Bad as that sounds, the Union of Concerned Scientists thinks there's even worse news. According to it, "We have strict laws governing the disposal of human waste, but the regulations are lax, or often nonexistent, for animal waste" (Robbins 2011, p. 243).

The absence of strict oversight for the mountains of animal waste—an absence actively encouraged by lobbyists for the meat and poultry industries[2]—contributes hugely to the pollution of both land and water. Waste held in storage lagoons leaches into the ground, and manure too generously spread over pastures and fields, ostensibly to fertilize them but actually to get rid of some of the tons of muck laying about, turns into soluble compounds of ammonia and nitrate which wash into wells, groundwater, streams, and rivers. Once the manure hits living water, it accelerates the growth of algae, the algae deoxygenate the water, and aquatic life perishes. Thanks in large part to chicken waste from the Delmarva Peninsula and manure fertilizing along Pennsylvania's Susquehanna River, the Chesapeake Bay has been inundated for years with phosphorus and nitrogen runoff that's seriously damaged its aquatic life capacity. South of Louisiana, in the Gulf of Mexico, a 7,000 square mile dead zone is the result of deoxygenation caused in large part by animal waste runoff. Nor are factory-farmed land animals the only contributors to manure pollution. Densely populated industrial fish cages also befoul the waters. Caged salmon off the coast of Scotland contaminate coastal waters with waste equivalent to that produced by 8 million people. The human population of Scotland is just a bit over five million (New Internationalist 2000).

Manure pollution isn't the only way that water resources are depleted by the millions of animals we eat. Meat production is the single most significant user of water in the United States. A full 80 percent of the country's water consumption is traceable to animal food crops or direct consumption by the animals themselves (Hill 1996, p. 112). Nearly half of it is used for cattle (Robbins 2011, p. 238). The thousands of acres of soy and corn grown annually to feed animals must be irrigated, and this also takes immense quantities of water. In the western United States, one of the main sources of water for both irrigation and cattle is the Ogallala Aquifer, an immense underground lake that stretches from South Dakota to Texas. Each year, the aquifer loses 13 trillion tons of water, most of which is used to produce beef. Geologists worry that at the present rate of consumption, the aquifer will be dry before the end of this century. Wells that feed into it throughout Kansas, Nebraska, Oklahoma, Colorado, northwest Texas, and New Mexico are already at risk.

In her classic book *Diet for a Hungry Planet*, Frances Moore Lappe (1991) famously calculated that it takes as much water to bring a steer to maturity as would float a battleship. More specifically, about 2,500 gallons of water are needed to produce 1 pound of beef.[3] That's 15 times the amount needed to produce 1 pound of wheat, rice, or barley. Put another way, more water goes into a quarter-pound hamburger than the average human drinks directly in four years.

Water pollution and depletion are inevitable when food animals are factory farmed. But land suffers as well. The meat industry is dependent on industrial agriculture to grow the immense quantities of soy, corn, and other crops needed to bring animals to maturity. Industrial agriculture, dependent in turn on artificial fertilizers, pesticides, and insecticides to produce high yields and thus meet expectations, douses the soil with chemicals. It doesn't take too many growing seasons for the chemical-drenched earth to lose texture as well as topsoil. Topsoil accumulates slowly. It takes between 200 and 1,000 years, depending on region and climatic conditions, for the earth to produce one inch of the stuff. But in the United States, topsoil is blowing away at a rate of an inch every 16 years (Hill 1996, pp. 108–9). Seven billion tons of it, the equivalent of nearly 60,000 pounds per person, are lost every year, enough to cover the entire state of Connecticut. The amount of topsoil lost each year in Iowa alone is enough to fill 165,000 Mississippi River barges (Robbins 2011, p. 241).

Over half the total land mass (including mountains) in the continental United States is used for the production of meat and dairy products. A full 70 percent of land in the American West, 525 million acres, is used to graze young cattle before they're shipped off to factory farm feeding lots. That's two-thirds of the entire land area of Montana, Wyoming, Colorado, New Mexico, Arkansas, Nevada, Utah, and Idaho.

The irony is that the more arable land we use, the more arable land we need. Topsoil loss and soil degradation steadily decrease the productivity of American farm land. According to USDA calculations, the agricultural capacity of the continental United States has dropped by 70 percent in the last two hundred years. Even grazing land is jeopardized by the thousands of hard-hoofed beasts that trample plants and compact the soil, making it harder for the ground to absorb rain water and retain topsoil. One acre of wilderness is turned into industrial farmland every 5 seconds in the United States. For every acre of forest lost to roads, shopping centers, and houses, seven more become feed lots and animal cropland (Hill 1996, p. 108). As long as we continue feeding on factory-farmed beasts, we'll also feed on the soil.

The grazing and feeding of beef cattle tends to be the most voracious devourer of land. Central and South America have been particularly ravaged by the worldwide appetite, especially North American, for beef. Much of the beef eaten in the United States is imported from Costa Rica, Columbia, Brazil, and Argentina. Cattle grazing and the cultivation of cattle grain has slashed and burned away Latin American forestland at an alarming rate. Since 1960, over 25 percent of it has been cleared for cattle. Costa Rica has sacrificed 80 percent of its virgin forests. Mexico has lost 27 million acres of woodland. African forests are likewise toppling before the world's appetite for beef. In East Africa, over 50 percent of the land is now devoted to cattle (Hill 1996, p. 108). In all these areas, the environmental consequences typical of massive cattle grazing and animal crop cultivation follow: compacted grazing land, depleted soil nutrients, and loss of topsoil. And the sacrifice simply seems wildly disproportionate to the harvest. To get just one fast food hamburger harvested from Latin American beef, 55 square feet of tropical rainforest must be slashed and burned (Denslow and Padoch 1988, p. 69).

It's apparent that arable land, forests, and water are damaged by meat-eating. But recently environmentalists have begun to appreciate the danger that factory farming poses to the very atmosphere itself. The vast deforestation in Latin America and parts of Africa that's driven by cattle production contributes to rising levels of carbon dioxide, one of the gases responsible for the greenhouse effect. Moreover, the huge quantities of methane expelled by livestock, especially cattle, is another major contributor. The Environmental Protection Agency estimates that the world's livestock are responsible for up to one-quarter of the globe's human-caused or anthropogenic methane emissions (Halweil 1998), and methane is 24 times more potent a greenhouse gas than carbon dioxide. The atmospheric danger posed by animal methane is so grave that the Union of Concerned Scientists claim that driving vehicles with poor gas mileage and eating beef are two of the most damaging things US citizens do to the atmosphere (Brower and Leon 1999).

And speaking of gas-guzzling vehicles: because factory farms rely so heavily on industrial agriculture, eating meat—especially beef—indirectly encourages the use of huge quantities of carbon dioxide-emitting fossil fuels needed to run mega-planters, cultivators, and harvesters, as well as to transport crops from the fields to distributors. So much fossil fuel is required that the Worldwatch Institute claims that the feed grown for food animals "might as well be a petroleum byproduct" (Robbins 2011, p. 267). Additionally, the most common form of the nitrogen fertilizers used on livestock corn is ammonium nitrate, a fossil fuel product which contributes to the greenhouse effect. About one-quarter of all the ammonium nitrate used in the United States finds its way to cattle cornfields (Ryan and Durning 1997, p. 55).

Does the environment have moral standing?

Despite the protestations of special interest groups working for the meat industry, the facts on the ground are clear enough: large-scale factory farming of food animals is bad for the environment. It devastates rain forests, erodes topsoil, tramples grazing lands, depletes aquifers, pollutes streams, rivers, lakes, bays, and portions of oceans, kills flora and fauna, and is a strong player in the creation of greenhouse gases. The elimination of factory farms wouldn't, of course, spell an end to environmental degradation. But it would certainly slow it down.

Given this, many vegetarians adopt a meatless diet for prudential reasons. They see befouling one's own nest as an irrational lifestyle, and consequently make a conscious decision to wean themselves from a particular type of behavior—meat-eating—that contributes hugely to the unbalancing of ecological stability. One way of justifying this prudential choice is by arguing that human self-interest entails indirect duties to the environment.

Recall that in Chapter 4, we examined the contractarian model of rights which maintained that humans may have indirect duties to at least some animals. The only creatures capable of possessing rights are those who can freely and intelligently enter into contractual arrangements with similar creatures—so "creatures" in this context, is of course limited to humans. The agreement or contract between them spells out reciprocal rights and duties. Only humans, then, possess rights, and it's only to humans that we can be said to have direct duties. But if the contract mandates respect for private property, for example, we may have an obligation not to harm the animals belonging to other humans. This, as we saw, constitutes an indirect duty to the animals themselves. We refrain from violating them, but only out of respect for their human owners.[4]

One of the more common arguments for granting moral standing to the environment proceeds along similar lines. Defended by authors such as Blackstone (1972), Gewirth (2001), and O'Neill (1997), the argument contends that even though we owe no direct duties to the natural world, we *are* morally obliged to look out for the well-being of fellow humans. The stronger version of this duty obliges us to strive actively for their physical and psychological flourishing. The minimal version calls on us to at least refrain from engaging in private or public actions that would interfere with their well-being.

Now, the health of the ecosystem is something that affects all humans for good or ill. To the extent that our actions are capable of deteriorating its health and thus potentially harming the well-being of our fellow humans, we're obliged at least to refrain from any environmentally damaging behavior which we can reasonably forgo without causing undue immediate harm to ourselves. Thus we have an indirect duty to the natural environment not to degrade it, a duty that arises only because of our direct duties to humans. The vegetarian who embraces this way of thinking concludes that factory farming damages the environment, and so behavior like meat-eating which encourages factory farming ought to be forgone if doing so doesn't entail undue harm to humans. Those people who rely upon the factory farm system for meat but who can easily acquire both nutrition and gustatory pleasure from a meatless diet are morally obliged to become vegetarians.

But many other vegetarians—and nonvegetarians as well, for that matter—are concerned about environmental degradation for reasons other than prudent self-interest. They sense, even if only vaguely, that there are additional grounds for cherishing and protecting ecological integrity. For them, the natural world possesses a kind of value that establishes claims against us for our moral consideration. Exactly what that value is, and precisely what our obligations to protect it are, remain perplexing questions that generate much discussion and much disagreement. But many vegetarians who are concerned about the environment tend to endorse one or more of a number of arguments that try to establish the moral standing of the natural world. What most of these arguments have in common is a set of assumptions nicely spelled out by philosopher Peter Wenz. "Healthy ecosystems are of value, the value of an ecosystem is positively related to its degree of health, and at least part of this value is independent of the interests of human and other sentient beings." Wenz believes that if one accepts the independent value of ecosystems, then one must likewise "accept the prescription to become a vegetarian" (Wenz 1999, p. 190). But he admits that the sticking point is in showing that the ecosystems *do* have independent value. So let's turn to four arguments that try to justify the claim.

Ecofeminist and social ecology arguments

A couple of distinct but related arguments that defend the claim that the environment possesses value are offered by ecofeminists on the one hand and social ecologists on the other. In the last chapter, we saw that the ecofeminist attitude towards the natural environment is that it, like historically oppressed groups such as women, peoples of color, and animals, has been victimized by patriarchal domination structures. The rescue of nature from its status as a mere repository of raw material goes hand in hand with the liberation of women, peoples of color, and animals because it helps to erode patriarchal hegemony. But ethical models based on universal and abstract norms of justice and rights won't do because they merely duplicate the dualistic assumptions and adversarial attitude embedded in patriarchy. Much more effective is the nurturance of caring relationships which allow the genuine value of that which is cared for to reveal itself. Just as it's essential to allow the embodied being of an animal to speak for itself and to value the disclosure for what it is rather than trying to force human categories such as rights and duties upon it, so it's also important to allow the natural world to be what it is, valuing it for its beauty, intricacy, and even occasional ferocity rather than reducing it to a ready-to-hand repository of raw material. Adopting this kind of attitude to nature necessarily entails recognizing its value and refraining from inflicting harm upon it, not merely for our sake, but out of respect for it as well. And for an ecofeminist vegetarian, that means refraining from a diet that not only encourages the abuse of animals but the degradation of the natural world.

Social ecology, especially as defended by Murray Bookchin (Bookchin 1982; Bookchin and Foreman 1991), agrees with the ecofeminist assumption that there's a strong relationship between social oppression and the abuse of the environment. But Bookchin's target isn't patriarchal structures so much as the capitalist ethos that values the natural world only insofar as its resources can be manipulated as exchangeable commodities. Along with ecofeminists, social ecologists argue that this commodification creates hierarchies of power which guarantee the exploitation of peoples and things that occupy subordinate positions. In the capitalist hierarchy, the natural world is always subordinate, and so always exploitable as commodifiable raw material.

Bookchin argues that breaking the hierarchies of oppression requires a shift in perspective that recognizes humans as embedded within nature rather than distinct from it. Members of an ecosystem are interrelated and mutually dependent on one another. No single individual or species is of more value than another. The capitalist-generated gaps between humans and nature on the one hand and between dominant and subordinate humans on the other can be seen for the socially constructed artificialities they are once the nonhierarchical character of the natural world is appreciated. A social ecology vegetarian, then, can easily see factory farming as the widespread commodification of animals, an economic exploitation which in turn both accepts and reinforces the assumption that nature is properly subordinate to human will. One way of rebelling against the exploitation and affirming the claim that no member of an ecosystem is more valuable than another is by adopting a meatless diet.

The land ethic

Some critics (especially deep ecologists, whose position we'll examine shortly) maintain that both ecofeminism and social ecology approach the environment from an anthrocentric perspective. They charge that proponents of either model take the oppression of humans as the lens through which they then examine the human abuse of nature, and adopt modes of human liberation (from patriarchal, dualistic domination structures in the one case and capitalist exploitation in the other) as templates for establishing proper relationships with animals and the natural world. These critics conclude that ecofeminists and social ecologists, despite their claims of moving away from traditional moral analysis, are more conventional than they think.

One model that grants moral standing to the environment that is much less human-centered is the well-known "land ethic" defended by environmentalist Aldo Leopold. For Leopold, the land isn't simply "dirt." It's the source of energy that flows through plants and animals and maintains the delicate balance necessary for a healthy environment. The land, therefore, is the necessary condition for the flourishing of ecosystems, and as such ought to be valued rather than treated as mere resource. As Leopold famously writes, "A thing is right when it tends to preserve the integrity, stability, and beauty of the biotic community. It is wrong when it tends otherwise" (Leopold 1966, p. 262). Leopold was no vegetarian himself (and in fact was an advocate of game hunting). But he didn't live (he died in 1948) to witness the full-fledged emergence of factory farming. Had he observed the way food animals have come to be produced in the United States, it's likely he would've seen factory farms as destructive of the biotic community he believed deserved moral standing.

Debate over both interpretation and correctness of Leopold's land ethic is lively. Many philosophers accuse him of unwarrantedly jumping from description to prescription, from a statement of fact—that the land is essential to the health of the biotic community—to a statement of value—that there is a moral obligation to protect its "integrity, stability, and beauty." Such a move is called the "naturalistic fallacy." It's not entirely clear that moving from fact to value is a fallacy, although many philosophers, following David Hume, have believed it is. What basis other than facts about the world might we have for inferring value? Certainly the arguments for vegetarianism based on animal welfare move from description—sentient creatures fail to flourish when they endure physical or psychological suffering—to prescription—sentient creatures ought not to have unnecessary suffering inflicted on them.

Even if one takes the naturalistic fallacy seriously, it may not mean that Leopold's model is destroyed. J. Baird Callicott (1989) argues, for example, that Leopold is best read as encouraging us to interpret our feelings of affection for the environment as noteworthy moral intuitions. We value and wish to protect a beautiful work of art because it moves us. Why not a similar response to the beauty of the biotic community? Under this reading, Leopold's land ethic is a reminder that our feelings can have moral significance and ought not to be dismissed as mere emotionality or sentimentality. Affection for the land bridges the gap between fact and value.

But another defender of Leopold's land ethic (Johnson 1993) worries that Callicott's argument doesn't bridge the gap at all. Many people feel no more affection for the land than they do for animals. For them, it's absurd to suggest that inanimate objects, even beautiful works of art, somehow deserve moral consideration just because we like them. But if we suppose that something can have interests which are essential to its flourishing even if it isn't consciously aware of those interests, and if we have moral obligations to facilitate or at least not impede interests essential to flourishing (which we certainly do in the case, for example, of human infants), and if finally we agree with Leopold that it's in the interest of the biotic community not to have its integrity disrupted, then it makes perfect sense to bestow moral standing on the environment.

So if the factory farming system violates biotic integrity, then vegetarianism seems an appropriate, and at least in some contexts an obligatory, response.[5]

Deep ecology

The least anthrocentric argument for the bestowal of moral standing on the environment (although Leopold's land ethic runs a close second) is known as "deep ecology." Pioneered by philosopher and environmentalist Arne Naess (1973, 1993, 2008), deep ecology (or "ecosophy," as it's sometimes called) takes the position that traditional ways of thinking about ethics are inadequate when it comes to the environment.[6] "Shallow" ecology is content with hanging onto the conventional assumption that humans comprise a superior and privileged class of beings in the natural world whose interests always trump the environment's. "Deep" ecology, on the other hand, argues that humans have no more ecological value than any other member of the biotic community. Consequently, we need to develop a new type of moral consciousness about our place in the natural world.

In accordance with this radical equalization, deep ecologists contend that *all* life possesses value, regardless of its usefulness to humans, and that human interference with the diversity of life forms, except in situations of dire need or emergency, is morally unwarranted. Public policies and moral norms that respect the well-being of all members of the biotic community should be adopted. Human overpopulation, for example, is a threat to the ecological integrity of the planet which calls for a drastic reduction in reproduction patterns. The notion that "bigger is better," which the Western world especially has adopted as the recipe for growth, needs to be replaced with a commitment to "small is beautiful" sustainability (Schumacher 1999). But above all, a radical revisioning of what it means to be a human member of the biosphere is needed. At the very least, such a rethinking demotes humans from the morally privileged position we've historically assigned ourselves and encourages as deep an identification with the rest of nature as possible.

Deep ecology has been criticized on the grounds that it tends to be vague when it comes to handling conflicts between different life forms. If all life is valuable, does this mean that all life deserves equal treatment? If so, then we are amiss in attacking bacteria with antibiotics, a position that on the surface seems absurd. If not, are we forced back to a traditional sliding scale assignation of value to different life forms, with humans at the top, which deep ecologists condemn? It's simply not clear. As we'll see in Chapter 8, these are questions that can also be asked of Albert Schweitzer's reverence for life ethic.

It's not the case that deep ecology entails vegetarianism, since it doesn't necessarily forbid the killing of animals. Some species are naturally predatory, and the integrity of the ecosystem in which they're situated depends on their keeping the populations on which they prey from overreproducing. Similarly, the hunting of animals by humans, so long as the hunting is done sustainably rather than wantonly and for food rather than mere sport, is likewise compatible with deep ecology's moral regard for the environment. But it's obvious that factory farming falls outside any morally acceptable predation cycle. The practice not only reflects the hubris that humans are morally superior to animals, since we would roundly condemn treating humans in the way we treat factory-farmed food animals; it also wreaks havoc upon the natural environment, thereby disrespecting the value of other flora and fauna species. If the food which one eats comes from factory farms, then, deep ecology's moral recommendation would be to abstain from meat at the personal level and to work toward raising ecological sensibilities at the public one.

Objections

In addition to the specific criticisms of the various arguments for granting the natural world moral standing that we've already examined, some environmentalists argue that vegetarianism is potentially destructive to the environment, reflecting as it does a naïve worldview completely out of touch with the actual world of nature "red in tooth and claw."

In Chapter 4, we saw philosopher Steven Davis (2003) challenge Tom Regan's defense of animal rights by claiming that the cultivation of food crops for human consumption inflicts more damage on

the environment than the cultivation of pasture lands for large grazing food animals. His argument was that clearing land and planting
crops disrupts the natural habitats of scores of animal and plant
species, and the actual harvesting of the crops kills hundreds of
individual animals and plants. A much more environment friendly
policy would be to leave the land untilled and suitable for domesticated animals such as cattle or sheep. Eating them would result in
fewer deaths and less degradation of the environment.

J. Baird Callicott, a defender of Leopold's land ethic, agrees with
Davis but takes the environmental argument against vegetarianism
even further.[7] He contends that "a vegetarian human population"
isn't merely damaging to the environment, but would likely be "ecologically catastrophic" (Callicott 1989, p. 35). Callicott's argument
focuses on a cycle of destructive events he thinks a global vegetarian diet could set in motion. While acknowledging that worldwide
vegetarianism will most likely increase the food resources available
to humans, he warns that

> [t]he human population would probably, as past trends
> overwhelmingly suggest, expand in accordance with the potential
> thus afforded. The new result would be fewer nonhuman beings
> and more human beings who, of course, have requirements of
> life far more elaborate than even those of domestic animals,
> requirements which would tax other "natural resources"
> (trees for shelter, minerals mined at the expense of topsoil and
> its vegetation, etc.) more than under present circumstances.
> (Callicott 1989, pp. 34–5)

Callicott recognizes that the average vegetarian's diet is less burdensome on the environment than the omnivore's, and he believes that
humans have a moral obligation to reduce their negative impact on
the biotic community as much as they reasonably can. His point,
however, is that what seems morally acceptable for individuals or
small groups of individuals may morph into something destructive
of the very environment it seeks to protect if adopted as public
policy. At the very least, this calls into question the alleged ethical
superiority of a vegetarian diet over one that includes meat.

The arguments offered by Davis and Callicott are reasonable,
but neither has gone unanswered by vegetarians concerned with

the environmental impact of meat-eating. In order for Davis' challenge to the planting and harvesting of human food crops to stick, it would be necessary to demonstrate that doing so inflicts more harm upon the environment than the cultivation of monocultural crops, mainly corn and soy, fed to food animals. There's little doubt that ecosystems are nearly always adversely affected when land is cultivated. But given the necessity to cultivate land if humans are to be fed, the question then becomes what sort of cultivation does the least damage. Given the fact that most plant protein fails to transfer proportionately to food animals when they ingest it, thus obliging farmers to grow huge quantities of corn and soy to produce small quantities of meat, a good case can be made that less land could feed more people if the "middle-men"—animals—were dropped. According to one estimate (Francione 2000, p. 15), the typical omnivore's diet in the United States requires the use of 3.5 acres of cropland per year, whereas a vegetarian diet needs only one-fifth of an acre. Thus cultivating food crops for people is, all things considered, less burdensome on the environment (Auxter 1999).

Peter Wenz responds to Callicott's Malthusian antivegetarian warning of overpopulation and ecological disaster by arguing that the real culprit is overpopulation, not diet. Unlike Callicott, Wenz sees no reason to suppose that overpopulation and a vegetarian diet are necessarily connected. He reasons that human populations which are ecologically minded enough to give up meat for the sake of the environment aren't likely to "apply the money they save on food to the birth and rearing of a child they would not otherwise have" (Wenz 1999, p. 198). Birthing extra children imposes both a personal and an ecological burden that, in this context, is simply "psychologically implausible."

A stronger objection to Callicott's position is Wenz's claim that the same argument Callicott makes against vegetarianism can be made against any lifestyle if the population increases. If human beings overreproduce, "all roads . . . lead to perdition" regardless of how or what they eat. Consequently, Callicott's case is underdetermined.

Whether people were vegetarians or omnivores, whether industry were powered by solar energy or nuclear energy, whether there were disarmament or a continued arms race, population increase would destroy the biosphere. The danger of ecological disaster would, therefore, not serve to favor any one course of action over its opposite, and so would not favor either an omnivorous or a vegetarian diet over the other. (Wenz 1999, p. 199)

It's worth mentioning that neither Davis nor Callicott support the factory farm system. Since Davis defends eating large pasture-grazing ruminants as a strategy for saving the lives of a far greater number of plants and small animals, it's not likely that he would endorse the unnecessary slaughter of billions and billions of factory-farmed animals, much less the environmental impact of doing so. Callicott explicitly condemns factory farming, arguing that the "transmogrification" of flora through intensive farming is just as unacceptable from the perspective of the land ethic as is the "transmogrification" of animals though the factory farming of them. He still refuses to endorse widespread vegetarianism. But he opines that "[t]he important thing, I would think, is not to eat vegetables as opposed to animal flesh, but to resist factory farming in all its manifestations, including especially its liberal application of pesticides, herbicides, and chemical fertilizers to maximize the production of vegetable crops," whether the crops are raised as food for animals or humans (Callicott 1989, pp. 35–6).

A different sort of objection to environmental vegetarianism is the claim that it's hopelessly out of touch with both nature as it actually operates and what's most beneficial for both humans and animals. Environmental ethicist Holmes Rolston[8], for example, confesses that he's "not sure a vegetarian even understands the way the world is built." Meat-eating humans "know their ecology and natural history in a way that vegetarians do not." They, unlike vegetarians, participate "in the logic and biology of [their] ecosystem" (Hettinger 2004, pp. 294–5).

The ecosystem's "logic and biology" that Rolston thinks vegetarians ignore is that the weak eat the strong. Sacrifice is part of the warp and woof of the natural world. Predation in nature is not only an incontestable fact, it's also one that benefits animals—including humans, whom evolution has placed at the top of the food chain. Without the additional protein provided by meat, claims Rolston, humans would never have developed into the intellectually sophisticated creatures we are. Indeed, it's not even obvious that the species would've survived. By eating meat—especially meat acquired by hunting—we reaffirm our essentially carnivorous, predatory nature. Rolston for one is unapologetic about his embrace of what he sees as a legacy of predation. "Nature is bloody," he declares, "the top trophic rungs are always raptors, cats, wolves, hunters, and I'm one of those, and unashamed of it" (Hettinger 2004, p. 297).

Nett Hettinger agrees. Predation, he claims, "should be understood holistically as the process of advancement and flourishing of life that it is." Granted, "from the perspective of the prey who loses, predation does appear evil" (Hettinger 2004, p. 298). But examined in the context of the biotic community, the death of the prey is balanced out by the sustenance of the predator. The problem that vegetarians make is in sentimentally focusing on the good of the individual rather than the good of the biosphere. But doing so "is in serious tension with a healthy respect for the sometimes violent, painful, and life-sacrificing processes of nature" (p. 296).

Both Rolston and Hettinger fret that even though environmental vegetarians claim to renounce meat because they value the biotic community, their condemnation of animal killing actually shows them to hate the natural world because of its ubiquitous predation. This creates a dilemma which vegetarians are unable to navigate. Either they must morally condemn natural predation, or they must concede that it's either ecologically good or at least one of those facts of life that's morally neutral. If they prefer the first option, they're obliged to protect prey animals from predators, a duty which, as we saw in Chapter 4, seems both morally counterintuitive and practically impossible,[9] as well as answer to the charge that they hate nature. But if they choose the second option, consistency requires them to accept human predation as likewise ecologically beneficial or at least morally neutral.

Environmentally concerned vegetarians remain unimpressed by these criticisms. Instead, they express bewilderment, as philosopher Jennifer Everett puts it, that Rolston, Hettinger, and similar minded individuals should see an incompatibility with environmentalism and vegetarianism. "[V]egetarians, like environmentalists, seek a new moral relationship between humans and extra-human animals. In place of exploitation, cruelty, and indifference toward other species . . ., we envision a future in which humanity recognizes and honors the inherent worth of all creatures." If vegetarians refuse to look at animals as "lunch meat," it's because they are convinced that "human dominance over the rest of nature is not only imprudent but also morally wrong" (Everett 2004, p. 305). How could this be anti-environmentalist?

More specifically, Everett and others argue that no morally relevant analogy can be drawn between animal and human predation. Consequently, it's not at all inconsistent to condemn the latter but not the former. Carnivorous predators in the wild *must* eat meat to survive. They just can't flourish on a vegetable diet. Humans, on the other hand, don't require meat, being perfectly able from a biological (not to mention psychological and cultural) point of view to thrive without meat. Additionally, because humans are moral agents, it's reasonable to expect more of them than we do from animals, who are, after all, only moral patients. Simply because wolves kill and eat cattle is no license for humans doing so, as we saw when we examined the Benjamin Franklin argument in Chapter 4. Finally, except in the case of hunting, the typical "prey" of a human isn't a wild animal but instead a domesticated one whose factory-farmed life is probably more brutal than anything a wild animal experiences.

Hettinger and Rolston might respond to Everett's claim that humans don't need animal flesh to survive by arguing that we're still hardwired, by virtue of our evolutionary development, to eat meat. But as we'll see in the next chapter, this is a flimsy justification for meat-eating.

From the environment to humans

One thing is incontestable: given the way in which the vast bulk of the meat we eat is produced, an omnivorous diet is bad for the environment. But as we've seen, the precise nature of our obligations to the environment is open to question. Some contend that prudence is the only check upon our treatment of nature. Others argue from a number of perspectives for the bestowal of moral standing on the environment. None of these attempts to defend moral consideration of the biosphere is without its conceptual and practical difficulties, and some environmentalists who otherwise endorse one or the other of them deny that vegetarianism is a necessary corollary. Even stronger, some environmentalists argue that environmentalism and vegetarianism are incompatible.

In light of this uncertainty, even those vegetarians who see their choice of diet as part of a larger concern for the welfare of the environment may well be perplexed about exactly what their moral obligations to the biosphere are. It's not simply that there are philosophical difficulties in attributing moral standing to land, water, and the atmosphere. It's also difficult to wrap one's imagination around so great a departure from the traditional way of thinking of what is in and what is outside of the moral community. In the next chapter, we turn to more familiar ground by examining unapologetically human-centered arguments for vegetarianism.

CHAPTER SEVEN

The anthrocentric argument

It is the position of the American Dietetic Association that appropriately planned vegetarian diets, including total vegetarian or vegan diets, are healthful, nutritionally adequate, and may provide health benefits in the prevention and treatment of certain diseases.

AMERICAN DIETETIC ASSOCIATION

Everyone has the right to a standard of living adequate for the health and well-being of himself and his family, including food.

UNIVERSAL DECLARATION OF HUMAN RIGHTS

The word "anthrocentrism" frequently carries negative connotations. Normatively, critics charge that anthrocentrism arrogantly presumes that humans are ethically privileged in comparison to all other organisms. As we've seen in previous chapters, defenders of both animal- and environment-focused vegetarianism reject this as a form of species chauvinism. From a logical perspective, critics argue that anthrocentrism is a hasty generalization. As John Stuart Mill contended in his *System of Logic*, it is the fallacy of presuming that human language and reason are the standards to which everything in the universe necessarily conforms (Mill 1884).

But one person's anthrocentrism is another person's humanism. There is a long philosophical tradition in the West which argues that humans indeed *are* superior to animals when it comes to the things that matter—intelligence and creativity—and that consequently it isn't arrogant at all to view human needs and desires as morally privileged and human reason as a sufficient tool for the exploration and explanation of reality. On the contrary, it's an entirely reasonable position.

There are many vegetarians whose primary reason for adopting a meatless diet is human-centered or anthrocentric. They may feel compassion for the plight of factory-farmed animals, and may even believe that it's morally indecent to mistreat any sentient creature. Or, on the contrary, they may be indifferent to animals and feel no moral obligation to them. But whether they do or don't, the primary focus of anthrocentric vegetarianism is the empirical claim that abstaining from animal food benefits humans and indulging in it harms them, and the moral conclusion that we *should* therefore abstain. The first and foremost reason for refusing to eat animals, therefore, is our moral responsibility to ourselves and our fellow-humans. If we have a moral responsibility to animals, it's indirect or secondary. That human abstention from meat will benefit animals is a pleasing by-product, perhaps, but it's not the moral target.

As we saw in the last chapter, contractarian vegetarians can be especially interested in the environmental impact of meat-eating, although their concern isn't for nature per se but rather for the deleterious effects environmental degradation has on human well-being. In this chapter, we'll concentrate on three other arguments commonly invoked by them: that meat-eating harms personal health, brutalizes us psychologically and morally, and contributes to world hunger. Taken individually or collectively, they constitute, for anthrocentric vegetarians, sufficient reasons to adopt a meatless diet.

You are what you eat

Anthrocentric vegetarians agree that, from the standpoint of physical health, "you are what you eat," and that meat-eating, all things being equal, is less healthy than a vegetarian or vegan diet. But it's one thing to claim that vegetarianism is healthier than omnivorism. It's quite another to derive a moral prescription from the fact, if fact it be. There are, after all, all kinds of behavior which are either potentially dangerous or actually harmful to personal physical health. Mountain-climbing and bungee-jumping fall into the first category; smoking cigarettes and drinking alcohol to excess fall into the second. But so long as the behaviors are legal, what except mere prudence could be invoked to persuade me against indulging in them? In other words, do I have a moral obligation to refrain from activity that harms myself?[1]

One obvious response is a libertarian one which argues that so long as my actions don't affect anyone else, I'm morally free to do whatever I wish, even if what I indulge in is self-destructive. This is an ethical position that fits well with a worldview that highly values individualism, but ill accords with others (such as, for example, ecofeminism) that focus on relational interconnection. But even rugged individualists must admit that in an increasingly shrinking world, there simply aren't a lot of personal activities which are also so private that they don't affect others for good or ill. Much behavior which we may think of as private can have consequences that radiate far beyond our own private sphere. If I choose to smoke or drink excessively, for example, I may ruin my health, and this in turn can impose burdens on my family and fellow citizens to care for me, foot the bill for my medical treatment, shoulder indirect financial loss because of my inability to work, and so on. If what we eat is one of those activities that potentially or actually imposes burdens on others, thereby interfering with their freedom, then our choice of diet is no more private than our choice to smoke. As we'll explore in detail a bit later in this chapter, anthrocentric vegetarians defend precisely this conclusion.

So even on libertarian grounds, my personal freedom is limited by its impact on others. But what about behavior that, arguably, harms me alone? This is a much more difficult question. It's clear to most of us that we have obligations to not harm others, either directly or indirectly, when we can avoid doing so. But do we have an obligation to not harm ourselves as well?

What makes this a perplexing question is the conventional assumption that ethics examines the ways human beings ought to treat one another. I have certain rights that others have a moral duty to honor, just as they have similar rights against me to act dutifully toward them. According to this way of thinking, moral duties are always interpersonal, directed outwards to other people. When it comes to my intrapersonal relationship with myself, there are no analogous duties. So it follows that I'm under no moral obligation not to harm myself, so long as others aren't affected.

But it's not at all clear that I can't have moral duties to myself. In fact, philosopher Elizabeth Telfer (1996) offers a very compelling case for the claim that I do. When we consider our obligations to other people, we discover that they're grounded in a fundamental duty not to act in any way that unwarrantedly diminishes their autonomy, self-development, and well-being. But if we value these qualities in others to the extent that we accept a responsibility not to interfere with them—and, furthermore, may even acknowledge a responsibility to promote them—then consistency demands that we likewise value the same qualities in ourselves. And if we have a duty to honor them in others, there's no reason to deny that we have a duty to honor them in ourselves as well. So it's not unreasonable to presume that humans have intrapersonal duties, connected to but not identical to their duties to others, to promote their own autonomy, self-development, and well-being.

Now, if we tie this into diet, it becomes apparent that we have a duty to ourselves to eat in ways that promote our own well-being. Even if we stipulate for the sake of discussion that my filling up on junk food and soda pop harms no one else but me, Telfer's analysis concludes that I've still acted immorally, because to the extent that the junk food diminishes my ability to further my personal gifts and talents, I've broken a duty to myself. The obligation to myself is even more complex if I accept that I also have an obligation to others to eat healthily, not simply, as the libertarian would say, so my illness doesn't burden them, but because I have a positive duty to flourish so I can help them flourish as well. Note that this argument against eating certain foods isn't based on mere prudence, although prudence is certainly a factor. Instead, it's based on the much stronger claim that I have ethical obligations to treat myself in such a way as to maximize my chances of flourishing as a human being as well as my ability to help others do likewise.

If Telfer is correct, I have no right to indulge in private behavior which affects no one else but harms me. On the contrary, I have a positive duty, first to myself and then to others, to maintain my well-being as best I can. Given this, the question of whether certain kinds of diet are healthier than others carries moral as well as hygienic weight. Vegetarians argue that the data strongly point to the conclusion that a vegetable-based diet is healthier than one which includes meat. But before we take a look at those data, we need to examine and dispose of a popular but irrelevant objection to the claim that humans are better off abstaining from meat.

The objection has it that humans are "natural" omnivores. Our distant ancestors may've once subsisted on a vegetable diet, but at some point they began eating meat. The infusion of protein that resulted from the dietary switch in turn increased physical strength and brain size, and the end result was the transition from earlier hominid species to homo sapiens. Meat-eating comes naturally to us because it made us who we are. A corollary of this argument is that abstention from meat is actually harmful to health because it "goes against" human nature.

Although this objection is commonplace, it's neither as strong nor as pertinent as its defenders maintain. In the first place, the jury is out as to whether we're "naturally" omnivores. Many anthropologists point out, for example, that humans lack the typically short colons of meat-eaters and that our canine teeth, which proponents of the meat-eating-is-natural thesis frequently cite as evidence, are too underdeveloped to be of much use in ripping apart animal flesh.

But even if it's true that our ancestors ate meat, it's a huge jump from that fact to the normative inference that we *ought* to continue eating meat today. Simply because an act is "natural"—sidestepping the thorny issue of what we mean by the very word—is no guarantee that it's right. Even stronger, many acts that are "natural," at least in the sense that our ancestors regularly performed them, may be harmful if not morally repellant. Our ancestors, for example, believed that illnesses were caused by malevolent spirits or gods and that magical rituals were appropriate medicines. But surely this ancient practice shouldn't be thought of as prescriptive. Moreover, it may be perfectly "natural" for humans to die of burst appendixes, in that death is the natural culmination of peritonitis. But today we certainly consider it imprudent and, depending on the circumstances, even immoral to refuse to use modern surgery and antibiotics in cases of appendicitis. As philosopher Jennifer Everett points out, the claim that meat-eating is evolutionarily natural "goes absolutely no distance toward providing a moral defense of meat-eating, for clearly, not everything 'deeply ingrained in human nature' is morally permissible" (Everett 2004, p. 304).

Aggressiveness, promiscuity, and bullying, after all, may be equally hardwired, but they're certainly not ethically acceptable attitudes or behavior. In short, says Everett, "we should not regard as permissible, value as good, or want to emulate today every behavior, activity, or trait that happened to play a formative role in our species' genesis" (p. 310).

Now that the "eating meat is natural" argument is out of the way, let's examine the anthrocentric vegetarianism claim that a diet which includes animal products is less healthy than a meatless one. Defenders of this position generally point to three areas of special concern: the linkage of meat to heart disease and cancer; the risk of food contamination in industrial slaughtering and meat-packaging; and the animal pandemics that factory farming practices encourage.

In the United States, heart disease is the number one killer. Forty million people are afflicted by it. One million and a half people suffer heart attacks every year, and seven hundred thousand Americans, a quarter of them under 65 years of age, die from heart disease annually (Cohn and Kannel 1995; Diehl 1995). There is a well-established correlation between high blood cholesterol and coronary disease. In fact, the medical community has known for over 20 years that high cholesterol, along with smoking and hypertension, is a major indicator of the risk of heart attack (LaRosa 1990).

Cholesterol, a substance necessary for animal life, is naturally produced by the human liver, which in effect produces all the cholesterol we need. So when we eat foods rich in cholesterol and saturated fats—foods such as meat, eggs, and dairy products—we're essentially pumping unnecessary cholesterol into our systems. Given the correlation between cholesterol and heart disease, any additional cholesterol is probably too much. As one Harvard nutritionist research team warns, the optimal intake of cholesterol is most likely zero (Ascherio and Willett 1995). But given the prevalence of carbohydrates, sugars, and meat and dairy products in what Peter Singer and Jim Mason (2006) call the "standard American diet," the average American omnivore consumes way more saturated fats, more calories, and more protein than is good for heart health.[2] By contrast, countries in which people typically eat only small amounts of meat and dairy have much lower rates of heart disease. In China, for example, the risk of heart disease in citizens is only a fraction of what it is in North America and Europe, although it increases for Chinese who immigrate to the West and adopt a Western, meat-heavy diet (Kloer 1989).

Heart disease may not be the only human malady tied to high cholesterol levels. Although the data isn't as conclusive, there's evidence to suggest that elevated blood cholesterol is implicated in colon, lung, prostate, and breast cancers. Moreover, free radicals, molecules produced when meat is charred or cooked, break down healthy cells in search of oxygen atoms. In attacking the cells, free radicals damage DNA, which then are at higher risk of producing cancer cells. So meat-eating can introduce compounds into the body that hasten the development of malignancies (Marcus 2001, pp. 38–9).

Although the biochemical relationship between meat and cancer is still being studied, demographic evidence strongly suggests that vegetarians suffer less from cancers than omnivores. As William Castelli of the National Heart, Lung, and Blood Institute says, vegetarian men "have only 40 percent of [the national] cancer rate. On average they outlive other men by about six years" (Robbins 2011, p. 39). Not surprisingly, the National Cattlemen's Association disputes estimates such as these. In one of its public statements, the lobbying group maintains that increased longevity rather than meat consumption is responsible for the escalation of heart disease and cancer. And "[w]hat has allowed us to live long enough to run these risks? Meat, among other things" (Robbins 2011, p. 39). While it's reasonable to presume that increased life span does play a role in the rise of coronary disease and cancer, the National Cattlemen's Association blanket denial that meat is a factor ignores demographic comparisons of disease rates between high meat-eating and low meat-eating populations.

Even if there was absolutely no medical linkage between meat and heart disease and cancer, the factory farm origin of most of the meat consumed in the United States makes eating it a human health hazard. The ways in which cattle, pigs, and chickens are raised and slaughtered encourage contamination of their flesh by bacteria such as *E. coli* and *Campylobacter*. The squalid and crowded conditions endured by the animals ensure that their digestive tracts are breeding grounds for such bugs, despite the huge amounts of antibiotics regularly mixed in with their food. When the animals are taken to industrial slaughterhouses, where the high volume of animals can only be handled by a rapid assembly line process, the meat quickly carved out of the animals is frequently spattered with feces and urine from nicked bowels and bladders. As consumer advocacy group Public Citizen describes the process when it comes to cattle,

> [M]any cows are raised in dirty conditions in huge, city-sized feedlots where they become smeared with fecal matter and other filth. In this condition, they are transported to slaughterhouses, where rapid processing takes place. Workers are under pressure to work as quickly as possible, killing and gutting as many as 330 animals per hour. In such an intensive operation, a cow's body cavity is slit open, and if any errors occur in cutting, the intestines can be punctured and feces released. The carcasses are immediately dipped in a cold water bath, which becomes a fecal stew. (Public Citizen Foundation 2000, p. 13)

Similar conditions hold for the slaughter of pigs and chickens. The cold water bath for their carcasses is one of the major causes of fecal contamination.[3] As a former US Department of Agriculture microbiologist said in reference to chicken that's purchased in supermarkets, the final product "is no different than if you stuck it in the toilet and ate it"[4] (Eisnitz 1997, p. 169). An estimated 70 percent of chickens and 90 percent of turkeys are contaminated with enough campylobacter to cause illness in humans when eaten. Beef purchased in supermarkets is just as filthy. The USDA estimates that 89 percent of all US ground beef patties contain "traces" of E. coli (Robbins 2011, p. 126). Given that ground beef is typically made of the mixed-together meat of around one hundred different beasts, it's not surprising that so much of it should be contaminated. A single infected cow can cross-contaminate 16 tons of beef. Nor are eggs from factory farm hen batteries much of an improvement. Salmonella contaminated eggs are so prevalent—more than 650,000 Americans sicken from them each year—that the Centers for Disease Control strongly advise consumers to avoid eating raw or even undercooked eggs (Robbins 2011, pp. 130–1).

One of the reasons so much meat from industrial slaughterhouses is contaminated is the inability of federal meat inspectors, stationed in every slaughterhouse in the nation, to keep up with the head-spinning flow of animals. Approximately six thousand inspectors must scrutinize the billions of animal carcasses that whip past them each year. They typically do nothing more than eyeball the meat for the visible presence of fecal material or disease, despite the National Academy of Sciences' 1985 warning that it's "virtually impossible" to spot contaminants "with current inspection methods" (Eisnitz 1997, p. 161). To make matters worse, the US Department of Agriculture (USDA) has shown an alarming willingness to cut corners in order to take some of the pressure off its inspectors. In 1978, for example, the agency allowed the poultry industry to reclassify fecal contamination as a mere "cosmetic blemish" that requires nothing more than a simple rinsing—like a cold water bath—to pass inspection (Eisnitz 1997, p. 167).

Despite its public denials that the very way in which meat is produced increases its likelihood of contamination, the meat industry has enthusiastically endorsed the use of what's sometimes called "electron beam pasteurization." This is a fancy term for irradiating processed meat to kill pathogens on it. While it's true that the irradiation *does* kill bacteria, the practice ignores and thereby implicitly condones the unsanitary factory farm and slaughterhouse conditions that contaminate meat in the first place. Nor does it remove fecal material, urine, and pus from the meat itself. As the Center for Science in the Public Interest notes, irradiated meat is "irradiated filth" (Robbins 2011, p. 122).

An additional health hazard associated with meat-eating involves the enormous amounts of antibiotics and hormones typically fed to factory-farmed animals. Antibiotics are given to food animals both when they become ill and as a prophylactic measure against potential infections caused by their filthy living conditions. Each year in the United States, nearly 25 million pounds of preventive antibiotics are given to livestock, whereas humans ingest only 3 million pounds in the same time period (Mason and Finelli 2006, pp. 115–18; Robbins 2011, p. 141). In other words, the amount of antibiotics given to food animals each year accounts for 70 percent of the total use in the United States.

We know that bacteria are becoming increasingly resistant to antibiotic treatment. In the years immediately following the 1928 discovery of penicillin, no strain of staphylococcus could resist the antibiotic. Today, penicillin is useless against more than 95 percent of staphylococci strains. In the words of World Health Organization pathologist Jeffrey Fisher, "[h]ospitals are in jeopardy of once again being overwhelmed with untreatable infectious diseases such as pneumonia, tuberculosis, meningitis, typhoid fever and dysentery"

(Fisher 1994, p. 30). The worry is that feeding massive quantities of antibiotics to food animals increases the level of bacterial resistance to them, seriously undermining the ability of antibiotics to treat or protect human patients. Both the World Health Organization and the US Centers for Disease Control have declared that the factory farming of antibiotic-stuffed animals is a contributing factor in the rise of drug-resistant bacterial infections in the human population (Robbins 2011, pp. 139–40).

Hormone supplements are also a dietary staple for food animals. Steroids are fed to increase bulk and speed up maturation in cattle, pigs, and chickens, and fed to dairy cows and chickens to increase milk and egg production. The meat industry insists that the use of hormones is harmless. As the National Cattlemen's Beef Association says, hormones are required for the "efficient production of beef that is safe" and asserts that they "have no physiological significance [to humans] whatsoever." But the European Union has completely banned the addition of hormones to animal feed on the grounds that many of them are known to cause several kinds of human cancer. As one EU report said about one hormone regularly given to beef raised in the United States, it is "a complete carcinogen" which both initiates and promotes the growth of malignant tumors. "In plain language this means that even small additional doses of residues of this hormone in meat, arising from its use as a growth promoter in cattle, has an inherent risk of causing cancer" (Robbins 2011, p. 143).

Another health hazard associated with the vast quantities of meat produced and eaten in both the United States and across the globe has received much attention in the past quarter century: the possibility of pandemic animal diseases crossing over into the human population. The best known of these is, of course, bovine spongiform encelphalopathy, popularly known as mad cow disease. Caused by feeding cattle the remains of sheep—cattle, to point out the obvious, are grass-eating, not omnivorous, animals—the human variety of mad cow disease, which can be caught by eating infected beef, is always fatal. There is a long incubation period for the disease, a particularly worrisome fact since we now know that it can also be transmitted through blood transfusions.

But mad cow disease isn't the only risk. Influenzas that affect fowl and pigs have also jumped across species to infect humans. It's likely that both swine and bird influenza originated in wild animals. But the factory farming of thousands of close-quartered birds and beasts gives infections adventitiously transmitted from wild to domesticate populations ideal conditions for mutation and growth. The fear of many scientists is that such influenzas, once they mutate with human viruses, could give rise to worldwide infections to which humans would have little if any resistance.

The indivisibility of violence

Eating meat is not only risky business when it comes to physical health. According to many vegetarians, anthrocentric and otherwise, it also damages psychological or spiritual well being by making us complicit in the systematic infliction of suffering and death upon billions of creatures. We saw in Chapter 1 that Isaac Bashevis Singer referred to the plight of factory-farmed animals as an "eternal Treblinka." If he's correct, then those of us who eat meat are analogous in at least one sense to Germans who benefited from the imprisonment and extermination of Jews: our moral sensitivity is coarsened and our capacity for sympathy calloused. Such an impoverishment of our inner life not only diminishes our ability to flourish as decent individuals. It also endangers other humans, because desensitization to the suffering of animals risks bleeding over into an indifference to human suffering as well.

Obvious signs of this coarsening can be found among men and women who actually work in factory farms and who are encouraged to view animals as thing-like units. Animal discomfort, distress, illness, and death are viewed more as inconveniences on the assembly line than as events to evoke compassion. A more likely emotional response on the part of workers is anger or impatience at the extra work caused by panicked or suffering beasts.

Anger as well as overt acts of physical cruelty are even more common in the frenzied pace of industrial slaughterhouses. Investigative journalist Gail Eisnitz interviewed dozens of men and women who work in them, and she was struck time and again at the extent to which their tasks of killing and butchering animals fostered indifference to suffering and, occasionally, downright pleasure in it. One union official told her, "[a]nimal abuse is so common that workers who've been in the industry for years get into a state of apathy about it. After a while it doesn't seem unusual anymore" (Eisnitz 1997,

p. 133). A "sticker," tasked with slitting the throats of animals, told her that his job had taken an "emotional toll" on him, by which he meant a deadening of his capacity for compassion. "If you work in the stick pit for any period of time," he said, "you develop an attitude that lets you kill things but doesn't let you care . . . Pigs down on the kill floor have come up and nuzzled me like a puppy. Two minutes later I had to kill them—beat them to death with a pipe. I can't care" (p. 87). Either indifference sets in, as with the worker who describes his coworker's practice of shoving prods up hogs' anuses to move them along the killing line, and whose only reaction is "I didn't appreciate that because it made the hogs twice as wild by the time they got to me" (p. 68), or workers begin to take a sadistic pleasure in abusing the animals they're about to kill. As another sticker told Eiznitz, if an animal "pisses" him off, he didn't "just kill it." Instead, "you go in hard, push hard, blow the windpipe, make it drown in its own blood. Split its nose . . . One time I took my knife and I sliced off the end of a hog's nose. [Then] I took a handful of salt brine and ground it into his nose . . . I still had a bunch of salt left . . . and I stuck the salt right up the hog's ass" (p. 93).

The type of bloody work slaughterhouse laborers do day after day coarsened their sensitivity to animal suffering while on the job. Many of them told Eisnitz that the anger and tension the work built in them bled over into their private lives. As one testified, "[e]very sticker I know carries a gun, and every one of them would shoot you. Most stickers I know have been arrested for assault. A lot of them have problems with alcohol. They have to drink, they have no other way of dealing with killing live, kicking animals all day long" (p. 88). Eisnitz also discovered that high incidents of spousal abuse are correlated with slaughterhouse work.[5]

The clear implication is that direct participation in the daily routine slaughter of thousands of terrified, screaming, and physically anguished animals is an unnatural act which does violence to the human psyche. Many of us can accept this as an abstract possibility. After all, we know that prison guards can become brutalized by the work they do, and it's a lot less sanguinary than killing and dismembering animals all day long. So it's not unreasonable to suppose that the factory farm and industrial slaughterhouse systems can also desensitize the people who work in them.

But many vegetarians worry that the circle of damage extends to the wider population. Author Victoria Moran (1985) argues, for example, that violence is indivisible. Depending upon its intensity, the effects of an act of violence radiate outwards, and few violent acts are more intense than the infliction of suffering and death on billions of food animals each year. The psychological effects of living in a culture that literally feeds upon suffering and death can't help but create a mindset that reinforces indifference to animal suffering and, perhaps, to human suffering as well.

Moran isn't the only commentator who worries about the moral and spiritual desensitization that a diet based on suffering and death breeds. Some authors are concerned that we literally ingest fear and violence when we eat the flesh of violently slain animals. John Robbins contends, for example, that we absorb "biochemical agents designed by nature to tell an animal that its life is in the gravest danger" (Robbins 1987, p. 156). That we literally eat the biologically poisonous fear of violently slain animals may be too much for skeptics to swallow. But there's greater consensus, stretching back centuries, about the negative moral effects of killing and eating animals. Pythagoras reasoned that "those who are accustomed to abominate the slaughter of other animals as iniquitous and unnatural will think it still more unjust and unlawful to kill a man" (Spencer 1995, p. 50). Porphyry complains that killing and eating animals encourages "a murderous disposition and a brutal nature" (Porphyry 1999, p. 43). David Hartley observed in the eighteenth century that "taking away the lives of animals in order to convert them into food does great violence to the principles of benevolence and compassion" (Hartley 1999, p. 57). A century later Leo Tolstoy argued that in order to kill food animals we must suppress "the highest spiritual capacity—that of sympathy and pity toward living creatures" (Tolstoy 1999, p. 99). Even some who argue against the moral necessity of vegetarianism worry that killing animals harms humans. Philosopher Tibor Machan, who in Chapter 4 unyieldingly denied that humans have ethical obligations to animals, concedes that mistreating them encourages a "lack of sensitivity, a certain callousness" (Machan 2004, p. 22). And Immanuel Kant, who famously refused to grant rights to animals, insisted that humans nonetheless corrupt their capacity for compassion if they harm them, and that a person's heart can be judged by his or her treatment of animals (Kant 2001, p. 212).

One of the more insightful analyses of the damaging moral and spiritual effects meat-eating can have on humans comes from philosopher Roger Scruton. Not a vegetarian himself, Scruton nonetheless believes that "the indifference of modern carnivores to the methods used to reduce the cost of their habit"—that is, the billions of food animals raised each year in factory farms and butchered in industrial slaughterhouses—"is a morally repulsive characteristic against which it is wholly natural to rebel." This willingness to kill so many animals to keep down the cost of a food that isn't necessary in the first place is bad enough. But the ethos of the developed world—a "solipsistic fast-food culture" which removes meat from its traditional role as a "focus of hospitality" and transforms it into a taken-for-granted commodity—only underscores our moral insouciance as meat-eaters. "[R]educe meat to an object of solitary greed like chocolate," writes Scruton, "and the question naturally arises: why should life be sacrificed, just for this?" (Scruton 2004, p. 89).

A few years ago, a reader of *Vegetarian Times* wrote a letter in which he complained about the magazine's dedication of so much space to the cruelty of the factory farm system. "I do not care what happens to a cow!" he protested. He himself was a vegetarian solely because he believed a vegetable diet good for his health (McGinnis 1993, p. 8). If anthrocentric vegetarians are correct in their allegation that the prevalence of factory farms and industrial slaughterhouses coarsens our capacity for sympathy and compassion, it may be that the letter-writer, although a vegetarian, was a victim of that very desensitization. Otherwise, he wouldn't have been so indifferent about "what happens to a cow."

You are what *I* eat

Food riots throughout the Middle East in 2011 that helped fuel political and social revolutions in Tunisia, Egypt, and Libya reminded North Americans and Europeans that the world suffers from a chronic shortage of food. The planet's human population topped seven billion in late 2011. Roughly 10 percent of that seven billion goes hungry every day. Forty to 60 million people die each year of hunger related illnesses. Approximately 14 million of them are children under the age of 5.

The problem of world hunger isn't likely to lessen any time soon, because human population is projected to expand rapidly for at least another generation. One out of three persons in the world is under 15 years of age, while only one out of ten is over 60. The average age of the current population is 28. So over the next 30 or so years, birth rates are bound to exceed death rates. Dismally, the United Nations predicts that the world's population will exceed a staggering ten billion by 2050 (Cone 1999).

The surge in population means that there will be greater need for arable land on which to grow crops. But as we saw in Chapter 6, we're running out of it. The intensive farming methods of agribusiness erode topsoil 16 to 300 times faster (depending on the locale) than it can regenerate. Land already under cultivation is particularly susceptible to topsoil loss, suffering each year a reduction in its crop-bearing capacity. Moreover, new arable land is getting scarcer. One study (Kendall and Pimentel 1994) found that a full one-fourth of current farmland is so fragile that it's on the verge of turning into desert and ought to be allowed to go fallow. After excluding infertile regions such as desert, mountainous, and frozen land, the study concludes that available farmland can increase by no more than a third—period.

World hunger would simply be a tragic fact of life if the planet was incapable of producing enough food to supply an adequate amount of nourishment to each and every person. But most authorities on world hunger agree with Frances Moore Lappe's conclusion (Lappe 1998) that despite the shrinkage of arable land, it's still possible to feed everyone, including those who will swell the population in the coming four decades. The problem isn't that the planet is too small or too increasingly infertile to grow food. The problem is that the planet's arable land is being misused and wasted.

If this is the case, world hunger isn't just a tragic fact. It also becomes an ethical issue, first because good arguments can be made for the claim that it's immoral for some people to eat well at the expense of others, but also because Article 25 of the Universal Declaration of Human Rights (quoted as one of this chapter's epigraphs) declares that every person has a fundamental right to enough food to sustain the well-being of "himself and his family." Rights, as we saw in Chapter 4, are entitlements that posit claims against others. If I have a fundamental right to be fed, and others are being fed at my expense, then I have a moral claim against them and they, in turn, have a moral duty to me. When it comes to world hunger, the following case can be made. Presuming that the planet has the capacity to produce adequate food for everyone but that arable land is being misused such that a few benefit at the expense of the many, the few have a moral claim against the many to change their eating habits so that everyone has enough to eat.

One of the most obvious ways to ensure an adequate food supply is to reduce the amount of land used to grow food for the animals those of us in the developed world like to eat. A full one-third of the world's grain is fed to cattle and other livestock. In the United States alone, one-half of the total annual agricultural output goes to feed livestock. Two percent of the corn grown in the United States is eaten by people; 77 percent is consumed by livestock. Four million acres of the nation's farmland are devoted to growing vegetables; 56 million acres are set aside to grow hay for livestock (Robbins 2011, p. 293). Moreover, the worldwide percentage of grain earmarked for livestock is growing. In China alone, the share of grain fed to food animals more than trebled in just a 20 year period (p. 285).

Devoting so much land to growing food for animals is a major obstacle to eliminating hunger in the world. The same amount of grain and corn grown to raise livestock is more than adequate to feed every human.[6] One estimate has it that if the grain currently given to animals was instead diverted to humans, four tons of surplus could be given to each of the one billion hungry persons on the planet (Schleifer 1985, p. 68). The fact that it isn't, says one commentator, amounts to "a kind of mass reckless homicide on the international level" (Hill 1996, p. 127).

The question immediately arises: if we currently grow enough grain and corn to feed the planet, why are so many people in food distress? The answer, according to the anthrocentric vegetarian (as well as many nonvegetarians), lies in the fact that huge amounts of grain protein are wasted—up to 90 percent—when converted into animal protein. Most estimates, including the one endorsed by the USDA, conclude that it takes a full 16 pounds of grain to produce a single pound of beef. (The National Cattlemen's Beef Association predictably disputes this figure, offering in its place a 4.5 to 1 pound ratio [Robbins 2011, p. 293], a figure almost universally disputed.) The 16 pounds of grain, furthermore, is of more nutritional value than the meat into which it converts. It contains 21 times the calories and eight times the protein as a pound of beef. It also contains more fiber and no fat.

Given the large amounts of plant protein needed to produce animal protein, nations which consume large quantities of meat naturally get the lion's share of the world's plant protein as well. In the United States and Canada, for example, grain consumption is five times greater than in most developing nations. But only a small percentage of it is eaten directly. The bulk is consumed indirectly through meat. United States omnivores alone consume enough grain through the meat they eat to supply each human on earth with a daily cup of grain (Amato and Partridge 1989). The obvious conclusion, as the Worldwide Institute notes, is that "meat production is an inefficient use of grain—the grain is used more efficiently when consumed directly by humans." Continuing to divert grain from humans to food animals creates "competition for grain between affluent meat eaters and the world's poor" (Halweil 1998), and in that kind of contest, the poor generally lose.

From the standpoint of anthrocentric vegetarians, then, it's too simple merely to say that "I am what I eat." While it's true that my diet affects my personal health, it's equally true that my diet affects the well-being of others too, sometimes so significantly that it makes sense also to say that "*You* are what *I* eat." Meat-eating is one of the most obvious examples of how the dietary patterns of people in one part of the globe affect humans in other parts. Walden Bello of the Institute for Food and Development Policy puts it like this:

Every time you eat a hamburger you are having a relationship with thousands of people you never met. Not just people at the supermarket or fast food restaurant but possibly World Bank officials in Washington, D.C., and peasants from Central and South America. And many of these people are hungry. The fact is that there is enough food in the world for everyone. But tragically, much of the world's food and land resources are tied up in producing beef and other livestock—food for the well-off—while millions of children and adults suffer from malnutrition and starvation. (Robbins 2011, p. 289)

As we saw in the Introduction, eating in today's world is never merely a private affair, even though it can be intensely personal. In Chapters 1–5 of this book, we saw how eating a diet that includes meat, eggs, and dairy products almost inevitably affects animals for the worse. In Chapter 6, we saw that the way we eat impacts the environment. The proponents of anthrocentric vegetarianism once again remind us of the nonprivate nature of eating by underscoring the way in which dietary choices in one part of the world radiate outwards to influence the way people in other parts of the world eat—or don't eat, as the case may be.

A vegetarianism that's easy to swallow

Human nature being what it is, we tend to listen to ethical advice more carefully when we sense that it's in our best interest to do so. Many and perhaps most people sympathize to one degree or another with any animal that suffers because they see suffering as an evil. But those same people continue to eat animals, thus tacitly accepting complicity in their suffering. They pity, as Oliver Goldsmith observed, but they also eat, because to abstain from a food that gives them gustatory pleasure goes against their (perceived) self-interest. The tastiness of a chicken leg or a rump roast simply outweighs an abstract and frequently vague sense that it's wrong to cause animals to suffer simply for gustatory satisfaction.

Similarly, many people aren't particularly interested in the health of the environment until it affects them in immediate and obvious ways. They may intellectually acknowledge that manure from factory farms pollutes land and water without feeling a sense of moral urgency about it strong enough to change their eating habits. Even if they happen to live close enough to a hog factory farm to experience firsthand the effects of its pollution of land, water, and atmosphere, they're more likely to condemn the farm's owner than the consumer's demand for pig meat. And they probably won't stop eating pork themselves.

But anthrocentric vegetarianism, precisely because it focuses so heavily on immediately obvious self-interest, offers a reason to abstain from meat that most people get. Eating meat, eggs, and dairy products, especially in the excessive amounts that North Americans and Europeans do, is simply bad for physical health. Even people who refuse to give them up completely either have or want to cut back on their consumption of them. Personal health considerations often speak louder than moral concerns for animals or the environment.

But as we've seen, personal health considerations aren't just prudential. They're also normative. We have a duty to maintain our personal health so that we flourish. We have a duty to flourish so that we can be of service to other human beings who are likewise interested in achieving states of well-being. And finally, we have a moral obligation to temper our diets if they tend, as meat-eating does, to harm other people. For many people, this chain of reasoning is compelling, honing in as it does on both self-interest and the well-being of humans in general.

Still, it's neither necessary nor realistic to endorse one of the models we've examined thus far to the exclusion of all others. Although there are obvious disagreements between the interests, rights, and ecofeminist defenses of vegetarianism, proponents of each of them are certainly united in their broader concern for animal welfare, and all of them can easily concur with features of the environmental and anthrocentric arguments.[7] As we saw in the Introduction, when it comes to reasons for endorsing vegetarianism, one size needn't fit all, and an individual vegetarian can be motivated by multiple reasons.

But there remains one more way of advocating a meatless diet that, for many people, may not be as easy to swallow as the ones we've examined thus far. It's the position that life is sacred because of its causal link with a divine Creator, and that therefore the taking of life is wrong primarily because it's an offense against God. We turn to this argument next.

CHAPTER EIGHT

The reverence for life argument

The Christian argument for vegetarianism is simple: since animals belong to God, have value to God, and live for God, then their needless destruction is sinful.

ANDREW LINZEY

The first great vow: I renounce all killing of living beings, whether subtle or gross, whether movable or immovable. Nor shall I myself kill living beings nor cause others to do it, nor consent to it.

AKARANGA SUTRA

Veterinarian and author James Serpell argues that cultures which regularly hunt and eat animals nearly always contrive mechanisms for expiating guilt about taking their lives. When ancient Babylonian priests sacrificed animals, for example, they whispered in the slaughtered beast's ear, "This deed was done by all the gods; I did not do it." Japanese Ainu justify the killing and eating of bears by insisting that doing so sends the slain creatures to the spirit realm, a place they long to be. Hunters in many African tribes publicly apologize in elaborate purification ceremonies to the animals they kill. In short, expiatory myths and ceremonies abound, suggesting that human omnivores feel deep-seated uneasiness about slaying beasts (Serpell 1986). In modern cultures in which meat-eaters have no personal contact with animals, much less the process of slaughtering them, the guilt may be vestigial, tamped down below the level of conscious awareness and public ritual. But it can reveal itself in all sorts of ways, including, as we saw in the Introduction, in the anger and defensiveness that omnivores sometimes display when they think their dietary preferences are being challenged.

The guilt humans experience over the killing of food animals may be explained in moral terms. Eating animals could violate our normative sense of kinship with them, or stick in our craw because we believe we owe them some degree of moral consideration. Or we may feel uneasy because we believe that killing and eating animals harms the environment or exacerbates the problem of world hunger, thereby making us morally culpable for contributing to already bad situations. But the sense of discomfort that Serpell writes about is nearly always expiated by a religious myth and ritual of one sort or another rather than an ethical argument, suggesting that its roots go deeper than moral sensibility about right and wrong. The implication is that it is religious or spiritual in origin.

Some vegetarians take this suggestion seriously.[1] For them, the killing and eating of animals is wrong because they see all life as belonging to God. Consequently, it should be reverenced and protected rather than taken for granted, much less slain. Depending in part on which religious or spiritual tradition they identify with, these religious vegetarians offer several related justifications for their refusal to eat animals. One is that that animals, like all of creation, are created by a good and holy God, and all God's work should properly solicit our admiration, gratitude and respect. Another is that we are deeply akin to animals, not just in the sense of sharing with them the ability to experience pain and pleasure, as the basic argument for vegetarianism has it, but because we share a common divine Parent. Since they are literally our spiritual brothers and sisters, it's only proper that we extend compassion and kindness to them. A third justification is that everything which God created is imbued with a divine spark or principle, so to revere creatures is to revere the God within them. Yet another perspective is that humans, made in the likeness of God, are intended to serve as divinely appointed protective and compassionate stewards over creation, not its rulers.

But an obvious question immediately arises. If some vegetarians base their choice of diet on religious grounds—a position that I generically call the reverence for life argument—why is it that the world's major religions, especially the so-called Abrahamic ones, seem so indifferent to animal welfare? According to philosopher Paul Waldau, "it remains overwhelmingly true today that mainline religious institutions have left unchallenged virtually all practices of modern industrialized societies that are harmful to nonhuman animals" (Waldau 2006, p. 81). Waldau's accusation is not easily dismissible. And it also calls into question claims about deep-seated religious guilt over killing animals made by people like James Serpell.

Many religious vegetarians respond that major religious traditions have prescriptions against needlessly killing animals embedded within them, even if these ideals aren't often honored in practice. Although too often bypassed by cultural convention, individual gluttony, and sometimes outright physical necessity, the ideals nonetheless serve as reminders of what the proper human relationship with God and God's creation should be. Even Waldau admits that despite the present-day indifference on the part of religious traditions to animal welfare, "there remains vast potential for emergence of more informed and open-minded treatment of nonhuman animals in the doctrines, rituals, experiences, ethics, myths, social realities, and ecological perspectives of religious believers" (p. 80). Religious vegetarians maintain that this potential exists because their spiritual traditions fundamentally entail a reverence for God-created life, even if that reverence is all but forgotten by many adherents today. They also argue that the dim memories of this reverence are the sources of the guilt discussed by Serpell.[2]

In the rest of this chapter, we'll examine different defenses of vegetarianism based on what proponents see as their religious traditions' "vast potential" for grounding a diet that properly honors God by revering the life God creates. We'll begin by taking a look at Albert Schweitzer's well-known defense of the position, move on to consider the Hindu and Buddhist traditions, and conclude with an examination of the Abrahamic religions of Judaism, Christianity, and Islam.

"Life as such is sacred"

Curiously, one of the best-known modern defenses of a reverence for life perspective, Albert Schweitzer's, is difficult to place comfortably in any discrete religious tradition. Schweitzer was a trained Christian theologian, ordained Protestant pastor, and missionary physician in present-day Gabon. But his reverence for life position, although he refers to it as "the ethic of Jesus brought to philosophical expression," (Schweitzer 1999, p. 149) is an amalgamation of biblical theology, the atheistic metaphysics of the nineteenth-century philosopher Arthur Schopenhauer, and the Indian notion of *ahimsa* or nonviolence to living creatures. (*Ahimsa* will be explored more fully in the next section of this chapter.) Moreover, Schweitzer seems to have been an on-again off-again vegetarian. Some of his acquaintances report that he dined primarily on fruits and vegetables. Others maintain that he always ate with gusto whatever was put in front of him, even if the dish was meat (International Vegetarian Union 2010).

Schweitzer's starting point is his realization that a fundamental impetus or motive lay behind all of his own actions in the world: a will-to-live, or "a yearning for more life" (Schweitzer 1999, p. 146). He found this urge so overwhelming in himself that he assumed other humans must have it as well. The will-to-live especially reveals itself when life and well-being are threatened, but manifests itself in any number of ways at other times. In whatever we do, we're largely motivated by the desire to continue living.

Schweitzer went on to infer that every living thing is likewise imbued with a deep-seated urge to live. The very nature of living things is to resist decay and dissolution. Animals display extraordinary aversion to threats of death, and even plants which seem on the edge of death can be revived with a minimum of care. Everything that lives struggles to remain alive. It follows that if I value my own life, wish to continue to live, and object to anything that threatens my life, consistency demands that I likewise value all life and object to actions which threaten it. From this argument, Schweitzer derives the "fundamental principle of morality": "it is good to maintain and cherish life; it is evil to destroy and to check life" (p. 146). This cherishing of life displays itself as more than mere sympathy, which Schweitzer dismisses as "too narrow a concept." Instead, cherishing life demands full-bodied love, a "fellowship" with all life forms in their will-to-live and an eagerness to aid them in their endeavor to maintain life.

Read casually, Schweitzer's model seems a straightforward ethic based on a characteristic—the will to live—shared by all living beings, and the normative claim that the characteristic creates a kinship between humans and animals such that what we value for ourselves we ought also to value for them. And in his best known discussion of his thesis, a 1935 essay entitled "The Ethics of Reverence for Life," Schweitzer for the most part defends his position without appealing to God. But toward the end of the essay he tips his hand and makes clear to readers why he uses the word "reverence"—which often, after all, carries a religious connotation. According to Schweitzer, every form of life "emanates" from a divine "Creative Will," and our felt will-to-live is a reflection of the Creative Will's vitality. In respecting all manifestations of life, we reverence the Creative Will present in them, and thus cultivate a lifestyle in "harmony" with the divine.

It's precisely this presence of the Creative Will in all life that, according to Schweitzer, makes "life as such . . . sacred" (p. 146). Loving protection of all living forms displays reverence for the divine Spirit that births and indwells them. At times it may be tragically necessary to take life. But two things need always to be kept in mind. First, even if circumstances sometimes force us to injure life, we "ought never to pass the limits of the unavoidable, even in apparently insignificant cases" (p. 149). Second, we should cultivate such mindfulness of the sacred nature of life that we "tear no leaf from its tree, break off no flower, and [are] careful not to crush any insect as [we] walk." This is not, insists Schweitzer, mere "sentimentality" (pp. 146–7). It is an expression of awe at the sheer fact of life and gratitude to its Creator and Sustainer.[3]

Vegetarians who refrain from meat on religious grounds but who don't subscribe to any specific faith tradition may find Schweitzer's model especially appealing. Although he claims that his ethics exemplifies Jesus' teaching, the sort of divinity he invokes—the Creative Will—is open-ended enough to be acceptable to a wide range of God-believers. But Schweitzer's open-endedness when it comes to his fundamental principle—it's "good to maintain and cherish life" and "evil to destroy and to check life"—has generated a great deal of criticism from vegetarians and nonvegetarians alike.

Tom Regan is one vegetarian who expresses reservations about it. To begin with, he notes that Schweitzer seems to collapse the boundary between the living and the nonliving in one of his most-cited passages. After telling us that all life is sacred, Schweitzer goes on to say that a person who reverences life will refrain from even shattering an ice crystal sparkling in the sun. Schweitzer is either misspeaking here, since an ice crystal obviously isn't alive and has no will-to-live, or he's conflating the beauty of the inanimate natural order and life. Regan thinks that the second move is the most likely explanation. After all, it makes sense, given Schweitzer's claim that the Creative Will is present in all living things, that it's also present in every *created* thing. If this is the case, it follows that humans honor the Creative Will when we treat all creation respectfully. But if this is what Schweitzer is driving at, then his "fundamental" moral principle isn't fundamental at all, and so "we are in need," Regan concludes, "of a more general principle than that of 'reverence for (all) life' " (Regan 1983, p. 242).

Even if we give Schweitzer the benefit of the doubt by assuming that he misspoke about the ice crystals, more than one critic (including Regan) has pointed out that his fundamental moral principle is still too inclusive. If taken literally, it throws all life forms, from human beings to microbes, into the same ethical category. As Regan says, it's difficult to see how we can reasonably be said to have moral responsibilities to individual blades of grass, potatoes, and cancer cells or to lawns, potato fields, and cancerous tumors (Regan 1983, p. 242). Surely we ought to be more discriminating. Along similar lines, nonvegetarian Tibor Machan notes that the simple invocation of "life" is too vague.

If one asks whether life is to be revered, one must know what sort of life is at issue. Are we speaking of ants, cockroaches, viruses, bacteria, cats, dogs, horses, or human beings? Are we speaking of life at any stage of its development, in any of its manifestations? (Machan 2004, p. 29)

There's another problem with Schweitzer's refusal to draw normative distinctions between various life forms, one that he himself seemed uncomfortably aware of. Life not only competes with life, it also predatorily feeds upon life. The world is an arena in which wills-to-live prey and are preyed upon. This raises all sorts of logistical problems, as Regan and Machan suggest, about how actually to go about reverencing life. When we reverence one life form, our action almost inevitably means that we wind up not reverencing others. This tragic inevitability suggests that Schweitzer defends an ethic that's impossible to live up to. It also suggests that the Creative Will which gave rise to the state of affairs in which some life survives at the expense of another cares less about life than Schweitzer.

What this means is that someone who conscientiously tries to live up to Schweitzer's reverence for life ethic is in for a great deal of frustration. Schweitzer himself admits the impossibility of his position noting that every day of his life, in thousands of ways, he brings destruction and pain to living beings. But instead of rethinking his fundamental principle, Schweitzer rather romantically rides into battle knowing that he will be defeated. He accepts that he will inevitably tread upon earthworms, absentmindedly swat at mosquitoes, kill with antibiotics bacteria infecting his patients, and occasionally eat meat with gusto. The task of removing the self-contradiction that arises from a reverence for life position simply can't be accomplished.

Still, Schweitzer's position does remind vegetarians and nonvegetarians alike that humans are in many respects accountable for the plight of food animals. In thwarting their wills-to-live, especially when we do so unnecessarily, we fail in our responsibility to prevent, insofar as we can, pain and suffering. A critic might argue that one doesn't need to drag in vague references to a divine Creative Will in order to make the point. Proponents of the basic argument for vegetarianism do quite well without them. But for Schweitzer and religious-minded vegetarians, the invocation of God imparts what they consider to be an essential gravity to the human responsibility to care for other forms of life, a gravity that otherwise, in their estimation, would be missing.

The Hindu and Buddhist traditions

Of all living religious traditions, Indian Hinduism is both the oldest and takes pride of place when it comes to defending vegetarianism as a spiritual duty. The earliest religious writings associated with

Hinduism, known as the Vedas, were composed over a vast period of time, probably beginning around 2500 BCE and ending around 600 BCE. Even in the oldest Vedas, traces of the religious vision commonly and properly associated with Hinduism—belief in a divine One both transcendent and imminent in all living things—can be found. By the time the later Vedic texts known as the Upanishads were written, this understanding of the One or "Brahma" as the supreme creative principle capable of infinite material manifestations or "descents," was well established.

The Hindu worldview is essentially monistic. Because everything that exists is indwelt by Brahma, no sharp and impenetrable distinctions can be drawn between beings. Part of the spiritual goal of the devout Hindu is to come to an enlightened awareness of the divine essence in all things, thereby achieving liberation (or *moksha*) from the illusion (*maya*) of differentiation and fragmentation. The normative implication that arises from viewing all physical forms as manifestations of Brahma is the duty to treat all things with the reverence that is Brahma's due. Self-control, or *yoga*, dictates the practice of *ahimsa*, or nonviolence, to all living beings. This doesn't mean that the devout Hindu sees humans as equal to animals. The reincarnation of a human as an animal is seen as a karmic step backwards in the journey to enlightenment and liberation. Moreover, mistreatment of animals is typically denounced more from worry over the spiritual harm human perpetrators inflict upon themselves through their cruelty than from compassion for animals. But it *is* the case that human life is seen on a continuum with other Brahma-indwelling forms of life rather than as enjoying a radically different and radically privileged status. Humans are different from animals in degree, but not in kind.

Even though, as we saw in the Introduction, slightly less than a third of Indian Hindus actually practice vegetarianism, a meatless diet is especially compatible with the deepest Indian religious traditions. Abstention from the flesh of animals is explicitly advocated in the Laws of Manu, codified between 200 BCE and 100 BCE. The Laws are a set of prescriptions for the conduct of life based on the belief that ethical propriety and spiritual liberation are inseparably linked to nonviolent reverence for all living creatures. Purporting to be a record of the words of Brahma, the Laws were invested with an authority that set the stage for subsequent Hindu defenses of vegetarianism. True to the tradition, their emphasis is on the spiritual purity of humans rather than the welfare of animals. "He who injures innoxious beings from a wish to give himself pleasure," we read, "never finds happiness, neither living nor dead" (Walters and Portmess 2001, p. 41). As if this isn't warning enough, the Laws of Manu underscore it with this: "Meat can never be obtained without injury to living creatures, and injury to sentient beings is detrimental to the attainment of heavenly bliss" (p. 41).

Apparently Hindus were trying to find loopholes in Hinduism's proscription of meat-eating even as early as the Laws of Manu. One tactic was to argue that only those people who actually killed animals were in spiritual danger, thereby absolving everyone else associated with meat-eating. This can be inferred from another stern and unambiguous warning recorded in the Laws:

He who permits the slaughter of an animal, he who cuts it up, he who kills it, he who buys or sells meat, he who cooks it, he who serves it up, and he who eats it, must all be considered as the slayers of the animal. (p. 42)

According to the Laws of Manu, it's impossible to participate in any way with the slaughter of food animals and come away with clean hands.

The willingness of some Hindus to cut corners when it came to violence against animals inspired the holy man Vardhamana, known to his followers as Mahavira or "Great Hero," to found the sixth century BCE reform movement known as Jainism. Mahavira's teachings refocused attention on the presence of Brahma in every living thing and the doctrines of karma and reincarnation. Consequently, his reform entailed a scrupulous attention to the presence and protection of all life, from the microscopic to the human. In the Akaranga Sutra, written nearly a millennium after Mahavira's death, the Jain way of life is codified. Ostensibly a manual for Jain monks, the Sutra is also a model of ideal conduct for Jain laity. Wisdom, it teaches, is refraining from "act[ing] sinfully toward animals" or "caus[ing] others to act so" (Walters and Portmess 2001, p. 44). In order to cultivate this kind of wisdom, which leads to purity of life and, ultimately, liberation from *maya*, the Jain monk takes a series of vows that regulate his or her behavior. The first "great vow" is a pledge to practice *ahimsa:* "I renounce all killing of living beings, whether subtle or gross, whether movable or immovable. Nor shall I myself kill living beings nor cause others to do it, nor consent to it" (p. 45). To this end, the monk pledges to be "careful in his walk," lest he thoughtlessly "hurt or displace or injure or kill living beings" with his feet. He also pledges to purge his thought and speech of any thoughts or words that incite violence against living creatures, to be careful where he places his begging bowl lest he crush an insect, and to carefully inspect his food and drink so as not to accidentally ingest microbial creatures (pp. 44–5).

In modern times, Vivekananda (1863–1902), a monk of the Ramakrishna Order, nicely captured the dietary implications of the traditional Hindu and Jain conviction that Brahma indwells all life forms. "Oneness," he wrote, "includes all animals . . . The amoeba and I are the same; the difference is only one of degree." Consequently, to eat the flesh of animals is wrong.

> Even if I am bound to eat it under certain circumstances, I know it is cruel. I must not drag my ideal down to the actual and give excuses for my weak conduct. The ideal is not to eat flesh, not to injure any being; for all animals are my brothers. (Walters and Portmess 2001, pp. 50–1)

Jainism was one reform movement in Hinduism. Buddhism, which eventually became an independent tradition, originated as another. Its founder, Siddhartha, born in the fifth century BCE in present-day Nepal, renounced his royal birth to practice the wandering life of a Hindu ascetic. Failing to achieve liberation through extreme self-mortification, he eventually concluded that it wasn't enough to exhaust desire by punishing the yearning body. Desire itself had to be forsworn if humans were ever to escape illusion and rebirth, and this release was more likely once one realized the causal connection between restless desire and suffering. This insight brought enlightenment and transformed Siddhartha into the Buddha, or "Awakened One."

Buddhism, like Hinduism, teaches the interconnectedness of all things—what the Vietnamese Buddhist Thich Nhat Hanh refers to as "interbeing" (Nhat Hanh 1987)—and thus the kinship between humans and all other creatures. (Whereas Hindus think of this bond as the shared presence of Brahma, Buddhists think of it as the shared presence of Buddha-nature.) Realization that desire is the cause of one's own suffering necessarily leads to the realization that other sentient creatures likewise desire and hence suffer. Recognition that animals and humans share the burden of suffering awakens a high regard for compassion codified in a fundamental Buddhist precept: take no life. Like Hindus and Jains, Buddhists value the ideal of *ahimsa,* even if they don't always practice it.

Buddhist defenses of vegetarianism tend to focus on either the kinship of all living things or on compassion for animal suffering. The former approach is particularly stressed in the Mahayana branch of Buddhism practiced in China, Japan, Vietnam, Korea, Nepal, and Tibet. The latter approach is favored by the Theravada branch, found predominately in Southeast Asia, Sri Lanka, Malaysia, and Indonesia. The Mahayana or "Greater Vehicle" school emphasizes the Buddha-nature of all sentient beings, thereby focusing on the normative equality of all creatures and the transmigration of souls, which accentuates the cosmic kinship of all creatures with the more intimate possibility of a family connection to beasts who are actually reincarnated loved ones. The Theravada or "Lesser Vehicle" school focuses on the duty of pitying and coming to the aid of all suffering creatures. Curiously, however, it tends to be more lax in dietary proscriptions than the "Greater Vehicle."

The fifth-century Lankavatara Sutra is representative of Buddhist defenses of vegetarianism. In it, the Buddha tells his followers[4] that, given the doctrine of reincarnation, "there is not one living being that, having assumed the form of a living being, has not been your mother, or father, or brother, or sister, or son, or daughter, or the one or the other, in various degrees of kinship" (Walters and Portmess 2001, p. 67). This familial kinship, coupled with the fact that the Buddha-nature shared by all creatures means that the person seeking liberation should "approach all living beings as if they were himself," prohibits "eat[ing] the flesh of any living being that is of the same nature as himself" (p. 67). Once again, as we've already seen in both Albert Schweitzer's ethic of the reverence for life and the Hindu religious tradition, the notion of kinship here runs much deeper than the bond of sentience defended by proponents of the basic argument for vegetarianism.

In the last chapter, author John Robbins claimed that when we eat the flesh of violently slain food animals, we literally ingest biochemical agents of fear churned up in the animal during its final traumatic moments. The author of the Lankavatara Sutra seems to have a similar intuition. Meat-eating, we're told, leads to a deterioration of physical and spiritual equilibrium. A corpse generally has an offensive odor that suggests impurity. When we eat the flesh of a corpse, we absorb its physical corruption, and our "visceras are filled with worms and other impure creatures and harbor the cause of leprosy" (p. 69). It's little wonder that the meat-eater's sleep is uneasy and his wakeful hours anxious. He is frequently and bewilderingly "struck with terror," (p. 69) not realizing that in eating flesh he takes into his own body the terror experienced by the animal who was slain to provide his meal. After awhile, the physical and spiritual impurity of flesh-eating becomes so corrosive that any capacity for compassion toward living beings, beasts or humans, atrophies (p. 71).

The Surangama Sutra, a text written sometime between the first century BCE and the sixth century CE, continues the theme of the impurity that flows from meat-eating. In it, the Buddha asks his followers, "How can those who practice great compassion feed on the flesh and blood of living things?" (Surangama Sutra 2001, p. 65). The question is rhetorical, because the point is that compassion and meat-eating are incompatible. To eat meat is to participate, directly or indirectly, in the taking of life, thereby contradicting the hope of enlightenment that is the goal of every Buddhist. It is like "shutting one's ears while crying in the hope that people will not hear one's voice." (p. 65) But the real cost of eating slain animals isn't simply mental confusion. Moral and spiritual impurity also follows. The Surangama Sutra even contends that human meat-eaters who fail to control their murderous appetites in life become insatiable blood-drinking, flesh-eating predatory demons, or *raksasas*, when they die.

Although he doesn't speak of *raksasas*, the twentieth-century Zen Buddhist Roshi Philip Kapleau likewise argues that meat-eating leads to spiritual and moral impurity because of its disruption of our natural (Buddha-nature) reverence for life.

> It is in Buddha-nature that all existences, animate and inanimate, are unified and harmonized. All organisms seek to maintain this unity in terms of their own karma. To willfully take life, therefore, means to disrupt and destroy this inherent wholeness and to blunt feelings of reverence and compassion arising from

our Buddha-mind. The first precept of not killing is really a call to life and creation even as it is a condemnation of death and destruction.[5] (Kapleau 1986, p. 19)

The Abrahamic traditions

The Abrahamic religions are the three monotheistic faiths of Judaism, Christianity, and Islam that all trace their origins back to the patriarch Abraham and accept Hebrew scripture as authoritative. Christians and Muslims supplement it, of course, with the New Testament and the Qur'an.

For the most part, the Abrahamic religions lack the long tradition of vegetarianism seen in Hinduism and Buddhism. There are doubtlessly historical reasons that partly, at least, explain this, the chief being the relatively arid geographical regions from which the three religions emerged. There is no reason to suppose that the founders of each religion—Abraham and Moses, Jesus, and Mohammed—refrained from eating the meat of animals. In the case of Jesus, the New Testament explicitly states that he ate fish. Moreover, spiritual leaders in the three traditions have only rarely taught that their religious beliefs prescribed a meatless diet. Typically, vegetarianism has been limited to subgroups such as the Essenes in the Jewish tradition, the monks and nuns of certain religious orders in the Christian tradition, and Sufis in the Muslim tradition.

What vegetarians from all three traditions can agree on—and it's a point that's frequently discussed by Jewish and Christian defenders of a meatless diet, although less so by Muslims—is that even though their scriptures were most likely written by nonvegetarians, and even though historically most Jews, Christians, and Muslims have also been nonvegetarians, the Hebrew Book of Genesis suggests that vegetarianism was part of God's original plan for humans, and apparently for animals as well. The authority for this is Gen. 1:29–30, the first of the two creation accounts found in the Hebrew Bible. In these two verses, God tells Adam and Eve (she remains unnamed in this account) that even though they have dominion over all living things, their food is "every plant yielding seed that is upon the face of all the earth, and every tree with seed in its fruit." There's no textual suggestion that they may also eat animals.

Similarly, God announces that "to every beast of the earth, and to every bird of the air, and to everything that creeps on the earth, everything that has the breath of life, I have given every green plant for food." Again, there's no mention of meat as food, suggesting that predation wasn't part of God's original plan.

It isn't until the story of Cain's murder of Abel (Gen. 4) that any mention of humans slaying animals is made, and it's only after five more chapters that God expressly allows humans to eat flesh: "every moving thing that lives shall be food for you; and just as I gave you the green plants, I give you everything" (Gen. 9:3). But this dispensation takes place only after God has destroyed humankind in the great Noaic flood, thus ending one chapter in human history and beginning another. Even then God insists on a rather curious qualification to the permission to eat meat: "you shall not eat flesh with its life, that is, its blood" (Gen. 9:4).

Jewish vegetarians—and Christian and Muslim ones generally follow their lead—argue that this concession is revealing. Rashi, the influential medieval Talmudic scholar, contended that the story of the food riot described in Num. 11:1–35, when the Hebrews in the desert demanded meat, clearly demonstrated that meat is the "food of lust," and that "it was right for God to punish the Hebrews for their demand for meat, for we can live without meat, but we cannot live without bread" (Kalechofsky 2004, p. 171). Abraham Isaac Kook, the first chief rabbi of Mandate Palestine, agreed. The vegetarian diet of Genesis was a harbinger, he wrote, of the future messianic age when a proper relationship between humans and nature and humans and God would be reestablished. God's permission to eat meat after the Noaic flood was an acknowledgment that humans weren't yet ready to live as God intended them to (Kook 2001). But even though allowing them to eat meat while they matured spiritually, God imposed the ban against eating blood as a reminder that meat is not natural food for humans. *Kashrut*, the system of dietary laws that evolved from the blood ban, and *shehitah*, ritual slaughter that minimizes pain, serve as continuous reminders of what humans once were and what they will be again. They remind us, as Stephen Fuchs puts it, "of the magnitude of what we do each time we kill a living being" for food (Fuchs 1995, p. 16), and that all life ultimately belongs to God.

But Jewish vegetarians argue that *kashrut* and *shehitah* are only first steps to "proclaiming the autonomy of all living creatures," a principle that Rabbi Arthur Hertzgerb contends lies at the heart of the Jewish creation story (Kalechofsky 2004, p. 174). Rabbi Arthur Green agrees that reverence for life is a defining Jewish value, especially since the Holocaust. "We Jews," he writes:

> who have always looked upon killing for sport or pleasure as something alien and repulsive, should now, out of our own experience, be reaching the point where we find even the slaughter of animals for food morally beyond the range of the acceptable . . . A vegetarian Judaism would be more whole in its ability to embrace the presence of God in all of Creation. (Green 1995, p. 27)

Drawing from both the Torah and Talmudic tradition, Jewish vegetarian Roberta Kalechofsky argues that vegetarianism is actually a requirement rather than a dietary choice. Biblical commandments to guard one's health, to avoid causing pain to any living creature, to not squander anything of value, and to come to the aid of the needy all point to vegetarianism as the only proper diet of observant Jews. These, of course, can be seen as pragmatic and normative points rather than strictly religious ones. But Kalechofsky argues that they have a religious foundation, namely the requirement to reverence God and God's creation[6] (Kalechofsky 1998).

Jewish, Christian, and Muslim critics of the claim that meat-eating is a divine concession to human weakness argue that religious vegetarians are cherry-picking biblical verses in defense of their dietary preferences. In fact, these critics maintain, the Book of Genesis clearly gives the earth and everything in it to humans to subdue and exercise dominion over (Gen. 1:28), and this divine mandate is symbolized by God bestowal upon Adam the authority to name every living creature (Gen. 2:19). Humans, made in the likeness of God, are the pinnacle of creation. We have souls and animals don't. It's only proper that we exercise suzerainty over the earth. No violation of divine intention is committed in eating animals, so long as they're raised and slaughtered in noncruel ways.

This dominion view has clearly been the norm in the Christian tradition, especially after it was wed with the typically Greek philosophical claim that the possession of reason makes humans superior to animals. So the fifth-century Augustine, for example, insists that there are "no common rights between us and the beasts," and to believe otherwise is "the height of superstition"[7] (Augustine 1966, p. 102). Seven centuries later, Thomas Aquinas defends a similar line when he says that it's no sin to kill an animal because the divinely designated purpose of animals is to serve and feed humans (Aquinas 1948, II.II.64.1). The historical record of Christianity's attitude toward animals is so bleak that nineteenth-century philosopher Arthur Schopenhauer could say with some truth that Christian morality has "outlawed" animals from the moral community. "Shame on such a morality," he thundered, "that fails to recognize the eternal essence that exists in every living thing" (Schopenhauer 1998, p. 96). In saying this, Schopenhauer seems closer to the vegetarian reverence for life argument than mainstream Christianity does.[8]

But from the very beginning, the dominion position has been challenged by some Christians. Ascetics throughout the history of Christianity have argued that meat-eating is indulgence in the sin of gluttony. Church Fathers such as John Chrysostom, Jerome, and Cassian, influenced by the Jewish tradition, maintained that meat-eating was a post-Fall concession to human sinfulness. The fourth-century Basil of Caesarea lamented that humans had little sense of fellowship with their "brothers the animals," and called upon the faithful to "remember in shame that in the past we have exercised the high dominion of man with ruthless cruelty" (Scully 2002, p. 13). In the thirteenth century, St. Richard of Chichester worried that human mistreatment of animals is so great that the beasts, could they but speak, "would curse us" (Linzey 2008, p. 292). John Henry Newman in the late nineteenth century deplored the "cruelty shown to poor beasts," (Scully 2002, p. 14), and in the following century, even C. S. Lewis, who relished a cut of meat as much as James Joyce's Leopold Bloom, worried about the suffering humans inflict on animals (Lewis 2001). In our own day, Pope Benedict XVI declares that treating animals as mere raw material or commodities contradicts the "relationship of mutuality" between humans and animals "that comes across in the Bible"[9] (Ratzinger 2002, p. 78).

The usual justification of this minority opinion hinges on what the author of Genesis means by "dominion." Although typically interpreted as "domination," the kind of authority granted to humans by God is better viewed, in the judgment of Christian vegetarians, as a "stewardship" which emphasizes human responsibility rather than privilege. Philosopher and theist Tom Regan puts it like this:

> To be given dominion by God is not to be given a blank check made out to satisfying our needs and satiating our desires. On the contrary, it is to be charged with the awesome responsibility of being the creator's agent within nature; in other words, we are called by God to be as loving and caring for what God has created as God was loving and caring in creating it. (Regan 2004b, p. 69)

On this reading, believes Regan, there's no good reason to make the conventional Christian assumption that humans are valuable because made in God's likeness and that animals, who (presumably) are not, are consequently valueless. "It is perfectly consistent with our unique status as God's chosen representative within creation that other creatures have inherent worth equal to our own," he writes (Regan 2004a, p. 178). (Readers will recall from Chapter 4 Regan's subject-of-a-life defense of inherent worth or value.) If we occupy a "higher" place in a moral hierarchy, our "superiority" is defined by the weight of our moral obligations, not by special entitlements.

British theologian Andrew Linzey, the leading contemporary proponent of Christian vegetarianism, agrees with Regan's claim that animals have inherent rights, or what Linzey refers to as "theos-rights," granted them because they are God's creatures. The reason we should treat animals with moral consideration is "simple": "since animals belong to God, have value to God, and live for God, then their needless destruction is sinful" (Linzey 1991, p. 146). Theos-rights proclaim that animals deserve moral consideration because their creation by a good and loving God shows them to be valuable and lovable. Honoring their theos-rights means acknowledging that their lives belong to God rather than to humans and allowing them to flourish in ways that God intends: "to live; to be free; and to live without suffering, distress, and injury"[10] (p. 104). Human lifestyles which needlessly inflict pain and death upon animals are contrary to "the establishing of God's right in creation and the liberation of nonhuman creation from the hand of tyranny" (p. 103). Eating meat supplied by factory farming and industrial slaughterhouses whose practices inflict cruelty on animals and degrade the environment obviously doesn't contribute to the "liberation of nonhuman creation."

Still, Linzey and most Christian vegetarians recognize that some-times eating meat is a necessity for human health and even life itself. Killing, argues Linzey, isn't entirely proscribed in the Bible. But it is always treated as a "grave matter." So if it's absolutely necessary to slay beasts for food, we may do so. But the killing should be done with an acute sense of regret. Nor does Linzey advocate a sudden, immediate cessation of meat-eating in cultures and places where meat isn't a necessary staple. Instead, he defends a gradual approach which is as peaceful in spirit as the humane diet he proposes. "What we need," he writes, "is progressive disengagement from injury to animals . . . If someone is prepared to abandon just meat and fish, at least some other creatures have a chance of living in peace. The enemy of progress is the view that everything must be changed before some real gains can be secured"[11] (Linzey 1991, p. 148).

When it comes to diet, many Jews and Christians conclude that honoring scriptural intent and fulfilling their religious obligations require them to abstain from meat. Even though theirs is a minority opinion, its very existence suggests that Judaism and Christianity are conflicted, at least to some extent, about killing animals for food. Islam, the third Abrahamic religion, is much less so, perhaps because the religion arose in the extremely arid Arabian Peninsula, and probably because most Muslims live today in relatively poor countries where meat is a usually unaffordable luxury. Although a few Muslims have advocated vegetarianism as a religious duty— Rumi in the thirteenth century (Rumi 2001), Al-Hafiz B. A. Masri in our own (Masri 2001), and a scattering of Sufi teachers throughout the centuries—the general Muslim outlook is that although animals shouldn't be treated cruelly, they are given to humans by God for "food, clothing, and transport" (Forward and Alam 1008, p. 296). When it comes to interpreting the meaning of human "dominion" in Genesis, Islam generally opts for the view that humans are utterly subordinate to Allah and animals subordinate to humans.

But this doesn't mean, of course, that Islam is indifferent to the welfare of animals. There are passages in the Qur'an which stress that Allah is at least aware, and perhaps beneficently so, of animals; Sura 6:38, in which it is said that animals and birds will be gath-ered to God in the end, is the most frequently quoted. In the post-Qur'anic collection of commentary known as Hadith, the Prophet Mohammed is quoted as saying that "Whoever is kind to the crea-tures of God is kind to himself" (Masri 2001, p. 191).

One practical consequence of Mohammed's Hadithic insistence on kindness to animals is *qurban*, the ritual slaughter of food animals that has obvious connections to the older Judaic *shehitah*. Because animals, like everything else in creation, are the property of Allah, they should be treated with some measure of respect and gratitude when killed for food. *Qurban* requires that their throats be cut with mercifully swift strokes as an invocation of God is pronounced over them.[12] Doing so reminds the slayer that he can kill one of God's creatures only because God graciously gives him permission to do so.

But none of this makes a strong case for a claim that the seeds of vegetarianism are as deeply planted in Islam as in Judaism or Christianity. As two contemporary Muslims note, "Islam is not a sentimental religion" when it comes to animals. "By God's permission, human beings have power over the animals, as over all creation, and they can be used for various purposes"[13] (Forward and Alam 2008, p. 294).

Reverence: Religious and otherwise

Most people who embrace a vegetarian diet do so for nonreligious reasons. This isn't to say that they aren't religious—they may or may not be—but only that their primary motives for going meatless aren't obviously based on any religious beliefs. Moreover, it's entirely conceivable that many people who are vegetarians primarily for religious reasons are additionally motivated by moral concerns for animal welfare, environmental integrity, and human well-being. We've seen that Hindu and Buddhist vegetarians emphasize the kinship of all living things, that Jewish and Christian vegetarians embrace a species of environmentalism in their emphasis on stewardship rather than dominion, and that Muslim vegetarians can appeal to Hadithic teaching on the virtue of compassion to animals.

But there are two features unique to religious reverence for life arguments. The first is the claim that kinship with animals is spiritually rooted, based not so much on shared biological features as on a common divine Parent. Animals are not alien "others," but siblings who properly elicit our respect and compassion. So the bonds uniting humans and animals are fundamental and unbreakable.

Secondly, the religious vegetarian holds that all life, coming as it does from the Creator, ultimately belongs to the Creator and not to us. Consequently, to abuse animals (or any other part of creation, for that matter) is to dishonor and steal from the Creator. To display reverence for life is to revere the God, the Creative Will, the indivisible One, who created, sustains, and owns life.

It would be a mistake to downplay the differences between secular and religious vegetarians—or, for that matter, between the seven different kinds of arguments for vegetarianism examined in this book. But one thing all of them might well have in common is an embrace of the virtue of reverence. We typically associate the word with religious belief—hence the "reverence for life" argument explored in this chapter—but there's no necessary linkage. As philosopher Paul Woodruff points out, reverence is simply "the capacity for a range of feelings and emotions that are linked: it is a sense that there is something larger than a human being, accompanied by capacities for awe, respect, and shame . . . when these are the right feelings to have" (Woodruff 2001, pp. 63, 8). For religious vegetarians, the "something larger than a human being" is God. For secular ones, ideals such as justice, truth, and compassion might be objects of reverence that help them transcend narrow ways of looking at the world and the place of humans in it. A secular vegetarian can feel awe for the intelligence and sensitivity of a food animal, respect for its interests or rights, and shame at violating those interests or rights. Similarly, she can be stirred by reverence for the intricate complexity and stunning beauty of the environment, or by shame at the way in which some humans are irreverently allowed to starve even though we have the capacity to feed everyone on the globe.

In the Introduction, I pointed out that what we eat goes far beyond a simple menu list of gustatory preferences. Our food choices always gesture at a gestalt, a general way of thinking about the world and one's place in it. They reflect some of our most deeply held commitments and values. For the vegetarian, regardless of whether or not she's conventionally religious, that gestalt is likely to be permeated by an abiding sense of awe at the world and respect for the creatures that dwell therein. This sense—this reverence—is the seasoning on every vegetarian meal.

NOTES

Introduction

Chapter epigraphs are from Joyce (1961, p. 55) and Plutarch (1999, p. 28).

1 I hope it's obvious that I'm speaking here of "first" or "developed" world inhabitants who aren't food-deprived. Millions of people around the world in developing countries are painfully aware of what (and when) their last meal was, precisely because food isn't a taken-for-granted feature of their everyday lives. A portion of Chapter 7 focuses on the problem of world hunger and the connection between it and dietary choices.

2 I have a good friend who makes a point of ordering the meatiest dish on the menu whenever we dine out together. I'm sure that his choice is a kind of speech act: in ordering a big hunk of meat, always served up rare and bloody, he implicitly pushes back against my vegetarianism.

3 Kathleen Madigan is a hilarious stand-up comic whose vegetarian quip can be viewed at www.youtube.com/watch?v=aqYk3KNliSA. Accessed July 7, 2011.

4 We'll take a look at two examples of them in subsequent chapters: Carl Cohen's negative response to Peter Singer's speciesism in Chapter 3 and Tibor Machan's criticism of Tom Regan's defense of animal rights in Chapter 4.

5 As we'll see in Chapter 5, ecofeminist Carol Adams argues that masculinity is also an integral aspect of the meat-eater's gestalt.

6 Further subdivisions of vegetarianism include raw vegetarianism, whose practitioners eat uncooked vegetables and fruits, and fruitarianism, whose practitioners eat only plant matter such as fruit and nuts that can be gathered without harming the plant. A vegetarian macrobiotic diet consists primarily of whole grains and beans.

Chapter One

The chapter epigraphs are from agriculture professor Wes Jamison (Mason and Singer 2006, p. 12) and ethologist Konrad Lorenz (Lorenz 1988, p. 14).

1 Shmoo and renew-a-bits meat (my name, not his) are from philosopher Michael Martin (1976). Chicken Little is the invention of Pohl and Kornbluth (1952).

2 The possibility of cultured meats may not be so fantastic. A decade ago, Dutch scientists succeeded in producing in vitro muscle (Singer and Mason 2006, p. 263). See also Specter (2011).

3 For representative illustrations of this "happy animal" advertising, see Adams (2004).

4 Far from defending vegetarianism, Fearnley-Whittingstall is the author of a cook book entitled *The River Cottage Meat Book*, from which the quoted passage is taken. But he obviously deplores factory farmed methods of producing food animals.

5 The debate about whether some animals can qualify as persons is complex. David Sztybel (2008) offers a very good introduction to it.

6 For more on nonhuman persons, see the essays in Cavalieri and Singer (1993).

7 Philosopher Stephen R. L. Clark (1983, p. 176) argues that the problem of other minds misses the whole point of how we pick up on the presence of mental states such as pain in both humans and animals. "Few philosophers would now describe 'mental states' as things uneasily inferred from purely impersonal descriptions, as though we could only see a creature twisting about, sweating, emitting high-pitched noises (and so on) and must thence infer that there is a mental cause of these motions, namely pain . . . I can recognize the latter directly. I cannot infer the existence of fire from the sight of smoke unless fire and smoke are at least sometimes observed together."

8 The USDA reports a recent slight decline in the numbers of food animals slaughtered in the United States. But the figures are still staggering. The 2009 tally: 35.6 million cattle, 116.5 million hogs, 4.3 million sheep and goats, 2.3 million rabbits, nearly 9 billion broilers, 154 million laying hens, 269 million turkeys, and 24 million ducks. www.farmusa.org/images/statistics9_lg.jpg. Accessed February 2010.

9 The documentary film "A Cow at the Table" (Abbott 1998) is a look at factory farming and the meat industry that includes interviews

with some of the people—Carol J. Adams, Jim Mason, Tom Regan, and Peter Singer—discussed in this book. Another noteworthy film is "The Auction Block" (Compassion Over Killing 2001), which offers an "inside look at farmed animal sales." A third helpful documentary is "A River of Waste" (McCorkell 2009).

10 The documentary film "Hope for the Hopeless" (Compassion Over Killing 2001) offers an inside look at an egg battery.

11 The European Union also banned veal crates in 2007 and battery hen cages in 2012.

12 The documentary films "Midwest Pig Farm Investigation" (PETA no date) and "Death on a Factory Farm" (HBO 2009) offer an inside look at the life of hogs on factory farms.

13 The PBS documentary "Modern Meat" (Frontline 2002) is a thoughtful examination of the public health risks of meat processed at industrial slaughterhouses.

14 According to Pollan (2002b, p. 48), "Forgetting, or willed ignorance, is the preferred strategy of many beef-eaters." Leo Tolstoy (1999, p. 104), made a similar point at the end of the nineteenth century. Referring to the suffering of food animals, he wrote, "we cannot pretend that we do not know this. We are not ostriches, and cannot believe that if we refuse to look at what we do not wish to see, it will not exist."

Chapter Two

The Chapter epigraphs are from Scully (2002, p. 95) and Burns (1909, p. 119).

1 Although Lamartine (1999, p. 79) ate meat as an adult, he confessed uneasiness about it his entire life.

2 The film Regan (2004b, p. 2) watched is entitled "To Love or Kill: Man vs. Animals." His description of the treatment of the cat is, if anything, understated. The truly horrendous clip to which he refers, the third of five parts, may be viewed on Youtube: www.youtube.com/watch?v=PXad55RQQ1k&NR=1. Accessed July 23, 2010.

3 Schopenhauer's argument for sympathetic kinship as the heart of morality is quite different from that of Enlightenment thinkers such as David Hume and Adam Smith. The latter saw sympathy as a psychological sharing in the passions of others, which in turn creates a normative bond between them. For Schopenhauer, sympathy with

animals is a corollary of his belief that each living thing is imbued with and bound together by Creative Will.

4 Rowlands takes this example from Regan (1983, p. 334).

Chapter Three

The chapter epigraph from Bentham is part of a footnote from (1823, pp. 235–6): "The day may come when the rest of the animal creation may acquire those rights which never could have been withholden from them but by the hand of tyranny. The French have already discovered that the blackness of the skin is no reason that a human being should be abandoned without redress to the caprice of a tormentor. It may one day come to be recognized that the number of legs, the villosity of the skin, or the termination of the os sacrum are reasons equally insufficient for abandoning a sensitive being to the same fate. What else is it that should trace the insuperable line? Is it the faculty of reason, or perhaps the faculty of discourse? But a full-grown horse or dog is beyond comparison a more rational, as well as a more conversable animal, than an infant of a day or a week or even month, old. But suppose they were otherwise, what would it avail? The question is not, Can they reason? nor Can they talk? but, Can they suffer." The chapter epigraph from Singer is from (2008, p. 22).

1 As Singer puts it elsewhere (2009, p. 19), "To avoid speciesism we must allow that beings who are similar in all relevant respects have a similar right to life—and mere membership in our own biological species cannot be a morally relevant criterion for this right."

2 Singer's endorsement, however ambivalent he may be about it, is consistent with his acknowledged indebtedness to the nineteenth-century utilitarian Henry Sidgwick. In *Animal Liberation* (2009, p. 5), he approvingly cites this passage from Sidgwick: "The good of any one individual is of no more importance, from the point of view (if I may say so) of the Universe, then the good of any other." (The quote is from Sidgwick's 1907 *The Methods of Ethics*.) What is valuable is the kinds of experience individuals have.

3 In addition to the coarsening effects of eating animals that have been killed, Singer (2009, pp. 159–60) worries that a Goldsmithian inconsistency bordering on moral hypocrisy is also possible. "If one is opposed to inflicting suffering on animals, but not to the painless killing of animals, one could consistently eat animals who had lived free of all suffering and been instantly, painlessly slaughtered. Yet

practically and psychologically it is impossible to be consistent in one's concern for nonhuman animals while continuing to dine on them. If we are prepared to take the life of another being merely in order to satisfy our taste for a particular type of food, then that being is no more than a means to our end . . . The factory farm is nothing more than the application of technology to the idea that animals are means to our ends."

4 If Frey is correct, it might be argued, animals would have a difficult time surviving in the wild since they would be able to discern a genuine (true) situation of danger from a merely apparent (false) one.

5 A representative expression of it comes from farmer Joel Salatin: "People have a soul. Animals don't. It's a bedrock belief of mine. Unlike us, animals are not created in God's image, so when they die, they just die" (Singer and Mason 2006, p. 252). Secularists often substitute "have no reason or self-consciousness" for God-believer Salatin's "are not created in God's image."

Chapter Four

The chapter epigraphs are from Plutarch (1999, p. 32) and Regan (1983, p. 280).

1 This of course places Scully (2002, p. 287) squarely in the basic argument for vegetarianism camp.

2 Elsewhere, Regan asserts that "the idea of animal rights has reason, not just emotion, on its side" (Regan 1985, p. 14).

3 Thomas Auxter (1999, p. 185) also defends a telic model of animal rights. Jon Lowry (1975) similarly argues that natural rights are based upon basic needs required for flourishing. Even if different standards of flourishing are appropriate to different species, which certainly is the case, a need (and accompanying) right to life is fundamental to them all.

4 Brian Luke (2007) also believes that Regan has failed to show sufficient "relevant similarity" between human and animal capacities.

5 Another philosopher who might accuse Regan of pulling a shell game, although his language is much more temperate than Cohen's, is Duane Willard (1982), who argues that rights aren't predicated on natural properties, such as those Regan attributes to subjects-of-a-life, but are instead based on value judgments about what ought or ought not to be permitted. He concludes, in other words, that Regan is guilty of the naturalistic fallacy of deriving a value from a fact.

6 Others who argue that animals are incapable of making moral choices and hence lack rights include Burch (1977), Cebik (1981), Leahy (1994), McCloskey (1979), Reichman (2000), and Scruton (2003).

7 A tu quoque is a fallacious move in which I try to justify my wrong actions by claiming that everyone else acts similarly. I don't try to deny my malfeasance, but rather appeal to a perverse sense of fair play: if others do wrong, why mayn't I?

8 Elizabeth Telfer suggests (1996, p. 79), however, that a hypothetical contract between humans and domesticated animals, in which the quid pro quo is a pleasant life for the animal's flesh, might be reasonable.

Chapter Five

Chapter epigraphs are from Warren (1990, p. 126) and Adams (2007b, pp. 33–4).

1 According to Marti Kheel, ecofeminism replaces top-down patriarchal dualism with a "holistic vision of reality in which everything is integrally interconnected and thus part of a large whole," and in doing so affirms the "oneness of the universe" (Kheel 2007, p. 40).

2 According to Gilligan, "The moral imperative that emerges repeatedly in interviews with women is an injunction to care, a responsibility to discern and alleviate the real and recognizable trouble of this world . . . The reconstruction of the dilemma in its contextual particularity allows the understanding of cause and consequence which engages the compassion and tolerance [that] distinguish[es] the moral judgments of women." Men, on the other hand, subordinate relationships "to rules . . ., and rules to universal principles of justice." Their moral imperative "is geared to arriving at an objectively fair or just resolution to moral dilemmas upon which all rational persons could agree" (Gilligan 1982, pp. 21–2, 100).

3 Although not an ecofeminist, distinguished philosopher Mary Midgley is not unsympathetic with ecofeminist criticisms leveled against Singer and Regan. She argues that the notion of rights is too narrow to be helpful in thinking about animals because it's too tied to self-interested contractarianism. Networks of relations, not individual rights, ought to be the nuclei of ethical reflection (Midgley 1983).

4 It should be pointed out that not all feminists endorse an ethic of caring. Keller (1995) argues that it can encourage subordination of wives to husbands. Davion (1993) worries that it does nothing to

mitigate racism or homophobia. Both of them agree that an ethics of care whittles away at autonomy, which they think essential to a viable ethics.

5 Lori Gruen (Gruen 1993) goes so far as to argue that our privileging of our own species prevents us from judging between humans and animals impartially. If we're more concerned about a human in danger of drowning than we are of a dog in the same situation, it's just because we insist on viewing the situation from a human perspective. A dog's desire to escape drowning so that it can run by the river may be just as strong and legitimate as the human's desire to escape drowning in order to create art.

6 A significant difference between the absent referencing of women and the absent referencing of animals is that women are in danger of internalizing and hence collaborating with their objectification.

7 Adams argues that the patriarchal cycle which makes animals and women vanish is one of "objectification, fragmentation, and consumption, which links butchering and sexual violence in our culture. Objectification permits an oppressor to view another being as an object. The oppressor then violates this being by object-like treatment . . . Consumption is the fulfillment of oppression, the annihilation of will, of separate identity. So too with language: a subject first is viewed, or objectified, through metaphor. Through fragmentation, the object is severed from its ontological meaning. Finally, consumed, it exists only through what is represented. The consumption of the referent reiterates its annihilation as a subject of importance in itself" (Adams 1995b, p. 47).

8 Gruen (2004, pp. 287–8) also objects to applying language specifically intended to describe the abuse of women to the environment. "Consider the widespread use of the term 'rape' to describe environmental destruction. In describing clear-cutting as the rape of a forest, the very real trauma that women who are raped must live with when they survive the experience is ignored. This trauma and the anger, fear, doubt, and other emotions that rape survivors have to deal with are not—indeed, cannot be—experienced by trees. When rape is used to describe anything violent and horrible, the particular violence and horror of a man raping a woman is obscured." Although Gruen's point is worth considering, it seems overblown. Using the word "rape" to refer to clear-cutting doesn't entail that compassion for women victims of rape is compromised, although it may be. On the contrary, it might be argued that the use of "rape" to describe "anything violent and horrible," far from trivializing the rape of women, helps to underscore its horrific nature.

9 As Brian Luke puts it, "My opposition to the institutionalized exploitation of animals is not based on a comparison between human and animal treatment, but on a consideration of the abuse of the animal in and of itself. I respond directly to the needs and the plight of the animals . . ." (Luke 2007, pp. 129–30).

10 Even ecofeminist Deane Curtin admits that an ethics of care is open to the charge of privatism and localism (Curtin 2004, p. 277).

11 As Donovan writes, "natural rights and utilitarianism present impressive and useful philosophical arguments for the ethical treatment of animals. Yet, it is also possible—indeed, necessary—to ground that ethic in an emotional and spiritual conversation with nonhuman life-forms" (Donovan 2007a, p. 76).

Chapter Six

Chapter epigraphs are from Cheeke (1999, p. 19) and Wenz (1999, p. 191).

1 By way of comparison, the Exxon-Valdez oil spill was 12 million gallons.

2 The meat industries consistently maintain, even in the face of compelling evidence to the contrary, that the factory farm production of animals is environmentally friendly. The National Cattlemen's Beef Association, for example, claims that "Essentially all livestock and poultry manure winds up as a natural fertilizer on the land . . . without polluting water supplies" (Robbins 2011, p. 247).

3 True to form, the National Cattleman's Beef Association disputes this figure, arguing that one pound of beef requires only 441 gallons of water (Robbins 2011, p. 237). But all disinterested researchers agree that the Association is low-balling.

4 Recall from Chapter 4 that at least one contractarian (Rowlands 2009) offers an alternative understanding of the moral relationship between animals and humans.

5 This argument is similar to the one Bernard Rollin's (2006) offers (Chapter 4) in defense of moral consideration of animals.

6 Devall and Sessions (1985) offer insightful commentary on Naess' deep ecology.

7 Callicott subsequently tempers his argument. See Callicott (1989, pp. 49–59).

8 For Holmes' complete argument, see Holmes (1988). The passages quoted in the text are from personal correspondence between Holmes and Hettinger.

9 Philosopher Steve Sapontzis, an advocate of ethical vegetarianism, doesn't shrink from the claim that his position entails an ethical obligation to do something about predation. We are morally obliged, he argues, "to prevent predation whenever we can do so without occasioning as much or more unjustified suffering than the predation would create" (Sapontzis 1987, p. 247). Peter Singer, on the other hand, isn't so sure. "We may regret that this is the way the world is," he writes, "but it makes no sense to hold nonhuman animals morally responsible" (Singer 2009, p. 232).

Chapter Seven

Chapter epigraphs are from American Dietetic Association (2009, p. 1266) and United Nations (1948, Article 25.1).

1 This is of course similar to the conundrum we saw when examining environmental vegetarianism in Chapter 6.

2 The standard American diet is especially overly-rich in protein, which exceeds recommended levels by 45 percent. Some estimates claim that meat-eating Americans consume two to four times as much protein as their bodies need (Singer 2009, p. 181).

3 The cold water washing also adds water weight to the meat, thereby increasing the meat industry's margin of profit. According to Gail Eisnitz (1997, p. 168), "Federal regulations permit each carcass to soak up water" in the washing baths. "This in effect enables the industry to sell hundreds of gallons of germ-filled water at poultry-meat prices. US poultry consumers spend more than $1 billion on added water per year."

4 USDA meat inspector David Carney put it less delicately. "We used to trim the shit off the meat," he told investigative reporter Gail Eisnitz (1997, p. 155). "Then we washed the shit off the meat. Now the consumer eats the shit off the meat."

5 A separate but related issue is the abuse of factory farm and slaughterhouse workers by the corporations for whom they work. Both jobs have high accident and illness rates. Workers, who are often undocumented immigrants, are paid poorly and generally have no benefits. See Eisnitz (1997) and Singer and Mason (2006).

6 Most of the grain and corn raised to feed animals is suitable for livestock but not humans. So vegetarians don't mean to suggest that the same kinds of grain and corn currently fed to animals could easily feed the world's human population, but only the same amounts.

7 Of course there are different levels of agreement. An ecofeminist would dislike the anthrocentric argument's top-heavy focus on human welfare, but could certainly concur that meat-eating immorally disadvantages already underprivileged and hungry people in the world. Similarly, someone focused on animal welfare would readily agree that factory farms damage the environment, even if he or she chooses to focus on the suffering endured by animals in factory farms.

Chapter Eight

Chapter epigraphs are from Linzey (1991, p. 146) and Akaranga Sutra (Walters and Portmess 2001, p. 45).

1 But as we saw in the Introduction, they're a distinct minority among vegetarians in the United States. In Hindu and Buddhist cultures, the percentages are much higher, but still in the minority.

2 It's ironic—and also revealing—that the embedded reverence for life ignored by so many religious traditions was recently invoked by the American Meat Institute as a device for getting around consumer guilt over eating animals. In one of its "Fact Sheets," the AMI assures consumers that "One common theme among all faiths has been a respect for animals, avoidance of animal suffering and appreciation for the nourishment that they provide. These themes permeate the practices of the meat packing industry" (American Meat Industry 2011).

3 Schweitzer's ethics of reverence for life has enjoyed a revival in recent years. Especially good recent analyses of it include Barsam (2008) and Ives and Valone (2007). A useful collection of Schweitzer's writings on reverence for life is Meyer and Bergel (2002).

4 It's unknown, of course, whether the discourse attributed to the Buddha is actually from him or from later disciples speaking in his name. Buddhist tradition is divided as to whether the Buddha in fact ate meat and whether Buddhists should or shouldn't. One legend has it that the Buddha actually died from eating tainted pork, an ambiguous story that can be interpreted as either a condemnation of meat-eating or a granting of permission to dine on animals.

5 Further discussions of vegetarianism in the Hindu and Buddhist traditions may be found in Alsdorg (2010), Bodhipaksa (2010), Phelps (2004), Rosen (1997, 2004, 2011), Shabkar (2004), and Spencer (1995). Although focused specifically on the use of animals in scientific research rather than on vegetarianism, some of the essays in Regan (1986) provide insight into Asian perspectives on animals.

6 For more on Jewish vegetarianism, see Berman (1982), Dresner (1959), Pick (1978), and Schwartz (1988).

7 Dombrowski (1984) has some interesting things to say about Augustine's view of diet. His book also offers an excellent survey of ancient Greek and Latin views on vegetarianism.

8 In an often reprinted article, Lynn White (1967) argues that the other-worldliness of Christianity has historically made it hostile to the natural world and animals. Although White's thesis has been rightfully criticized for drawing too general a conclusion, it can hardly be denied that there are significant periods in Christianity's history in which the world has been seen as a place of temptation and evil.

9 For a good collection of Christian vegetarian voices, see Linzey and Regan (1990).

10 The perceptive reader will note that Linzey's defense of animal theos-rights provokes the same sorts of questions raised by ecologists against interests- or rights-based vegetarian models in Chapters 3 and 4. If animals in the wild have a right "to live; to be free; and to live without suffering, distress, and injury," does this mean that humans have an obligation to honor those rights by (e.g.) building heated winter shelters or scattering food for wild creatures?

11 Additional defenses of Christian vegetarianism include Linzey (1998), Spalde and Strindlund (2008), Webb (2001), and Young (1999).

12 The invocation is *bi-smillahi, allahu akbar*, "in the name of God, God is most great."

13 Resources on Muslim vegetarianism are scarce. But see Foltz (2006), Masri (1987, 2009), and Rosen (1997, 2011).

WORKS CITED

Many of the articles I cite or quote were originally published in academic journals not easily accessible to the general reader. Similarly, many of the pre-twentieth century books cited or quoted are also difficult to find. Accordingly, whenever possible, I have chosen to reference their recent reprinting, either in whole or in part, in more readily available anthologies.

Abbott, Jennifer (Director) (1998), "A Cow at My Table," Video. Flying Eye Productions.

Adams, Carol J. (1993a), "Feeding on Grace: Institutional Violence, Christianity, and Vegetarianism," in Charles Pinches and Jay B. McDaniel (eds), *Good News for Animals? Christian Approaches to Animal Well-Being*. Maryknoll, NY: Orbis Books, pp. 142–59.

— (1993b), "The Feminist Traffic in Animals," in Greta Gaard (ed.), *Ecofeminism: Women, Animals, Nature*. Philadelphia, PA: Temple University Press, pp. 195–218.

— (1995a), "Comment on George's 'Should Feminists Be Vegetarians?'," *Signs* 21: 221–5.

— (1995b), *The Sexual Politics of Meat: A Feminist-Vegetarian Critical Theory*. New York: Continuum.

— (2004), *The Pornography of Meat*. New York: Continuum.

— (2007a), "Caring about Suffering: A Feminist Exploration," in Josephine Donovan and Carol J. Adams (eds), *The Feminist Care Tradition in Animal Ethics*. New York: Columbia University Press, pp. 198–226.

— (2007b), "The War on Compassion," in Josephine Donovan and Carol J. Adams (eds), *The Feminist Care Tradition in Animal Ethics*. New York: Columbia University Press, pp. 21–36.

Alsdorf, Ludwig (2010), *The History of Vegetarianism and Cow-Veneration in India*. New York: Routledge.

Amato, Paul and Sonia A. Partridge (1989), *The New Vegetarians: Promoting Health and Protecting Life*. New York: Plenum Press.

American Dietetic Association (2009), "Position of American Dietetic Association on Vegetarian Diets," *Journal of the American Dietetic Association* 109: 1266–82.

American Meat Industry (2011), "AMI Fact Sheet. Animal Welfare in Packing Plants: An Overview." http://www.meatami.com/ht/a/ GetDocumentAction/i/71697. Accessed September 14, 2011.

Anti-Vegetarian Society of Meat Eaters (2009), "Introduction." http://www.freewebs.com/avsme/. Accessed January 12, 2011.

Aquinas, Thomas (1948), *Summa Theologica*, Fathers of the English Dominican Province (trans). London: Benzinger Brothers.

Ascherio, Alberto and Walter Willett (1995), "New Directions in Dietary Studies of Coronary Heart Disease," *Journal of Nutrition* 125: 647S–55S.

"The Auction Block" (2001). Video. Compassion over Killing.

Augustine (1966), *The Catholic and Manichaean Ways of Life,* G. D. Gallagher and I. J. Gallagher (trans). Boston, MA: The Catholic University Press.

Auxter, Thomas (1999), "The Right Not to be Eaten," in Kerry Walters and Lisa Portmess (eds), *Ethical Vegetarianism from Pythagoras to Peter Singer.* Albany, NY: State University Press of New York, pp. 177–87.

Bailey, Cathryn (2007), "On the Backs of Animals: The Valorization of Reason in Contemporary Animal Ethics," in Josephine Donovan and Carol J. Adams (eds), *The Feminist Care Tradition in Animal Ethics.* New York: Columbia University Press, pp. 344–59.

Barsam, Ara Paul (2008), *Reverence for Life: Albert Schweitzer's Great Contribution to Ethical Thought.* New York: Oxford University Press.

Bekoff, Marc (2010), *The Animal Manifesto: Six Reasons for Expanding Our Compassion Footprint.* Novato, CA: New World Library.

Bentham, Jeremy (1823), "Anarchical Fallacies," in *The Works of Jeremy Bentham,* Vol. 2. Edinburgh: William Tait.

Berman, Louis (1982), *Vegetarianism and the Jewish Tradition.* Jersey City, NY: K'tav.

Bernstein, Mark H. (2004), *Without a Tear: Our Tragic Relationship with Animals.* Urbana, IL: University of Illinois Press.

Birke, Lynda (1994), *Feminism, Animals, and Science: The Naming of the Shrew.* Buckingham, UK: Open University Press.

Blackstone, William T. (1972), "Ethics and Ecology," in William T. Blackstone (ed.), *Philosophy and Environmental Crisis.* Athens, GA: University of Georgia Press, pp. 16–42.

Bodhipaksa (2010), *Vegetarianism: A Buddhist View.* Cambridge, UK: Windhorse Publications.

Bookchin, Murray (1982), *The Ecology of Freedom: The Emergence and Dissolution of Hierarchy*. Palo Alto, CA: Cheshire Books.

Bookchin, Murray and Dave Foreman (1991), *Defending the Earth*. New York: Black Rose Books.

Boswell, James (2008), *The Life of Samuel Johnson*. New York: Penguin.

Brower, Michael and Warren Leon (1999), *The Consumer's Guide to Effective Environmental Choices: Practical Advice from the Union of Concern Scientists*. New York: Three Rivers Press.

Brown, Les (1988), *Cruelty to Animals: The Moral Debt*. New York: Palgrave Macmillan.

Burch, Robert W. (1977), "Animals, Rights, and Claims," *Southwestern Journal of Philosophy* 8: 53–9.

Burns, Robert (1909), *The Poems and Songs of Robert Burns*. New York: P.F. Collier & Son.

Callicott, J. Baird (1993), "The Search for an Environmental Ethic," in Tom Regan (ed.), *Matters of Life and Death: New Introductory Essays in Moral Philosophy*, 3rd edn. New York: McGraw-Hill, pp. 322–82.

— (1989), *In Defense of the Land Ethic: Essays in Environmental Philosophy*. Albany, NY: State University of New York Press.

Card, Claudia (1990), "Pluralist Lesbian Separatism," in Jeffner Allen (ed.), *Lesbian Philosophies and Cultures*. Albany, NY: State University of New York Press, pp. 125–42.

Cargile, James (1983), "Comments on 'The Priority of Human Interests'," in Harlan B. Miller and William H. Williams (eds), *Ethics and Animals*. Clifton, NJ: Humana Press, pp. 243–50.

Carruthers, Peter (1994), *The Animals Issue: Moral Theory in Practice*. Cambridge: Cambridge University Press.

Cavaliere, Paola (2008), "Are Human Rights Human?," in Susan J. Armstrong and Richard G. Botzler (eds), *The Animal Ethics Reader*, 2nd edn. New York: Routledge, pp. 30–5.

Cavalieri, Paola and Peter Singer (eds) (1993), *The Great Ape Project: Equality Beyond Humanity*. New York: St Martin's Griffin.

Cebik, L. B. (1981), "Can Animals Have Rights? No and Yes," *The Philosophical Forum* 12: 251–68.

Cheeke, Peter (1999), *Contemporary Issues in Animal Agriculture*. Danville, IL: Interstate Publishers.

Clark, Stephen R. L. (1977), *The Moral Status of Animals*. Oxford: Oxford University Press.

— (1983), "Humans, Animals, and 'Animal Behavior'," in Harlan B. Miller and William H. Williams (eds), *Ethics and Animals*. Clifton, NJ: Humana Press, pp. 169–81.

— (1987), "Animals, Ecosystems and the Liberal Ethic," *Monist* 70: 114–32.

— (1997), *Animals and Their Moral Standing.* New York: Routledge.

— (1999), "The Pretext of 'Necessary Suffering'," in Kerry Walters and Lisa Portmess (eds), *Ethical Vegetarianism from Pythagoras to Peter Singer.* Albany, NY: State University Press of New York, pp. 203–7.

Cocks, Joan (1989), *The Oppositional Imagination.* London: Routledge.

Coetzee, J. M. (1999), *The Lives of Animals.* Princeton, NJ: Princeton University Press.

Cohen, Carl (1986), "The Case for the Use of Animals in Biomedical Research," *New England Journal of Medicine* 315 (October 2): 865–9.

Cohen, Carl and Tom Regan (2001), *The Animal Rights Debate.* Lanham, MD: Rowman & Littlefield.

Cohen, Carol (2004), "A Critique of the Alleged Moral Basis of Vegetarianism," in Steve F. Sapontzis (ed.), *Food for Thought: The Debate over Eating Meat.* Amherst, NY: Prometheus Books, pp. 152–66.

Cohn, Jay N. and William B. Kannel (1995), "Cardiovascular Medicine," in James T. Willerson and Jay N. Cohn (eds), *Preventative Cardiology.* New York: Churchill Livingstone, pp. 1809–27.

Cone, Maria (1999), "Growth Slows as Population Hits 6 Billion," *Los Angeles Times* (6 October): A1.

Cranston, Maurice (1991), "John Locke and the Case for Toleration," in John Horton and Susan Medus (eds), *John Locke's A Letter Concerning Toleration in Focus.* London: Routledge, pp. 78–97.

Crisp, Roger (2009), "Utilitarianism and Vegetarianism," in Eldon Soifer (ed.), *Ethical Issues: Perspectives for Canadians,* 3rd edn. Peterborough, ON: Broadview Press, pp. 35–44.

Curtin, Deane (2004), "Contextual Moral Vegetarianism," in Steve F. Sapontzis (ed.), *Food for Thought: The Debate over Eating Meat.* Amherst, NY: Prometheus Books, pp. 272–83.

— (2007), "Toward an Ecological Ethic of Care," in Josephine Donovan and Carol J. Adams (eds), *The Feminist Care Tradition in Animal Ethics.* New York: Columbia University Press, pp. 87–104.

Davion, Victoria (1993), "Autonomy, Integrity, and Care," *Social Theory and Practice* 19: 161–82.

Davis, Karen (1996), *Poisoned Chickens, Poisoned Eggs: An Inside Look at the Modern Poultry Industry.* Summertown, TN: Book Publishing Company.

Davis, Steven L. (2003), "The Least Harm Principle May Require that Humans Consume a Diet Containing Large Herbivores, Not a Vegan Diet," *Journal of Agriculture and Environmental Ethics* 16: 387–94.

Dawkins, Marian Stamp (2006), "The Scientific Basis for Assessing Suffering in Animals," in Peter Singer (ed.), *In Defense of Animals: The Second Wave*. Oxford: Blackwell, pp. 26–39.

DeGrazia, David (1996), *Taking Animals Seriously: Mental Life and Moral Status*. Cambridge: Cambridge University Press.

De Lamartine, Alphonse (1999), "A Shameful Human Infirmity," in Kerry Walters and Lisa Portmess (eds), *Ethical Vegetarianism from Pythagoras to Peter Singer*. Albany, NY: State University of New York Press, pp. 77–9.

Denslow, Julie and Christine Padoch (1988), *People of the Tropical Rainforest*. Berkeley, CA: University of California Press.

Derrida, Jacques (2008), *The Animal That Therefore I Am*, 3rd edn. Trans. David Wills. New York: Fordham University Press.

Descartes, Rene (1999), "Letter to Henry More" in Kerry Walters and Lisa Portmess (eds), *Ethical Vegetarianism from Pythagoras to Peter Singer*. Albany, NY: State University of New York Press, pp. 263–5.

Devall, Bill and George Sessions (1985), *Deep Ecology*. Salt Lake City, UT: Gibbs M. Smith.

Diamond, Cora (1978), "Eating Meat and Meating People," *Philosophy* 53 (October): 465–79.

Diehl, Hans (1995), "Reversing Coronary Heart Disease," in N. J. Temple and D. P. Burkitt (eds), *Western Diseases: Their Dietary Prevention and Reversibility*. Totowa, NJ: Humana Press, pp. 237–316.

Dixon, Beth A. (1996), "The Feminist Connection between Women and Animals," *Environmental Ethics* 18: 181–94.

Dombrowski, Daniel A. (1984), *The Philosophy of Vegetarianism*. Amherst, MA: The University Press of Massachusetts.

Donovan, Josephine (1995), "Comment on George's 'Should Feminists Be Vegetarians?'," *Signs* 21: 226–9.

— (2007a), "Animal Rights and Feminist Theory," in Josephine Donovan and Carol J. Adams (eds), *The Feminist Care Tradition in Animal Ethics*. New York: Columbia University Press, pp. 58–86.

— (2007b), "Attention to Suffering: Sympathy as a Basis for Ethical Treatment of animals," in Josephine Donovan and Carol J. Adams (eds), *The Feminist Care Tradition in Animal Ethics*. New York: Columbia University Press, pp. 174–97.

— (2007c), "Caring to Dialogue: Feminism and the Treatment of Animals," in Josephine Donovan and Carol J. Adams (eds), *The Feminist Care Tradition in Animal Ethics*. New York: Columbia University Press, pp. 360–9.

Dresner, Samuel H. (1959), *The Jewish Dietary Laws: Their Meaning for Our Time*. New York: Burning Bush Press.

Edwards, Rem B. (1993), "Tom Regan's Seafaring Dog and (Un)Equal Inherent Worth," *Between the Species* 9: 231–5.

Eisnitz, Gail A. (1997), *Slaughterhouse*. Amherst, NY: Prometheus Books.

Everett, Jennifer (2004), "Vegetarianism, Predation, and Respect for Nature," in Steve F. Sapontzis (ed.), *Food for Thought: The Debate over Eating Meat*. Amherst, NY: Prometheus Books, pp. 302–14.

Fearnley-Whittingstall, Hugh (2004), *The River Cottage Meat Book*. London: Hodder & Stoughton.

Feinberg, Joel (1974), "The Rights of Animals and Unborn Generations," in William T. Blackstone (ed.), *Philosophy and Environmental Crisis*. Athens, GA: University of Georgia Press, pp. 43–63.

Fisher, Jeffrey (1994), *The Plague Makers*. New York: Simon and Schuster.

Foltz, Richard C. (2006), *Animals in Islamic Tradition and Muslim Cultures*. London: Oneworld.

Forward, Martin and Mohamed Alam (2008), "Islam," in Susan J. Armstrong and Richard G. Botzler (eds), *The Animal Ethics Reader*, 2nd edn. New York: Routledge, pp. 294–6.

Fox, Michael Allen (1999), *Deep Vegetarianism*. Philadelphia, PA: Temple University Press.

Francione, Gary L. (1996), *Rain Without Thunder: The Ideology of the Animal Rights Movement*. Philadelphia, PA: Temple University Press.

— (2000), *Introduction to Animal Rights: Your Child or Your Dog?* Philadelphia, PA: Temple University Press.

Francis, Leslie Pickering and Richard Norman (1978), "Some Animals Are More Equal than Others," *Philosophy* 53: 507–27.

Franklin, Benjamin (2009), *Autobiography and Other Writings*, ed. Ormond Seavey. New York: Oxford University Press.

Frey, R. G. (1980), *Interests and Rights: The Case Against Animals*. New York: Oxford University Press.

— (2004), "Utilitarianism and Moral Vegetarianism Again: Protest or Effectiveness?" in Steve F. Sapontzis (ed.), *Food for Thought: The Debate over Eating Meat*. Amherst, NY: Prometheus, pp. 118–23.

— (2008), "Rights, Interests, Desires and Beliefs," in Susan J. Armstrong and Richard G. Botzier (eds), *The Animal Ethics Reader*, 2nd edn. New York: Routledge, pp. 55–8.

Frontline (2002), "Modern Meat." Video. Public Broadcasting System.

Fuchs, Stephen (1995), "Enhancing the Divine Image," in Roberta Kalechofsky (ed.), *Rabbis and Vegetarianism: An Evolving Tradition*. Marblehead, MA: Micah Publications, pp. 13–17.

Gaard, Greta and Lori Gruen (1995), "Comment on George's 'Should Feminists Be Vegetarians?'," *Signs* 21: 230–41.

George, Kathryn Paxton (1994), "Should Feminists Be Vegetarians?," *Signs* 19: 405–34.

— (2000), *Animal, Vegetable, or Woman? A Feminist Critique of Ethical Vegetarianism*. Albany, NY: State University of New York Press.

— (2004), "A Paradox of Ethical Vegetarianism: Unfairness to Women and Children," in Steve F. Sapontzis (ed.), *Food for Thought: The Debate over Eating Meat*. Amherst, NY: Prometheus Books, pp. 261–71.

Gewirth, Alan (2001), "Human Rights and Future Generations," in Michael Boylan (ed.), *Environmental Ethics*. Upper Saddle River, NJ: Prentice-Hall, pp. 207–11.

Gilligan, Carol (1982), *In a Different Voice: Psychological Theory and Women's Development*. Cambridge, MA: Cambridge University Press.

Goldsmith, Oliver (1999), "They Pity, and Eat the Objects of Their Compassion," in Kerry Walters and Lisa Portmess (eds), *Ethical Vegetarianism from Pythagoras to Peter Singer*. Albany, NY: State University of New York Press, pp. 61–3.

Gompertz, Lewis (1997), *Moral Inquiries on the Situation of Man and Brutes*, ed. Charles R. Magel. Lewiston, NY: Edwin Mellen Press.

Green, Arthur (1995), "'To Work It and Guard It': Preserving God's World," in Roberta Kalechofsky (ed.), *Rabbis and Vegetarianism: An Evolving Tradition*. Marblehead, MA: Micah Publications, pp. 23–7.

Gruen, Lori (1993), "Animals," in Peter Singer (ed.), *A Companion to Ethics*. Oxford: Basil Blackwell, pp. 343–53.

— (2004), "Empathy and Vegetarian Commitments," in Steve F. Sapontzis (ed.), *Food for Thought: The Debate over Eating Meat*. Amherst, NY: Prometheus Books, pp. 284–92.

Gruzalski, Bart (2004), "Why It's Wrong to Eat Animals Raised and Slaughtered for Food," in Steve F. Sapontzis (ed.), *Food for Thought: The Debate over Eating Meat*. Amherst, NY: Prometheus Books, pp. 124–37.

Halweil, Brian (1998), "United States Leads World in Meat Stampede," Worldwatch Press Briefing on the Global Trends in Meat Consumption. Washington, DC, July 2.

Harrison, Peter (1989), "Theodicy and Animal Pain," *Philosophy* 64: 79–92.

— (1991), "Do Animals Feel Pain?" *Philosophy* 66: 25–40.

— (1993), "The Neo-Cartesian Revival: A Response," *Between the Species* 9: 71–6.

Hartley, David (1999), "Carnivorous Callousness," in Kerry Walters and Lisa Portmess (eds), *Ethical Vegetarianism from Pythagoras to Peter Singer*. Albany, NY: State University of New York Press, pp. 57–9.

HBO (2009), "Death on a Factory Farm." Video. Home Box Office.

Hettinger, Ned (2004), "Bambi Lovers Versus Tree Huggers," in Steve F. Sapontzis (ed.), *Food for Thought: The Debate over Eating Meat.* Amherst, NY: Prometheus Books, pp. 294–301.

Hill, John Lawrence (1996), *The Case for Vegetarianism: Philosophy for a Small Planet.* Lanham, MD: Rowman & Littlefield.

Holmes, Rolston III (1988), *Environmental Ethics: Duties to and Values in the Natural World.* Philadelphia, PA: Temple University Press.

"Hope for the Hopeless: An Investigation and Rescue at a Battery Egg Facility" (2001). Video. Compassion over Killing.

Hume, David (1960), *An Enquiry Concerning the Principles of Morals.* La Salle, IL: Open Court.

International Vegetarian Union (2010), "Dr. Albert Schweitzer (1875–1965)." www.ivu.org/history/europe20a/schweitzer.html. Accessed October 1, 2011.

Ives, David and David Valone (2007), *Reverence for Life Revisited: Albert Schweitzer's Relevance Today.* Newcastle, UK: Cambridge Scholars Publishing.

Johnson, Lawrence E. (1993), *A Morally Deep World: An Essay on Moral Significance and Environmental Ethics.* New York: Cambridge University Press.

Joyce, James (1961), *Ulysses.* New York: Vintage Books.

Kaldewaij, Frederike (2008), "Animals and the Harm of Death," in Susan J. Armstrong and Richard G. Botzler (eds), *The Animal Ethics Reader,* 2nd edn. New York: Routledge, pp. 58–62.

Kalechofsky, Roberta (1998), *Vegetarian Judaism: A Guide for Everyone.* Marblehead, MA: Micah Publications.

— (2004), "The Jewish Diet and Vegetarianism," in Steve F. Sapontzis (ed.), *Food for Thought: The Debate over Eating Meat.* Amherst, NY: Prometheus Books.

Kant, Immanuel (2001), *Lectures on Ethics,* Peter Heath and J. B. Schneewind (eds). New York: Cambridge University Press.

Kapleau, Philip (1986), *To Cherish All Life: A Buddhist Case for Becoming Vegetarian,* 2nd edn. Rochester, NY: The Rochester Zen Center.

Keller, Jean (1995), "Autonomy, Relationality, and Feminist Ethics," *Hypatia* 12: 128–33.

Kendall, Henry W. and David Pimentel (1994), "Constraints on the Expansion of the Global Food Supply," *Ambio* 23: 198–205.

Kheel, Marti (2004), "Vegetarianism and Ecofeminism: Toppling Patriarch with a Fork," in Steve F. Sapontzis (ed.), *Food for Thought: The Debate over Eating Meat.* Amherst, NY: Prometheus Books, pp. 327–41.

— (2007), "The Liberation of Nature: A Circular Affair," in Josephine Donovan and Carol J. Adams (eds), *The Feminist Care Tradition in Animal Ethics.* New York: Columbia University Press, pp. 39–57.

Kloer, Hans U. (1989), "Diet and Coronary Heart Disease," *Archives of Internal Medicine* 65: S13–21.

Kook, Abraham Isaac (2001), "A Firm and Joyous Voice of Life," in Kerry Walters and Lisa Portmess (eds), *Religious Vegetarianism from Hesiod to the Dalai Lama*. Albany, NY: State University of New York Press, pp. 118–21.

Lappe, Frances Moore (1991), *Diet for a Small Planet*, 20th anniversary edition. New York: Ballantine.

— (1998), *World Hunger: Twelve Myths*. New York: Grove Press.

LaRosa, John C. (1990), "AHA Medical/Scientific Statement Special Report. The Cholesterol Facts: A Summary of the Evidence Relating Dietary Fats, Serum Cholesterol, and Coronary Heart Disease," *Circulation* 81(5): 1721–33.

Leahy, Michael P. T. (1994), *Against Liberation: Putting Animals in Perspective*. New York: Routledge.

Leopold, Aldo (1966), *A Sand County Almanac*. New York: Ballantine Books.

Lewis, C. S. (2001), *The Problem of Pain*. New York: HarperOne.

Li, Huey-li (1993), "A Cross-Cultural Critique of Ecofeminism," in Greta Gaard (ed.), *Ecofeminism: Women, Animals, Nature*. Philadelphia, PA: Temple University Press, pp. 272–94.

Linzey, Andrew (1991), *Christianity and the Rights of Animals*. New York: Crossroad.

— (1998), *Animal Gospel*. Louisville, KY: Westminster John Know Press.

— (2008), "The Bible and Killing for Food," in Susan J. Armstrong and Richard G. Botzler (eds), *The Animal Ethics Reader*, 2nd edn. New York: Routledge, pp. 286–93.

Linzey, Andrew and Tom Regan (eds) (1990), *Animals and Christianity: A Book of Readings*. New York: Crossroad.

Lorenz, Konrad (1988), *On Life and Living*. New York: St Martin's.

Lowry, Jon (1975), "Natural Rights: Men and Animals," *Southwestern Journal of Philosophy* 6: 109–22.

Luke, Brian (2007), "Justice, Caring, and Animal Liberation," in Josephine Donovan and Carol J. Adams (eds), *The Feminist Care Tradition in Animal Ethics*. New York: Columbia University Press, pp. 125–52.

Lyman, Howard (2001), *Mad Cowboy: Plain Truth from the Cattle Rancher Who won't Eat Meat*. New York: Scribner's.

Machan, Tibor R. (2004), *Putting Animals First: Why We Are Nature's Favorite*. Lanham, MD: Rowman & Littlefield.

Marcus, Erik (2001), *Vegan: The New Ethics of Eating*, revised edn. Ithaca, NY: McBooks Press.

Martin, Michael (1976), "A Critique of Moral Vegetarianism," *Reason Papers* 3: 19–21.

Mason, Jim and Mary Finelli (2006), "Brave New Farm?" in Peter Singer (ed.), *In Defense of Animals: The Second Wave*. Malden, MA: Blackwell, pp. 104–22.

Mason, Jim and Peter Singer (1990), *Animal Factories,* revised edn. New York: Harmony Books.

Masri, Al-Hafiz B. A. (1987), *Animals in Islam*. Petersfield, England: The Athena Trust.

— (2001), "They Are Communities Like You," in Kerry Walters and Lisa Portmess (eds), *Religious Vegetarianism from Hesiod to the Dalai Lama*. Albany, NY: State University of New York Press, pp. 181–91.

— (2009), *Animal Welfare in Islam*. Markfield, UK: Islamic Foundation.

Masson, Jeffrey Moussaieff (2003), *The Pig Who Sang to the Moon*. New York: Ballantine.

Matheny, Gaverick (2006), "Utilitarianism and Animals," in Peter Singer (ed.), *In Defense of Animals: The Second Wave*. Malden, MA: Blackwell, pp. 13–25.

Maurer, Donna (2002), *Vegetarianism: Movement or Moment?* Philadelphia, PA: Temple University Press.

McCloskey, H. J. (1979), "Moral Rights and Animals," *Inquiry* 22: 23–54.

McCorkell, Don (Director) (2009), "A River of Waste." Video. EarthNow.

McGinnis, Richard (1993), "Letter to the Editor," *Vegetarian Times* (August): 8.

Melden, A. I. (1988), *Rights in Moral Lives: A Historical-Philosophical Essay*. Berkeley, CA: University of California Press.

Merchant, Carolyn (1990), *The Death of Nature: Women, Ecology, and the Scientific Revolution*. New York: HarperOne.

Meyer, Marvin and Kurt Bergel (eds) (2002), *Reverence for Life: The Ethics of Albert Schweitzer for the Twenty-First Century*. Syracuse, NY: Syracuse University Press.

Meyerding, Jane (1982), "Feminist Criticism and Culture Imperialism Where Does One End and the Other Begin?" *Animals' Agenda* (November–December): 14–15, 22–3.

Midgley, Mary (1983), *Animals and Why They Matter*. New York: Penguin.

Mill, John Stuart (1884), *A System of Logic*. London: Longmans, Green.

Moran, Victoria (1985), *Compassion: The Ultimate Ethic*. Wellingborough, UK: Thorsons.

Naess, Arne (1973), "The Shallow and the Deep, Long-Range Ecology Movement: A Summary," *Inquiry* 16: 95–100.

— (1993), *Ecology, Community and Lifestyle: Outline of an Ecosophy*. New York: Cambridge University Press.

— (2008), *The Ecology of Wisdom*, Alan Drengson and Bill Devall (eds). Berkeley, CA: Counterpoint.

Nagel, Thomas (1974), "What Is it Like to be a Bat?," *Philosophical Review* 84 (October): 435–50.

Narveson, Jan (1977), "Animal Rights," *Canadian Journal of Philosophy* 7: 161–78.

— (1983), "Animal Rights Revisited," in Harlan B. Miller and William H. Williams (eds), *Ethics and Animals*. Clifton, NJ: Humana Press, pp. 45–59.

National Resources Defense Council (1998), "Environmental and Health Consequences of Factory Farms." http://devstaging.win.nrdcdev.org/water/pollution/factor/cons.asp. Accessed September 19, 2010.

New Internationalist (July 2000), "Fishy Business." www.newint.org/features/2000/07/05/keynote/. Accessed October 10, 2010.

New York Times (1995), "Huge Spill of Hog Waste Fuels an Old Debate in North Carolina." www.nytimes.com/1995/06/25/us/huge-spill-of-hog-waste-fuels-an-old-debate-in-north-carolina.html. Accessed December 4, 2010.

Nhat Hanh, Thich (1987), *Interbeing: Fourteen Guides for Engaged Buddhism*. Berkeley, CA: Parallax Press.

Noddings, Nel (1984), *Caring: A Feminine Approach to Ethics and Moral Education*. Berkeley, CA: University of California Press.

O'Neill, Onoro (1997), "Environmental Values, Anthropocentrism and Speciesism," *Environmental Values* 6: 127–42.

Onslow County, N. C. (2010), "Citizens Financial Report." http://onslowcountync.gov/uploadedFiles/Finance_Office/Financial_Documents/2010pafr.pdf. Accessed April 24, 2011.

Orwell, George (2003), *Animal Farm*, centennial edn. New York: Plume.

Patterson, Charles (2002), *Eternal Treblinka: Our Treatment of Animals and the Holocaust*. New York: Lantern Books.

PETA (no date), "Midwest Pig Farm Investigation." Video. People for the Ethical Treatment of Animals.

Petrinovich, Lewis (1999), *Darwinian Dominion: Animal Welfare and Human Interests*. Cambridge, MA: MIT Press.

Phelps, Norm (2004), *The Great Compassion: Buddhism and Animal Rights*. New York: Lantern Books.

Pick, Philip L. (ed.) (1978), *Tree of Life: An Anthology of Articles Appearing in the Jewish Vegetarianism*. New York: A.S. Barnes.

Pike, David R. (2004), "Pest Management Strategic Plan for Lactating (Dairy) Cattle." www.ipmcenters.org/pmsp/pdf/NCDairyCattlePMSP.pdf. Accessed November 2, 2010.

Pluhar, Evelyn (1992), "Who Can Be Morally Obligated to Be a Vegetarian?", *Journal of Agricultural and Environmental Ethics* 5: 189–215.

— (1993), "On Vegetarianism, Morality, and Science: A Counter Reply," *Journal of Agricultural and Environmental Ethics* 6: 185–213.

— (1995), *Beyond Prejudice: The Moral Significance of Human and Nonhuman Animals*. Durham, NC: Duke University Press.

— (2004), "The Right Not to Be Eaten," in Steve F. Sapontzis (ed.), *Food for Thought: The Debate over Eating Meat*. Amherst, NY: Prometheus Books, pp. 92–107.

Plutarch (1999), "On the Eating of Flesh," in Kerry Walters and Lisa Portmess (eds), *Ethical Vegetarianism from Pythagoras to Peter Singer*. Albany, NY: State University of New York Press, pp. 27–34.

Pohl, Frederick and C. M. Kornbluth (1952), *The Space Merchants*. New York: Ballantine.

Pojman, Louis P. (1995), "Animal Rights, Egalitarianism, and Nihilism," in John Howie and George Schedler (eds), *Ethical Issues in Contemporary Society*. Carbondale, IL: Southern Illinois University Press, pp. 108–54.

Pollan, Michael (2002a), "An Animal's Place," *The New York Times Sunday Magazine* (November 10). http://michaelpollan.com/articles-archive/an-animals-place/. Accessed August 1, 2011.

— (2002b), "This Steer's Life," *The New York Times Sunday Magazine* (March 31): 44–51, 68, 71–2, 76–7.

— (2007), *The Omnivore's Dilemma: A Natural History of Four Meals*. New York: Penguin.

Porphyry (1999), "On Abstinence from Animal Food," in Kerry Walters and Lisa Portmess (eds), *Ethical Vegetarianism from Pythagoras to Peter Singer*. Albany, NY: State University Press of New York, pp. 35–45.

Public Citizen Foundation (2000), *A Citizen's Guide to Fighting Food Irradiation*. Washington, DC: Public Citizen's Critical Mass Energy and Environment Program.

Pythagoras (1999), "The Kinship of All Life," in Kerry Walters and Lisa Portmess (eds), *Ethical Vegetarianism from Pythagoras to Peter Singer*. Albany, NY: State University of New York Press, pp. 13–22.

Rachels, James (1976), "Do Animals Have a Right to Liberty?" in Tom Regan and Peter Singer (eds), *Animal Rights and Human Obligations*. Englewood Cliffs, NJ: Prentice-Hall, pp. 205–23.

— (1990), *Created from Animals: The Moral Implications of Darwinism*. Oxford: Oxford University Press.

— (2004), "The Basic Argument for Vegetarianism," in Steve F. Sapontzis (ed.), *Food for Thought: The Debate over Eating Meat*. Amherst, NY: Prometheus.

Ratzinger, Joseph (2002), *God and the World: Believing and Living in Our Time. A Conversation with Peter Seewald*. San Francisco: Ignatius Press.

Rawls, John (1971), *A Theory of Justice*. Cambridge, MA: Harvard University Press.

Regan, Tom (1983), *The Case for Animal Rights*. Berkeley, CA: University of California Press.

— (1985), "The Case for Animal Rights," in Peter Singer (ed.), *In Defense of Animals*. New York: Harper & Row, pp. 13–26.

— (1986), *Animal Sacrifices: Religious Perspectives on the Use of Animals in Science*. Philadelphia, PA: Temple University Press.

— (1991), *The Thee Generation: Reflections on the Coming Revolution*. Philadelphia, PA: Temple University Press.

— (2004a), "Christians Are What Christians Eat," in Steve Sapontzis (ed.), *Food For Thought: The Debate over Eating Meat*. Amherst, NY: Prometheus Books, pp. 177–85.

— (2004b), *Empty Cages: Facing the Challenge of Animal Rights*. Lanham, MD: Rowman & Littlefield.

Reichmann, James B. (2000), *Evolution, Animal "Rights," and the Environment*. Washington, DC: Catholic University of America Press.

Rifkin, Jeremy (1992), *Beyond Beef: The Rise and Fall of the Cowboy Culture*. New York: Dutton.

Ritchie, David G. (1894), *Natural Rights*. London: George Allen and Unwin.

Robbins, John (1987), *Diet for a New America*. Waltham, MA: Stillpoint.

— (2011), *The Food Revolution*, 10th anniversary edn. San Francisco, CA: Conari Press.

Rollin, Bernard E. (1989), *The Unheeded Cry: Animal Consciousness, Animal Pain, and Science*. Oxford: Oxford University Press.

— (2006), *Animal Rights and Human Morality*, 3rd edn. Amherst, NY: Prometheus Books.

Rosen, Steven J. (1997), *Diet for Transcendence: Vegetarianism and the World Religions*. Badger, CA: Torchlight Publishing.

— (2004), *Holy Cow: The Hare Krishna Contribution to Vegetarianism and Animal Rights*. New York: Lantern Books.

— (2011), *Food for the Soul: Vegetarianism and Yoga Traditions*. Santa Barbara, CA: Praeger.

Rowlands, Mark (2009), *Animal Rights: Moral Theory and Practice*, 2nd edn. New York: Palgrave Macmillan.

Rumi (2001), "The Men Who Ate the Elephant," in Kerry Walters and Lisa Portmess (eds), *Religious Vegetarianism from Hesiod to the Dalai Lama*. Albany, NY: State University of New York, pp. 173–4.

Rylan, John and Alan Durning (1997), *Stuff: The Secret Lives of Everyday Things*. Seattle: Northwest Environment Watch.

Sagoff, Mark (1984), "Animal Liberation and Environmental Ethics: Bad Marriage, Quick Divorce," *Osgoode Hall Law Journal* 22: 297–307.

Salt, Henry S. (1980), *Animals' Rights, Considered in Relation to Social Progress*. Clarks Summit, PA: Society for Animal Rights.

— (1999), "The Humanities of Diet," in Kerry Walters and Lisa Portmess (eds), *Ethical Vegetarianism from Pythagoras to Peter Singer*. Albany, NY: State University of New York Press, pp. 115–25.

Sapontzis, Steve F. (1987), *Morals, Reason, and Animals*. Philadelphia, PA: Temple University Press.

Schleifer, Harriet (1985), "Images of Death and Life: Food Animal Production and the Vegetarian Option," in Peter Singer (ed.), *In Defense of Animals*. New York: Blackwell, pp. 63–73.

Schopenhauer, Arthur (1998), *On the Basis of Morality*, E. F. J. Payne (trans). Indianapolis, IN: Hackett.

Schumacher, E. F. (1999), *Small Is Beautiful: Economics as if People Mattered*, 25th anniversary edn. Port Roberts, WA: Hartley and Marks.

Schwartz, Richard H. (1988), *Judaism and Vegetarianism*. Marblehead, MA: Micah Publications.

Schweitzer, Albert (1999), "The Ethic of Reverence for Life," in Kerry Walters and Lisa Portmess (eds), *Ethical Vegetarianism from Pythagoras to Peter Singer*. Albany, NY: State University of New York Press, pp. 145–51.

Scruton, Roger (2003), *Animal Rights and Wrongs*. New York: Continuum.

— (2004), "The Conscientious Carnivore," in Steve F. Sapontzis (ed.), *Food for Thought: The Debate over Eating Meat*. Albany, NY: Prometheus, pp. 81–91.

Scully, Matthew (2002), *Dominion: The Power of Man, the Suffering of Animals, and the Call for Mercy*. New York: St Martin's Griffin.

Serpell, James (1986), *In the Company of Animals: A Study of Human–Animal Relationships*. New York: Blackwell.

Shabkar (2004), *Food of Bodhisattvas: Buddhist Teachings on Abstaining from Meat*. Boston: Shambhala.

Singer, Isaac Bashevis (1983), "The Letter Writer," *The Collected Stories of Isaac Bashevis Singer*. New York: Farrar, Straus and Giroux, pp. 250–76.

Singer, Peter (1987), "Animal Liberation or Animal Rights?," *The Monist* 70: 3–14.

— (2008), *Practical Ethics*, 2nd edn. Cambridge: Cambridge University Press.

— (2009), *Animal Liberation*, Updated Edition. New York: Harper Perennial.

Singer, Peter and Jim Mason (2006), *The Way We Eat; Why Our Food Choices Matter*. Emmaus, PA: Rodale.

Spalde, Annika and Pelle Strindlund (2008), *Every Creature a Word of God: Compassion for Animals as Christian Spirituality*. Cleveland, OH: Vegetarian Advocates Press.

Specter, Michael (2011), "Test-Tube Burgers," *The New Yorker* (23 May). www.newyorker.com/reporting/2011/05/23/110523fa_fact_specter. Accessed June 26, 2011.

Spencer, Colin (1995), *The Heretic's Feast: A History of Vegetarianism*. Hanover, NH: University Press of New England.

Spiegel, Mary (1997), *The Dreaded Comparison: Human and Animal Slavery*, 3rd edn. New York: Mirror.

Sztybel, David (2008), "Animals as Persons," in Jodey Castricano (ed.), *Animal Subjects: An Ethical Reader in a Posthuman World*. Waterloo, ON: Wilfrid Laurer University Press, pp. 241–57.

Taylor, Angus (2003), *Animals and Ethics*. Peterborough, ON: Broadview Press.

Telfer, Elizabeth (1996), *Food for Thought: Philosophy and Food*. New York: Routledge.

Tolstoy, Leo (1999), "The Immorality of Carnivorism," in Kerry Walters and Lisa Portmess (eds), *Ethical Vegetarianism from Pythagoras to Peter Singer*. Albany, NY: State University of New York Press, pp. 97–105.

Tuck, Richard (1982), *Natural Rights Theories: Their Origin and Development*. New York: Cambridge University Press.

United Nations (1948), *Universal Declaration of Human Rights*. www.un.org/en/documents/udhr/. Accessed October 1, 2011.

Vegetarian Times (2008), "Vegetarianism in America." www.vegetariantimes.com/features/archive_of_editorial/667. Accessed November 30, 2010.

Wagner, Richard (1999), "Fellow-Suffering," in Kerry Walters and Lisa Portmess (eds), *Ethical Vegetarianism from Pythagoras to Peter Singer*. Albany, NY: State University of New York Press, pp. 93–5.

Waldau, Paul (2006), "Religion and Animals," in Peter Singer (ed.), *In Defense of Animals: The Second Wave*. New York: Blackwell, pp. 69–83.

Walker, Alice (1988), "Am I Blue?," *Living by the Word: Selected Writings, 1973–1987*. San Diego, CA: Harcourt Brace Jovanovich, pp. 3–8.

Walsh, Bryan (2011), "The End of the Line," *Time Magazine* 178 (July 18): 28–36.

Walters, Kerry and Lisa Portmess (eds) (2001a), "Akaranga Sutra," *Religious Vegetarianism from Hesiod to the Dalai Lama*. Albany, NY: State University of New York Press, pp. 43–6.

— (2001b), "Lankavatara Sutra," *Religious Vegetarianism from Hesiod to the Dalai Lama*. Albany, NY: State University of New York Press, pp. 66–74.

— (2001c), "Laws of Manu," *Religious Vegetarianism from Hesiod to the Dalai Lama*. Albany, NY: State University of New York Press, pp. 41–2.

— (2001d), "Surangama Sutra," *Religious Vegetarianism from Hesiod to the Dalai Lama*. Albany, NY: State University of New York Press, pp. 64–5.

— (2001e), "Vivekananda," *Religious Vegetarianism from Hesiod to the Dalai Lama*. Albany, NY: State University of New York Press, pp. 50–2.

Warren, Karen (1990), "The Power and Promise of Ecological Feminism," *Environmental Ethics* 12: 125–46.

— (2009), "America's Food Crisis and how to Fix It," *Time Magazine* 174 (August 31): 30–7.

Warren, Mary Anne (1987), "Difficulties with the Strong Animal Rights Position," *Between the Species* 2: 163–73.

Watson, Richard A. (1979), "Self-Consciousness and the Rights of Nonhuman Animals and Nature," *Environmental Ethics* 1: 99–129.

Webb, Stephen H. (2001), *Good Eating*. Grand Rapids, MI: Brazos Press.

Wenz, Peter S. (1999), "An Ecological Argument for Vegetarianism," in Kerry Walters and Lisa Portmess (eds), *Ethical Vegetarianism from Pythagoras to Peter Singer*. Albany, NY: State University of New York Press, pp. 189–201.

White, Lynn Townsend, Jr (1967), "The Historical Roots of Our Ecologic Crisis," *Science* 155: 1203–7.

Willard, Duane L. (1982), "About Animals 'Having' Rights," *The Journal of Value Inquiry* 16: 177–87.

Woodruff, Paul (2001), *Reverence: Renewing a Forgotten Virtue*. New York: Oxford University Press.

Young, Richard Alan (1999), *Is God a Vegetarian? Christianity, Vegetarianism, and Animal Rights*. Chicago, IL: Open Court.

INDEX